In this collection, Napoleon tells about Waterloo, John Paul Jones about the "Bon Homme Richard," and Thucydides about the Battle of Syracuse. Lesser known personages are represented as well: a slave recounts the fighting in New Orleans, a general's wife writes of combat at Saratoga, and an unknown author of hieroglyphic writing on a temple wall describes the struggle at Kadish in 1288 B.C.

JOHN BETTENBENDER is Professor of Drama and Director of Theater at Oberlin College, Oberlin, Ohio. He has edited for Dell *Poetry Festival* and *Three English Comedies*. George Fleming is Chairman of the Department of History at St. Joseph's College, East Chicago, Indiana.

THE LAUREL-LEAF LIBRARY brings together under a single imprint outstanding works of fiction and nonfiction particularly suitable for young adult readers, both in and out of the classroom. This series is under the editorship of M. Jerry Weiss, Distinguished Professor of Communications, Jersey City State College, and Charles F. Reasoner, Associate Professor, Elementary Education, New York University. Dell's special consultant in the social studies is Jane Greenspan, Hunter College High School.

Also available from Dell

FAMOUS BATTLES

EDITED BY

John Bettenbender

AND

George Fleming

Published by
Dell Publishing Co., Inc.
750 Third Avenue, New York, N.Y. 10017

Printed in the United States of America
First Laurel printing—June 1970

ACKNOWLEDGMENTS

"Gettysburg (Confederate Account)" by John Dooley: Reprinted from *John Dooley, Confederate Soldier* by Joseph
T. Durkin, by permission of Georgetown University Press
and the author.

"Gettysburg (Union Account)" by Frank A. Haskell: Reprinted
from *The Battle of Gettysburg* by Frank A. Haskell, by permission of Houghton Mifflin Company.

"Masada" by Flavius Josephus: Reprinted by permission of the
publishers and The Loeb Classical Library from Josephus,
The Jewish Wars, Volume III, H. St. J. Thackeray, trans-
lator. Cambridge, Mass.: Harvard University Press.

"Orléans": Reprinted from *The Trial of Joan of Arc* translated
by W. S. Scott, by permission of The Folio Society Ltd.,
London.

"Saratoga" by Baroness von Riedesel: Reprinted from *Baroness
von Riedesel and the American Revolution*, edited by Mervin
L. Brown and published by the University of North Carolina

Press for the Institute of Early American History and Culture. Used by permission of the University of North Carolina Press.

"Malta" by Francesco Balbi di Correggio: Reprinted from *The Siege of Malta* translated by H. A. Balbi, Copenhagen, 1961. Used by permission of the publishers, Ole Rostock and O. F. Gollcher.

"Midway" by William W. Smith: From *Midway* by William Ward Smith. Copyright © 1966 by William Ward Smith. Reprinted by permission of the publishers, Thomas Y. Crowell Company, New York.

"Waterloo" by Napoleon Bonaparte: From *The Waterloo Campaign,* ed. and translated by Somerset de Chair, The Folio Society, London, 1957. Reprinted by permission of A. Watkins, Inc. and David Higham Associates, Ltd.

"Alesia" by Julius Caesar: Reprinted by permission of the publisher and The Loeb Classical Library from Caesar, *The Gallic War* translated by H. J. Edwards, Cambridge, Mass.: Harvard University Press.

"Berlin" by Marshal Vasili I. Chuikov: From *The Fall of Berlin* by Marshal Vasili I. Chuikov. English translation copyright © 1967 by MacGibbon & Kee Ltd. Reprinted by permission of Holt, Rinehart & Winston, Inc., and MacGibbon & Kee Ltd.

"Solferino" by J. Henry Dumont: Reprinted from *A Memory of Solferino* by J. Henry Dumont. Copyright © 1959, The American National Red Cross and used by permission.

CONTENTS

Introduction

Whatever may be our feelings about it, warfare has occupied a large part of the history of man. From the earliest days of civilization—and long before civilization in all probability—human skill, energy, genius and heroism have been spent on the pursuit of war. For all its violence, destructive power, misery, and horror, war remains a subject of great fascination to most human beings. The first great epic poem of the Western world, Homer's *Iliad*, is about war and heroes of war. In fact the great epics of most nations, European, or not, are about deeds of valor performed in battle.

Almost no generation has been free of war. Even today when we have reached a stage where the danger of total human destruction is so great, we are still plagued by war. If we find no alternative to it, we may well perish.

Some men maintain that war has been a great boon to civilization as well as a curse. It has fostered scientific advancement at the same time it has destroyed. How many techniques in surgery and medicine have been perfected to aid the military? How long would we have waited for the development of atomic energy if war had not made this development urgent? And is not our space program being developed largely because we feel that military reasons dictate that we must not let another nation have unbridled control of space? Surely, though, there must come a time when we are able to advance without the barbaric motivations of war.

One reason for our fascination with war may be that we tend to glorify what is long past—to cover it with a romantic aura. Casualties become statistics and human suffering becomes remote. But there is great drama inherent in a battle. Dynamic forces are aligned against each other. The outcome is in doubt. We can watch these forces struggle in a great contest to determine who will prevail.

Those who hate war and those who are excited by the idea of it both seek to know what it is really like. Some of us have been in battle, but most of us have to rely on the reports of others for our information. And none of us can know directly about the great battles of the past. What was it like to ride with Richard the Lion-Hearted or with the swift horses of Saladin? What thoughts ran through the minds of the men as they charged Cemetery Ridge at Gettysburg? How do men stand up under long sieges? Or artillery barrages?

There are many histories of battles, but in this book we have the words of the men who were actually there or who knew the men who were there. These are firsthand accounts—from private soldiers, officers, generals, chroniclers, chaplains, reporters, soldiers' wives, and civilians. We have here the stories of twenty-four of the famous battles of history. The battles are not all of equal importance in size or significance, and some of the most famous battles are not represented. There are no satisfactory firsthand accounts, for instance, of such battles as Hastings or Tours. We have favored battles of the Western world—Europe and America—over others. This choice was dictated by the availability of material and by the fact that our educational and cultural tradition is Western, although many of us share an Asian or African heritage.

We have tried to present a variety of points of view as well as a variety of types of battles. These accounts are written by men who sing of the glories of war and men who tell of its horrors, by men who make war and men who are its victims. The excitement and the heroes are here. The ugliness is here. The waste is here.

Our fondest hope is that this institution we are examining with great interest will vanish from the affairs of men.

JOHN BETTENBENDER
GEORGE FLEMING

CHRONOLOGICAL TABLE
OF BATTLES

Kadesh (1288 B.C.)
Thermopylae (480 B.C.)
Syracuse (413 B.C.)
Alesia (52 B.C.)
Masada (72 A.D.)
Arsuf (1191)
Crécy (1346)
Agincourt (1415)
Orléans (1429)
Malta (1565)
Armada (1588)
Lützen (1632)
Saratoga (1777)
"Bon Homme Richard" (1779)
New Orleans (1815)
Waterloo (1815)
Ayacucho (1824)
Mexico City (1847)
Balaklava (1854)
Solferino (1859)
Gettysburg (1863)
Château-Thierry and Belleau Wood (1918)
Midway (1942)
Berlin (1945)

I
TWO SIDES OF
THE QUESTION

GETTYSBURG
ARSUF

Gettysburg July (1-3,1863)

Prologue

The Civil War, after more than one hundred years, still excites and troubles Americans, and much of the rest of the world as well. The reason for the interest may well be that the war was, as Lincoln said, a great testing of the whole idea of democracy.

Gettysburg was in many ways the central battle of the war. It was the second of Lee's invasions of the North, and its success or failure (we can say looking backward) may well have determined the continuance of the Confederate effort. The two armies met, by accident, rather than plan, near the town of Gettysburg, Pennsylvania. The Union forces, commanded by General George G. Meade, took up positions along Cemetery Ridge, and withstood Confederate attacks first on one end and then on the other, for two days. On the third day, General Robert E. Lee launched an attack on the Union center. General George Pickett and his Virginia division, along with others, made the charge; it failed, and with it the battle and campaign.

John Dooley, who tells the story of Pickett's charge as he lived through it, was a young captain in the First Virginia Regiment, part of Pickett's command. He had left Georgetown University to join the Confederate army, and fought with the army of Northern Virginia in 1862–63. At Gettysburg, he was wounded, as the account suggests, and was made a prisoner of war.

Frank A. Haskell, who tells the story as it appeared from the other side, was a Wisconsin lawyer who became a commissioned first lieutenant in a

13

volunteer regiment. When the regiment became part of the "Iron Brigade," General John Gibbon, the brigade commander, gave Haskell a staff position, and kept him on his staff when Gibbon rose to division command. Haskell was still on Gibbon's staff at Gettysburg, where Gibbon's division held a key position in the face of Pickett's charge. Haskell later had command of a regiment, and was killed leading it at Cold Harbor in 1864. His account of Gettysburg was a private letter to his brother, written within days of the battle.

JOHN DOOLEY
CONFEDERATE ACCOUNT

The sun poured down his fiercest beams and added to our discomfort. Genl. Dearing was out in front with his flag waving defiance at the Yankees and now and then rushing forward to take the place of some unfortunate gunner stricken down at his post. The ammunition wagons fly back and forth bringing up fresh supplies of ammunition, and still the air is shaking from earth to sky with every missile of death fired from the cannon's mouth. Around, above, beneath, and on all sides they screech, sing, scream, whistle, roar, whirr, buzz, bang and whizz, and we are obliged to lie quietly tho' frightened out of our wits and unable to do anything in our own defence or any injury to our enemies.

Major Hutter tells me that he was conversing with a friend during the shelling, both having their faces close to the ground, and his friend making some remark, the Major asked him what he said; and after waiting a little while for an answer found on looking up that his friend was dead—dead by his side and he did not hear the blow that killed him.

Our artillery has now ceased to roar and the enemy have checked their fury, too. The time appointed for our charge is come.

I tell you, there is no romance in making one of these charges. You might think so from reading 'Charlie O'Malley,' that prodigy of valour, or in reading of any other gallant knight who would as little think of riding over *gunners and sich like* as they would of eating a dozen oysters. But when you rise to your feet as we did today, I tell you the enthusiasm of ardent breasts in many cases *ain't there,* and instead of burning to avenge the insults of our country, families and alters and firesides, the thought is most frequently, *Oh,* if I could just come out of this charge safely how thankful *would I be!*

We rose to our feet, but not all. There is a line of men still on the ground with their faces turned, men affected in 4 different ways. There are the gallant dead who will never charge again; the helpless wounded, many of whom desire to share the fortunes of this charge; the men who have charged on many a battlefield but who are now helpless from the heat of the sun; and the men in whom there is not sufficient courage to enable them to rise,—but of these last there are but few.

Up, brave men! Some are actually *fainting* from the heat and dread. They have fallen to the ground overpowered by the suffocating heat and the terrors of that hour. Onward —steady—dress to the right—give way to the left—steady, not too fast—don't press upon the center—how gentle the slope! steady—keep well in line—there is the line of guns we must take—right in front—but how far they appear! Nearly one third of a mile, off on Cemetery Ridge, and the line stretches round in almost a semicircle. Upon the center of this we must march. Behind the guns are strong lines of infantry. You may see them plainly and now they see us perhaps more plainly.

To the right of us and above the guns we are to capture, black heavy monsters from their lofty mountain sites belch forth their flame and smoke and storms of shot and shell upon our advancing line; while directly in front, breathing flame in our very faces, the long range of guns which must be taken thunder of our quivering melting ranks. Now truly does the work of death begin. The line becomes unsteady because at every step a gap must be closed and thus from left to right much ground is often lost.

Close up! Close up the ranks when a friend falls, while his life blood bespatters your cheek or throws a film over your eyes! Dress to left or right, while the bravest of the brave are sinking to rise no more! Still onward! Capt. Hallinan has fallen and I take his place. So many men have fallen now that I find myself within a few feet of my old Captain (Norton). His men are pressing mine out of place. I ask him to give way a little to the left, and scarcely has he done so than he leaps into the air, falling prostrate. Still we press on—oh, how long it seems before we reach those blazing guns. Our men are falling faster now, for the deadly musket is at work. Volley after volley of crashing musket balls sweeps through the line and mow us down like wheat before the scythe.

On! men, on! Thirty more yards and the guns are ours; but who can stand such a storm of hissing lead and iron? What a relief if earth, which almost seems to hurl these implements of death in our faces, would open now and afford a secure retreat from threatening death. Every officer is in front, Pickett with his long curls streaming in the fiery breath from the cannon's mouth. Garnett on the right, Kemper in the center and Armistead on the left; Cols.. Lieut. Cols., Majors, Captains, all press on and cheer the shattered lines.

Just here—from right to left the remnants of our braves pour in their long reserved fire; until now no shot had been fired, no shout of triumph had been raised; but as the cloud of smoke rises over the heads of the advancing divisions the well-known southern battle cry which marks the victory gained or nearly gained bursts wildly over the bloodstained field and *all that line of guns is ours*.

Shot through both thighs, I fall about 30 yards from the guns. By my side lies Lt. Kehoe, shot through the knee. Here we lie, he in excessive pain, I fearing to bleed to death, the dead and dying all around, while the division sweeps over the Yankee guns. Oh, how I long to know the result, the end of this fearful charge! We seem to have victory in our hands; but what can our poor remnant of a shattered division do if they meet beyond the guns an obstinate resistance?

There—listen—we hear a new shout, and cheer after cheer rends the air. Are those fresh troops advancing to our support? No! no! That huzza never broke from southern lips. Oh God! Virginia's bravest, noblest sons have perished here today and perished all in vain!

Oh, if there is anything capable of crushing and wringing the soldier's heart it was this day's tragic act and all in vain! But a little well-timed support and Gettysburg was ours. The Yankee army had been routed and Pickett's division earned a name and fame not inferior to that of the Old Guard of Bonaparte. I will not attempt to describe. . . .*

FRANK A. HASKELL
UNION ACCOUNT

What sound was that? There was no mistaking it. The distinct sharp sound of one of the enemy's guns, square over to the front, caused us to open our eyes and turn them in that direction, when we saw directly above the crest the smoke of the bursting shell, and heard its noise. In an instant, before a word was spoken, as if that was the signal gun for general work, loud, startling, booming, the report of gun after gun in rapid succession smote our ears and their shells plunged down and exploded all around us. We sprang to our feet. In briefest time the whole Rebel line to the West was pouring out its thunder and its iron upon our devoted crest. The wildest confusion for a few moments obtained sway among us. The shells came bursting all about. The servants ran terror-stricken for dear life and disappeared. The horses, hitched to the trees or held by the slack hands of the orderlies, neighed out in fright and broke away and plunged riderless through the fields. The General at the first had snatched his sword, and started on foot for the front. I called for my horse; nobody responded. I found him tied to a tree, nearby, eating oats, with an air of the greatest composure, which under the circumstances, even then struck me as exceedingly ridiculous. He alone, of all beasts or men near, was cool. I am not sure but that I learned a lesson then from a horse. Anxious alone for his oats, while I put on the bridle and adjusted the halter, he delayed me by keeping his head down, so I had time to see one of the horses of our mess wagon struck and torn by a shell. The pair plunge—the driver has

*At this point Dooley's original ends abruptly. Gettysburg had been fought and lost, and John Dooley had taken part in his last battle. During the night of the 3rd he lies in the open field with thousands of other wounded. He is now a prisoner of war.

lost the reins—horse, driver and wagon go into a heap by a tree. Two mules close at hand, packed with boxes of ammunition, are knocked all to pieces by a shell. General Gibbon's groom has just mounted his horse and is starting to take the General's horse to him when the flying iron meets him and tears open his breast. He drops dead and the horses gallop away. No more than a minute since the first shot was fired, and I am mounted and riding after the General.

The mighty din that now rises to heaven and shakes the earth is not all of it the voice of the rebellion; for our guns, the guardian lions of the crest, quick to awake when danger comes, have opened their fiery jaws and begun to roar —the great hoarse roar of battle. I overtake the General half way up to the line. Before we reach the crest his horse is brought by an orderly. Leaving our horses just behind a sharp declivity of the ridge, on foot we go up among the batteries. How the long streams of fire spout from the guns, how the rifled shells hiss, how the smoke deepens and rolls. But where is the infantry? Has it vanished in smoke? Is this a nightmare or a juggler's devilish trick? All too real. The men of the infantry have seized their arms, and behind their works, behind every rock, in every ditch, wherever there is any shelter, they hug the ground, silent, quiet, unterrified, little harmed. The enemy's guns now in action are in position at their front of the woods along the second ridge that I have before mentioned and towards their right, behind a small crest in the open field, where we saw the flags this morning. Their line is some two miles long, concave on the side towards us, and their range is from one thousand to eighteen hundred yards. A hundred and twenty-five rebel guns, we estimate, are now active, firing twenty-four pound, twenty, twelve, and ten pound projectiles, solid shot and shells, spherical, conical, spiral.

Who can describe such a conflict as is raging around us? To say that it was like a summer storm, with the crash of thunder, the glare of lightning, the shrieking of the wind, and the clatter of hailstones, would be weak. The thunder and lightning of these two hundred and fifty guns and their shells, whose smoke darkens the sky, are incessant, all pervading, in the air above our heads, on the ground at our feet, remote, near, deafening, ear-piercing, astounding; and these hailstones are massy iron, charged with exploding fire. And there is little of human interest in a storm; it is an absorbing element of this. You may see flame and smoke, and hurrying men, and human passion at a great conflagration; but they are all earthly and nothing more. These guns are great infuriate demons, not of the earth, whose mouths blaze with smoky tongues of living fire, and whose murky breath, sulphur-laden, rolls around them and along the ground, the smoke of Hades. These grimy men, rushing, shouting, their souls in frenzy, plying the dusky globes and the igniting spark, are in their league, and but their willing ministers. We thought that at the second Bull Run, at the Antietam and at Fredericksburg on the 11th of December, we had heard heavy cannonading; they were but holiday salutes compared with this. Besides the great ceaseless roar of the guns, which was but the background of the others, a million various minor sounds engaged the ear. The projectiles shriek long and sharp. They hiss, they scream, they growl, they sputter; all sounds of life and rage; and each has its different note, and all are discordant. Was ever such a chorus of sound before? We note the effect of the enemies' fire among the batteries and along the crest. We see the solid shot strike axle, or pole, or wheel, and the tough iron and heart of oak snap and fly like straws. The great oaks there by Woodruff's guns heave down their massy branches with a crash, as if the lightning smote them. The shells swoop down among the battery horses standing there apart. A half dozen horses start, they tumble, their legs stiffen, their vitals and blood smear the ground. And these shot and shells have no respect for men either. We see the poor fellows hobbling back from the crest, or unable to do so, pale and weak, lying on the ground with the mangled stump of an arm or leg, dripping their life-blood away; or with a cheek torn open or a shoulder mashed. And many, alas! hear not the roar as they stretch upon the ground with upturned faces and open eyes, though a shell should burst at their very ears. Their ears and their bodies this instant are only mud. We saw them but a moment since there among the flame, with brawny arms and muscles of iron, wielding the rammer and pushing home the cannon's plethoric load.

Not ten yards away from us a shell burst among some small bushes, where sat three or four orderlies holding horses. Two of the men and one horse was killed. Only a few yards off a shell exploded over an open limber box in Cushing's battery, and at the same instant, another shell over a neighboring box. In both the boxes the ammunition blew up with an explosion that shook the ground, throwing fire and splinters and shells far into the air and all around, and destroying several men. We watched the shells bursting in the air, as they came hissing in all directions. Their flash was a bright gleam of lightning radiating from a point, giving place in the thousandth part of a second to a small, white puffy cloud, like a fleece of the lightest, whitest wool. These clouds were very numerous. We could not often see the shell before it burst; the sometimes, as we faced towards the enemy, and looked above our heads, the approach would be heralded by a prolonged hiss, which always seemed to me to be a line of something tangible, terminating in a black globe, distinct to the eye, as the sound had been to the ear. The shell would seem to stop, and hang suspended in the air an instant, and then vanish in fire and smoke and noise.

An hour has droned its flight since the war began. There is no sign of weariness or abatement on either side. So long it seemed, that the din and crashing around began to appear the normal condition of nature there, and fighting man's element. The General proposed to go among the men and over to the front of the batteries, so at about two o'clock he and I started. We went along the lines of the infantry as they lay there flat upon the earth, a little to the front of the batteries. They were suffering little, and were quiet and cool. How glad we were that the enemy were no better gunners, and that they cut the shell fuses too long. To the question asked the men, "What do you think of this?" the replies would be, "O, this is bully," "We are getting to like it," "O, we don't mind this." And so they lay under the heaviest cannonade that ever shook the continent, and among them a thousand times more jokes than heads were cracked.

Half-past two o'clock, an hour and a half since the commencement, and still the cannonade did not in the least abate; but soon thereafter some signs of weariness and a little slacking of fire began to be apparent upon both sides. The stricken horses were numerous, and the dead and wounded men lay about, and as we passed these latter, their low, piteous call for water would invariably come to us, if they had yet any voice left.

Our infantry was still unshaken, and in all the cannon-ade suffered very little. The batteries had been handled much more severely. I am unable to give any figures. A great number of horses had been killed, in some batteries more than half of all. Guns had been dismounted. A great many caissons, limbers and carriages had been destroyed, and usually from ten to twenty-five men to each battery had been struck, at least along our part of the crest. All things must end, and the great cannonade was no exception to the general law of earth. In the number of guns active at one time, and in the duration and rapidity of their fire, this artillery engagement, up to this time, must stand alone and pre-eminent in this war. It has not been often, or many times, surpassed in the battles of the world. Two hundred and fifty guns, at least, rapidly fired for two mortal hours. Cipher out the number of tons of gunpowder and iron that made these two hours hideous. The artillery fight over, men began to breathe more freely, and to ask, What next, I wonder? The battery men were among their guns, some leaning to rest and wipe the sweat from their sooty faces, some were handling ammunition boxes and replenishing those that were empty. Some batteries from the artillery reserve were moving up to take the places of the disabled ones; the smoke was clearing from the crests. There was a pause between the acts, with the curtain down, soon to rise upon the great final act and catastrophe of Gettysburg.

None on that crest now need be told that *the enemy is advancing*. Every eye could see his legions, an overwhelm-ing resistless tide of an ocean of armed men sweeping upon us! Regiment after regiment and brigade after brigade move from the woods and rapidly take their places in the lines forming the assault. Pickett's proud division, with some additional troops, hold their right; Pettigrew's (Worth's) their left. The first line at short interval is fol-lowed by a second, and then a third succeeds; and columns between support the lines. More than half a mile their front extends; more than a thousand yards the dull gray masses deploy, man touching man, rank pressing rank, and line supporting line. The red flags wave, their horsemen gallop up and down; the arms of eighteen thousand men, barrel and bayonet, gleam in the sun, a sloping forest of flashing steel. Right on they move, as with one soul, in perfect order, without impediment of ditch, or wall or stream, over ridge and slope, through orchard and meadow, and cornfield, magnificent, grim, irresistible.

All was orderly and still upon our crest; no noise and no confusion. The men had little need of commands, for the survivors of a dozen battles knew well enough what this array portended, and, already in their places, they would be prepared to act when the right time should come. The click of the locks as each man raised the hammer to feel with his fingers that the cap was on the nipple; the sharp jar as a musket touched a stone upon the wall when thrust in aiming over it, and the clicking of the iron axles as the guns were rolled up by hand a little further to the front, were quite all the sounds that could be heard. Cap-boxes were slid around to the front of the body; cartridge boxes opened, officers opened their pistol-holster. Such preparations, little more was needed.

Our skirmishers open a spattering fire along the front, and fighting, retire upon the main line—the first drops, the heralds of the storm, sounding on our windows. Then the thunders of our guns, first Arnold's then Cushing's and Woodruff's and the rest, shake and reverberate again through the air, and their sounding shells smite the enemy. The General said I had better go and tell General Meade of this advance. To gallop to General Meade's headquarters, to learn there that he had changed them to another part of the field, to dispatch to him by the Signal Corps in General Gibbon's name the message, "The enemy is advancing his infantry in force upon my front," and to be again upon the crest, were but the work of a minute. All our available guns are now active, and from the fire of shells, as the range grows shorter and shorter, they change to shrapnel, and from shrapnel to canister; but in spite of shells, and shrapnel and canister, without wavering or halt, the hardy lines of the enemy continue to move on. The Rebel guns make no reply to ours, and no charging shout rings out to-day, as is the Rebel wont; but the courage of these silent men amid our shots seems not to need the stimulus of other noise. The enemy's right flank sweeps near Stannard's bushy crest, and his concealed Vermonters rake it with a well-delivered fire of musketry. The gray lines do not halt or reply, but withdrawing a little from that extreme, they still move on.

And so across all that broad open ground they have come, nearer and nearer, nearly half the way, with our guns bellowing in their faces, until now a hundred yards, no more divide our ready left from their advancing right. The eager men there are impatient to begin. Let them. First, Harrow's breastworks flame; then Hall's; then Webb's. As if our bullets were the fire coals that touched off their muskets, the enemy in front halts, and his countless level barrels blaze back upon us. The Second Division is struggling in battle. The rattling storm soon spreads to the right, and the blue trefoils are vieing with the white. All along each hostile front, a thousand yards, with narrowest space between, the volleys blaze and roll; as thick the sound as when a summer hail-storm pelts the city roofs; as thick the fire as when the incessant lightning fringes a summer cloud. When the Rebel infantry had opened fire our batteries soon became silent, and this without their fault, for they were foul by long previous use. They were the targets of the concentrated Rebel bullets, and some of them had expended all their canister. But they were not silent before Rorty was killed, Woodruff had fallen mortally wounded, and Cushing, firing almost his last canister, had dropped dead among his guns shot through the head by a bullet. The conflict is left to the infantry alone.

Webb's men are falling fast, and he is among them to direct and to encourage; but, however well they may now do, with the walled enemy in front, with more than a dozen flags to Webb's three, it soon becomes apparent that in not many minutes they will be overpowered, or that there will be none alive for the enemy to overpower.

Arsuf (1191)

Prologue

The conquest of Palestine by the Seljuk Turks in the eleventh century roused the antagonism of many in Christian Europe. The "Holy Land," scene of the life of Jesus, had been a great objective for European pilgrims. To have it in the possession of Moslems was for European Christians both a practical difficulty and a sacrilege. The Moslems, of course, believed the land was rightfully theirs. Jerusalem was a holy city to them as well as the Jews and Christians. Pope Urban II at Clermont preached the Crusade—the organized military effort under the auspices of the Papacy to retake the holy places. The First Crusade succeeded in taking Jerusalem and establishing a European Kingdom. Within a century, however, the Turks under Saladin had defeated the Christians at Hattin and seized Jerusalem.

The Third Crusade set out to restore Christian European rule. Its most famous leader was Richard I of England, the Lion-hearted. Richard and Saladin ultimately negotiated a peace, which gave Christians access to Jerusalem, but not control. On the way, the two forces fought a series of bloody sieges and battles.

The story of one of those battles is here told by two chroniclers. The first was a Christian whose identity is not certain, but who plainly had firsthand knowledge of the fighting. The original was in Latin prose, though there is a similar, and probably earlier, version in French verse. Most medieval chroniclers, including this one, were not careful or precise about such details as the numbers of troops

—they are clearly exaggerated—and were inclined to color their accounts.

Beha-ed-Din, who tells the story from the other side, was a lawyer and judge from Mosul (in present-day Iraq) who was in Saladin's service and with him at the battle.

Arsuf is near the coast, north of Jerusalem. The battle was fought September 7, 1191.

CHRISTIAN ACCOUNT
AUTHOR UNKNOWN

On the third day the army advanced slowly from the Dead River and, because they were unable to go by the sea-side, which was choked up by the luxuriant growth of the grass, they were compelled to march through a mountainous country of a most desolate character and destitute of everything. On its march the army kept itself in closer companies than usual. The Templars on that day had charge of the rear and they lost so many horses by the attacks of the Turks that they were almost reduced to despair. The Count of Saint Paul also lost many horses, for he himself opposed the Turks with great valour when they attacked and made incursions against us. By his exertions the rest got off in safety and he thus earned the thanks and favour of the whole army.

On that day the king was wounded in the side by a dart while he was driving the Turks; but this slight hurt only incited him to attack them more vehemently, for the smarting of the wound made him more eager for vengeance, and during the whole of the day he fought against them and drove them back.

The Turks, on the other hand, obstinately annoyed our men and, keeping by the side of our army, did them all the injury they could by throwing darts and arrows, which flew like hail. Alas! how many horses fell transfixed with darts! How many died afterwards of the wounds which they received! There was such a stream of darts and arrows that you could not find four feet of ground where the army passed free from them. This terrible tempest continued all day, until at night-fall the Turks returned to their tents and dwellings. Our people stopped near what was called the Salt River and passed the night there. They arrived on the Tuesday after the festival of Saint Giles, and tarried two days.

Here there was a great throng on account of the horses who died from their wounds; for the people were so eager to purchase the horse-flesh that they even had recourse to blows. The king, on hearing this, proclaimed by herald that he would give a live horse to whoever would distribute his dead one to the best men in his service who needed it; and thus they ate horse-flesh as if it was venison, and they reckoned it most savoury, for hunger served in the place of seasoning.

On the third day, about nine o'clock, our army marched in battle array from the Salt River, for there was a rumour that the Turks were lying in ambush for them in the forest of Arsuf and that they intended to set the wood on fire to prevent our troops from crossing it. But our men, advancing in order, passed unmolested the place where the ambuscade was said to be and, on quitting the wood, they came to a large plain that ran along it, and there they pitched their tents near the river commonly called Rochetailie. Here they sent spies to reconnoitre, who brought back news that the Turks were awaiting their approach in countless numbers; for their multitudes covered the whole face of the earth around, and were estimated at three hundred thousand men, while the Christians were only one hundred thousand strong. The Christian army arrived at the river Rochetailie on the Thursday before the Nativity of the blessed Virgin Mary and tarried there until the morrow.

On the Saturday, at earliest dawn, our men armed themselves with great care to receive the Turks, whose insolence nothing but a battle could check. The enemy had ranged themselves in order, drawing gradually nearer and nearer, and our men also took the utmost care to place themselves in as good order as possible.

King Richard, who was most experienced in military affairs, arranged the army in squadrons and directed who should march in front and who in the rear. He divided the army into twelve companies, and these again into five divisions, marshalled according as the men ranked in military

discipline; and none could be found more warlike if they
had only had confidence in God who is the giver of all
good things. On that day, the Templars formed the first
rank, and after them came in due order the Bretons and
men of Anjou; then followed King Guy, with the men of
Poitou; in the fourth line were the Normans and English,
who had the care of the royal standard; and last of all
marched the Hospitallers, a line composed of chosen warriors divided into companies. They kept together so closely
that an apple, if thrown, would not have fallen to the
ground without touching a man or a horse; and the army
stretched from the army of the Saracens to the sea-shore.

There you might have seen their most appropriate distinctions—standards and ensigns of various forms, and
hardy soldiers, fresh and full of spirits, and well fitted for
war. Henry, Count of Champagne, kept guard of the side
nearest the mountain, maintaining a constant look-out of
the flank; the foot-soldiers, bowmen and arbalesters were
on the outside, and the rear of the army was closed by the
pack-horses and waggons, which carried provisions and
other things, and journeyed along between the army and
the sea to avoid an attack from the enemy.

This was the order of the army as it advanced gradually
to prevent separation; for the less close the line of battle,
the less effective was it for resistance. King Richard and the
Duke of Burgundy, with a chosen retinue of warriors,
rode up and down, narrowly watching the position and
manner of the Turks, and correcting anything in their own
troops if they saw occasion; for they had need, at that
moment, of the utmost circumspection.

It was nearly nine o'clock when there appeared a large
body of the Turks, ten thousand strong, coming down upon
us at full charge, throwing darts and arrows as fast as they
could, while they mingled their voices in one horrible yell.
With them also were the Saracens who live in the desert,
called Bedouins. They are a savage race of men, blacker
than soot, who fight on foot and carry a bow, quiver, and
round shield, and are a light and active race. These men
dauntlessly attacked our army. Beyond them might be
seen the well-arranged phalanxes of the Turks, with ensigns fixed to their lances, and standards and banners of

separate distinctions. Their army was divided into troops, the troops into companies, and their numbers seemed to exceed twenty thousand.

In an irresistible charge, on horses swifter than eagles and urged on like lightning, they attacked our men; and as they advanced they raised a cloud of dust, so that the sky was darkened. In front came certain of their emirs, as was their duty, with clarions and trumpets; some had horns, others had pipes and tambourines, gongs, cymbals, and other instruments, producing a horrible noise and clamour. The earth vibrated from the loud and discordant sounds, so that the crash of thunder could not be heard amidst the tumultuous noise. They did this to excite their spirit and courage, for the more violent the clamour became, the more bold were they for the fray.

Thus the impious Turks threatened us both on the side towards the sea and from the side to the land; and for the space of two miles not so much earth as could be taken up in one's hand could be seen, on account of the hostile Turks who covered it. O how obstinately they pressed on and continued their stubborn attacks, so that our men suffered severe loss of horses, which were killed by their darts and arrows!

O how useful to us on that day were our arbalesters and bowmen, who closed the extremities of the lines and did their best to repel the obstinate Turks. The enemy came rushing down, like a torrent, to the attack; and many of our arbalesters, unable to sustain the weight of their terrible and calamitous charge, threw away their arms and, fearing lest they should be shut out, took refuge in crowds behind the dense lines of the army, yielding, through fear of death, to sufferings which they could not support. Those arbalesters whom shame forbade to yield, or the hope of an immortal crown sustained, were animated with greater boldness and courage to persevere in the contest, and fought with indefatigable valour face to face against the Turks, receding only step by step, and so securing their companions' retreat.

O how great was the strait we were in on that day! how great was our tribulation! when some were affected with fears, and no one had such confidence or spirit as not to wish, at that moment, that he had finished his pilgrimage and had returned home, instead of standing with trembling heart the chances of a doubtful battle. In truth, our people, so few in number, were hemmed in by such multitudes of the Saracens that they had no means of escape; neither did they seem to have valour sufficient to withstand so many foes—nay, they were shut in like a flock of sheep in the jaws of wolves, with nothing but the sky above and the enemy all around them.

What army was ever assailed by so mighty a force? There you might have seen our troopers, having lost their chargers, marching on foot with the foot-men, or casting missiles from arbalests, or arrows from bows, against the enemy, and repelling their attacks in the best manner they were able. The Turks, skilled in the bow, pressed unceasingly upon them: it rained darts; the air was filled with the shower of arrows, and the brightness of the sun was obscured by the multitude of missiles as if it had been darkened by a fall of winter's hail or snow.

The Turks pressed with such boldness that they nearly crushed the Hospitallers, on which the latter sent word to King Richard that they could not sustain the violence of the enemy's attack unless he would allow their knights to advance at full charge against them. This the king dissuaded them from doing, but advised them to keep in a close body; they therefore persevered and kept together, though scarcely able to breathe for the pressure. By these means they were able to proceed on their way, though the heat happened to be very great on that day, and the Christians sweated in the contest. He who could have seen them closed up in a narrow space, so patient under the heat and toil of the day and the attacks of the enemy (who exhorted each other to destroy the Christians), could not doubt in his mind that their straitened and perilous position, hemmed in as they were by so large a multitude, augured ill to our success.

The enemy thundered at their backs as if with mallets, so that having no room to use their bows, they fought hand to hand with swords, lances, and clubs; and the blows of the Turks, echoing from their metal armour, resounded as if they had been struck upon an anvil.

The battle fell heavily on the extreme line of the Hospitallers; the more so, as they were unable to resist, but moved forward with patience under their wounds, returning not even a word for the blows which fell upon them.

Then they pressed on for safety upon the centre of the army which was in front of them, to avoid the fury of the enemy who harassed them in the rear.

The strength of all Paganism had gathered together from Damascus and Persia, from the Mediterranean to the East; there was not left in the uttermost recesses of the earth one man of fame or power, one nation of valour, or one bold soldier, whom the sultan had not summoned to his aid, either by entreaty, by money, or by authority, to crush the Christian race; for he presumed to hope he could blot them from the face of the earth. But his hopes were vain, for their numbers were sufficient, through the assistance of God, to effect their purpose. The flower of the chosen youth and soldiers of Christendom had indeed assembled together and were united in one body, like ears of corn on their stalks, from every region; and if they had been utterly crushed and destroyed, there is no doubt that there were none left to make resistance.

A cloud of dust obscured the air as our men marched on and, in addition to the heat, they had an enemy pressing them in the rear, insolent, and rendered obstinate by the instigation of the Devil. Still the Christians proved good men and, secure in their unconquerable spirit, kept constantly advancing, while the Turks threatened them without ceasing in the rear; but their blows fell harmless upon the defensive armour, and this caused the Turks to slacken in courage at the failure of their attempts, and they began to murmur in whispers of disappointment, crying out in their rage that our people were of iron and would yield to no blow.

Then the Turks, about twenty thousand strong, rushed again upon our men pell-mell, annoying them in every possible manner; when, as if almost overcome by their savage fury, brother Garnier de Napes, one of the Hospitallers, suddenly exclaimed with a loud voice, 'O excellent Saint George! will you leave us to be thus put to confusion? The whole of Christendom is now on the point of perishing, because it fears to return a blow against this impious race.'

Upon this the master of the Hospitallers went to the king and said to him: 'My lord the king, we are violently pressed by the enemy and are in danger of eternal infamy, as if we did dare to return their blows; we are each of us

losing our horses one after another, and why should we
bear with them any further?' To whom the king replied:
'Good master, it is you who must sustain their attack: no
one can be everywhere at once.'

On the master returning, the Turks again made a fierce
attack on them from the rear, and there was not a prince or
count amongst them but blushed with shame, and they
said to each other: 'Why do we not charge them at full
gallop? Alas! alas! we shall forever deserve to be called
cowards, a thing which never happened to us before, for
never has such a disgrace befallen so great an army, even
from the unbelievers. Unless we defend ourselves by immediately charging the enemy, we shall gain everlasting
scandal, and so much the greater the longer we delay to
fight.'

While they were treating of this point and had come to
the same decision about charging the enemy, two knights,
who were impatient of delay, put everything in confusion.
It had been resolved by common consent that the sounding
of six trumpets in three different parts of the army should be
a signal for a charge, viz., two in front, two in the rear,
and two in the middle, to distinguish the sounds from those
of the Saracens, and to mark the distance of each. If
these orders had been attended to, the Turks would have
been utterly discomfited; but from the too great haste of
the aforesaid knights, the success of the affair was marred.

They rushed at full gallop upon the Turks and each of
them prostrated his man by piercing him with his lance.
One of them was the marshal of the Hospitallers, the other
was Baldwin de Carreo, a good and brave man, and the
companion of King Richard, who had brought him in his
retinue.

When the other Christians observed these two rushing
forward, and heard them calling with a clear voice on
Saint George for aid, they charged the Turks in a body
with all their strength; then the Hospitallers, who had been
distressed all day by their close array, followed the two
soldiers and charged the enemy in troops, so that the van
of the army became the rear, and the Hospitallers, who
had been the last, were the first to charge.

Those who were in the first line of the rear made a
united and furious charge; after them the men of Poitou,
the Bretons, and the men of Anjou, rushed swiftly onward,

and then came the rest of the army in a body: each troop showed its valour and boldly closed with the Turks, transfixing them with their lances and casting them to the ground. The sky grew black with the dust which was raised in the confusion of that encounter. The Turks, who had purposely dismounted from their horses in order to take better aim at our men with their darts and arrows, were slain on all sides in that charge, for on being prostrated by the horse-soldiers they were beheaded by the foot-men.

King Richard, on seeing his army in motion and in encounter with the Turks, flew rapidly on his horse at full speed through the Hospitallers who had led the charge, and to whom he was bringing assistance with all his retinue, and broke into the Turkish infantry who, astonished at his blows and those of his men, gave way to the right and to the left. Then might be seen numbers prostrated on the ground, horses without their riders in crowds, the wounded lamenting with groans their hard fate, others drawing their last breath weltering in their gore, and many lay headless whilst their lifeless forms were trodden under foot both by friend and foe.

O how different are the speculations of those who meditate amidst the columns of the cloister from the fearful exercise of war! There the king—the fierce, the extraordinary king—cut down the Turks in every direction, and none could escape the force of his arm; wherever he turned, brandishing his sword, he carved a wide path for himself, and as he advanced and gave repeated strokes with his sword (cutting them down like a reaper with his sickle) the rest, warned by the sight of the dying, gave him more ample space, for the corpses of the dead Turks which lay on the face of the earth extended over half a mile.

The dust which was raised by the conflict of the combatants proved very hurtful to our men, for, on becoming fatigued from slaying so many and on retiring to take fresh air, they could not recognize each other and struck their blows indiscriminately to the right and to the left; unable to distinguish friend from foe, they took their own men for enemies and cut them down without mercy.

Thus as the Christians pressed hard upon the Turks, the latter gave way before them. But for a long time the battle was doubtful; they still exchanged blows, and either party strove for the victory: on both sides some retreated, covered with wounds, while others fell slain to the ground.

O how many banners, standards, pennons and many-coloured ensigns might then be seen torn and fallen to the earth; swords of proved steel, lances of cane with iron heads, Turkish bows, maces bristling with sharp teeth, darts and arrows covered the ground, and missiles enough to load twenty waggons or more! There lay the headless trunks of the Turks who had perished, whilst others retained their courage for a time until our men increased in strength, when some of them concealed themselves in the copses, some climbed up trees and, being shot with arrows, fell with fearful groans to the earth; others, abandoning their horses, betook themselves by slippery foot-paths to the sea-side, and tumbled headlong into waves from the precipitous cliffs that were five poles in height.

The rest of the enemy were repulsed in so wonderful a manner that for the space of two miles nothing could be seen but fugitives, although before they had been so obstinate and fierce, and puffed up with pride: but by God's grace their pride was humbled, and they continued still to fly; for when our men ceased the pursuit, fear alone added wings to their feet.

Our army had been ranged in divisions when they attacked the Turks; the Normans and English also, who had the care of the standard, came up slowly towards the troops which were fighting with the Turks—for it was very difficult to disperse the enemy's strength—and they stopped at a short distance therefrom, that all might have a rallying point.

On the conclusion of the slaughter, our men paused; but the fugitives, to the number of twenty thousand, when they saw this immediately recovered their courage and, armed with maces, charged the hindmost of those who were retiring and rescued some from our men who had just struck them down.

O how dreadfully were our men then pressed! for the darts and arrows, thrown at them as they were falling back, broke the heads, arms, and other limbs of our horsemen, so that they bent, stunned, to their saddle-bows; but having quickly regained their spirits and resumed their strength, and thirsting for vengeance with greater eagerness (like a lioness when her whelps are stolen), they charged the enemy, and broke through them like a net.

Then you might have seen the horses with their saddles displaced, and Turks, who had but just now fled, returning and pressing upon our people with the utmost fury. Had our men kept marching and not stood still in a compact immovable body, every cast of their darts would have told.

The commander of the Turks was an emir, Tekedin by name, a kinsman of the sultan, and he had a banner with a remarkable device: namely, that of a pair of breeches carved thereon, a symbol well known to his men. He was a most cruel persecutor and a persevering enemy of the Christians, and he had under his command seven hundred chosen Turks of great valour of the household troops of Saladin, each of whose companies bore a yellow banner with pennons of a different colour.

These men, coming at full charge, with clamour and haughty bearing, attacked our men who were turning off from them towards the standard, cutting at them and piercing them severely, so that even the firmness of our chiefs wavered under the weight of the pressure; yet our men remained immovable, compelled to repel force by force, and the conflict grew thicker, the blows were redoubled, and the battle raged fiercer than before: the one side labouring to crush, the other to repel.

Both exerted their strength, and although our men were far the fewest in numbers, they made havoc of great multitudes of the enemy; but thus hemmed in and unable to return to the standard with ease, they began to flag in courage, and few dared to renew the attack on the enemy. In truth, the Turks were furious in the assault and greatly distressed our men, whose blood poured forth in a stream beneath their blows.

On perceiving them reel and give way, William de Barris, a renowned knight, breaking through the ranks, charged the Turks with his men; and such was the vigour of the onset that some fell by the edge of his sword, while others only saved themselves by rapid flight.

Then the king, mounted on a bay Cyprian steed which had not its match, bounded forward in the direction of the mountains and scattered those he met on all sides; for the enemy fled from his sword and gave way, while helmets tottered beneath it and sparks flew forth from its strokes. So great was the fury of his onset, and so many and deadly his blows that day in his conflict with the Turks, that in a short space of time the enemy were all scattered and our army allowed to proceed. Thus our men, having suffered somewhat, at last returned to the standard and proceeded in their march as far as Arsuf, and there they pitched their tents outside its walls.

While they were thus engaged, a large body of the Turks made an attack of the extreme rear of our army. On hearing the noise of the assailants, King Richard, encouraging his men to battle, rushed at full speed, with only fifteen companions, against the Turks, crying out with a loud voice, 'Aid us, O God! and the Holy Sepulchre!' and this he exclaimed a second and third time; and when our men heard it, they made haste to follow him and attack, routed, and put the Turks to flight, pursuing them as far as Arsuf (whence they had first come out), cutting them down and subduing them.

Then the king returned from the slaughter of the fugitives to his camp; and that night the men, overcome with the fatigues and exertions of the day, rested quietly.

Whoever was greedy of gain and wished to plunder the booty, returned to the place of battle and loaded himself to his heart's desire; and those who returned from thence reported that they had counted thirty-two Turkish chiefs found slain on that day, whom, from the splendour of their armour and the costliness of their apparel, they supposed to be men of great influence and power. The Turks also made search for them to carry them away, as being of the most importance; and as well as these, the Turks carried off seven thousand mangled bodies of those who were next in rank, besides the wounded, who went off in straggling parties and, when their strength failed, lay about the fields and died. But by the protection of God we did not lose a tenth, nor a hundredth part of those that fell in the Turkish army.

But we had to mourn greatly the loss of James d'Avennes, who was overpowered by the numbers of the Turks; he was thrown by a grievous fall of his horse while bravely fighting, and the Turks, gathering round him, after much labour put him to death. But before breathing his last he slew fifteen of the Turks, according to the report of those who were sent to bring his body to the camp and who found so many Turkish soldiers lying dead around him. There were also found dead along with him three of his kinsmen, to whom some of our men did not give the assistance which they ought, but (shame to say) deserted them in their struggle against the attack of the Turks; on this account the Count of Dreux and others who were present obtained the infamy and detestation which they deserved.

The sultan, hearing that his choice troops, in whom he had placed so much confidence, were routed in this manner by the Christians, was filled with anger and excitement. Calling together his emirs he said to them, 'Are these the deeds of my brave troops, once so boastful, and whom I have so loaded with gifts? Lo! the Christians traverse the whole country at their pleasure, for there is no one to oppose them!' The emirs held down their heads at these words, but one of them returned this answer: 'Most sacred sultan, saving your majesty, this charge is unjust, for we fought with all our strength and did our best to destroy them. But they are armed in impenetrable armour which no weapon can pierce, so that all our blows fell, as it were, upon a rock of flint. And, further, there is one among their number superior to any man we have ever seen: they call him Meleck Ric (King Richard). Such a king as he seems born to command the whole earth; what then could we do more against so formidable an enemy?'

Saladin, in the heat of his indignation, called to him his brother Saphadin. 'It is my wish,' said he, 'to try what reliance can be placed on my men in this extremity: go and destroy without delay the walls of Ascalon and Gaza, but deliver Deir-el-Belar into the custody of my people, to ensure safety to those who pass that way. Destroy Galatia, Blancheward and Jaffa, the castles of Plans, Maen, Lydda, and Ramle, Belmont, Toron, the castles of Ernald, Beauverie and Mirabel: destroy all the mountain fortresses—spare neither city, castle, nor fort, except Krak and Jerusalem.'

Saphadin obeyed these commands and destroyed all these fortresses without delay.

MOSLEM ACCOUNT
BEHA-ED-DIN

When the King of England learnt that el-Melek el-'Adel
had come to the outposts, he sent to him to ask for an
interview. El-'Adel consented, and the two princes met,
each attended by a magnificent cortege. The son of Hon-
feri, a man of high rank in the countries on the coast, acted
as their interpreter. I had an opportunity of seeing this
young man of the day when peace was concluded; he was,
in truth, a fine young fellow, but his beard was shaved after
the manner of his nation. The King of England opened the
conversation by expressing his desire for the conclusion of
peace, and el-'Adel replied: 'If you wish to obtain peace
and desire me to act as your agent with the Sultan, you
must tell me the conditions you have in view.' 'The basis
of the treaty,' said the king, 'must be this: You must return
all our territory to us and withdraw into your own country.' El-'Adel replied with scorn, and a discussion ensued,
which resulted in their each withdrawing to his own camp.
When the Sultan saw that the enemy was on the move, he
dispatched his baggage, but remained where he was himself
to draw up his troops in order of battle. The small baggage had already started, and was on the point of overtak-
ing the heavy, when the Sultan sent an order for its
return; but as night had now closed in, the people were
in great confusion all that night. The Sultan then sent for
his brother to know what had passed between him and the
king, and had a private conversation with him. This was
on the night preceding Friday, the 13th of the month. The
enemy resumed their march and encamped in another
place called el-Birka, from which they could see the sea.
During the morning of Friday the Sultan went out to get
news of the Franks. On his ride they brought him two men
who had been taken prisoners by the advanced guard, and
he ordered their heads to be struck off. When he had ascertained that the enemy would not leave their camp that day,
he dismounted, and had a talk with his brother on the unwillingness of the Franks to move, and discussed the mea-

sures that should be taken. He spent the night in the same halting-place.

On Saturday, the 14th of Sh'aban [September 7, 1191], the Sultan was informed that the enemy were marching on Arsuf. He mounted forthwith, and drew up his troops in order of battle, being resolved to come to close quarters with the enemy that day. The marksmen drawn from each battalion went out in advance, and rained a shower of arrows on the enemy, who were approaching the thickets and gardens of Arsuf. The Moslem troops harassed them on every side, some advancing, led by the Sultan in person, others remaining in position to cover them in case of retreat. They charged the enemy furiously; the fire of war burst from the marksmen, and killed and wounded. The enemy were obliged to hurry forward to try and reach the place where they were to halt and encamp, and they then found that they were in a most galling position, and that we had them at our mercy. The Sultan rode from the right wing to the left, urging his men to fight for the Faith. I several times saw him, attended by only two pages, who were each leading a horse; I met his brother also with no greater a following, and they could both see the enemy's arrows falling to right and left of them. The enemy's progress was forced to become slower and slower, and the Moslems were flattering themselves that it would prove an easy victory, when the first ranks of the enemy's foot reached the wood and the gardens of Arsuf. Then the enemy's cavalry formed in one body, and, knowing that nothing but a supreme effort could save them, they resolved to charge. I myself saw their knights gathered together in the midst of a protecting circle of infantry; they put their lances in rest, uttered a mighty war-cry, and the ranks of infantry parted to allow them to pass; then they rushed out, and charged in all directions. One division hurled itself on our right wing, another on our left, and a third on our centre, throwing our whole force into confusion. I was in the centre, and when that body fled in the wildest disorder, it occurred to me that I might take refuge in the left wing, which was the nearest to me. But when I came up with it, I found that it, too, was struck with panic, and had taken to its heels even quicker than the other. Then I turned to the right wing; but when I reached it, I found it in still greater confusion than the left. I then turned to the position occupied, according to custom, by the Sultan's squadron, which was always a rallying-point for the others. I there found only seventeen men; but the standards were still flying, and the drum continued to beat. When the Sultan saw the dire discomfiture of the Moslems, he returned to his squadron, and found but very few men. He stopped here, and, perceiving that the whole neighbourhood was filled with fugitives, he ordered the drums to beat without ceasing, and had all whom he saw escaping brought to him. But, in truth, he could not stop the people in their flight; when the enemy charged, they gave way, and when he drew rein for fear of an ambush, they also came to a stand, and did battle with him. During the second charge, they fought even while they fled, and halted as soon as their pursuers stopped; and in the third, in which the enemy reached the top of the hillocks and rising ground that happened to be in his way, they fled once more, but, seeing him draw up, they also came to a stand. All those who saw that the Sultan's squadron was still at its post, and who heard the drum beating, were ashamed to go on, and, dreading the consequences if they continued their flight, they came up, and joined that body of troops. A number of soldiers had now rallied in the centre, and the enemy, who had reached the top of the hillocks [tells], halted, and turned to face their ranks. The Sultan, for his part, occupied the centre of his squadron, and displayed such energy in rallying the fugitives that he finally succeeded in collecting the whole of his army together again. The enemy, fearing that some ambush was concealed in the woods, retired towards their halting-place, and the Sultan regained some rising ground close to the edge of the wood, and there drew up his troops; having no tent to take shelter in, he stood in the shadow of a piece of cloth. I stood beside him, endeavouring to console him, but he would not listen to me—he was so overwhelmed by the events of the day; however, he took a little food that we offered him. He remained in this position, awaiting the return of the horses that had been taken to water at some considerable distance, and while we were thus drawn up, he had the wounded brought to him to comfort them, and to see that their wounds were dressed. He gave his own horses to those who had lost theirs. There were a great number of killed and wounded this day on both sides. Amongst the leaders who stood firm, the chief

were el-Melek el-'Adel, Kaimaz en-Nejmi the eunuch, and
el-Melek el-Afdal, the Sultan's son. El-Afdal charged so
furiously that a tumour he had in the face burst, and his
face was drenched with blood; but he suffered it with remarkable patience. The squadron from Mosul displayed
the greatest bravery, and won the Sultan's thanks for its
leader, 'Ala ed-Din. Our people sought for their comrades,
and found many a one who had died a martyr on the battlefield. The bodies of persons of note were found, especially
that of Musek, the grand emir [of the Kurds], a chief renowned for his bravery; that of Kaimaz el-'Adeli, who
was also celebrated; and that of Lighush, a brave officer,
whose death was a cause of great grief to the Sultan. We
had a large number of men and horses wounded, and the
enemy on their side had a great many casualties. We took
only one prisoner, who was brought to the Sultan, and beheaded by his command. We also captured four horses
from them. The Sultan then ordered the baggage forward
[to the river] el-'Auja, and I obtained his permission to follow it, and to precede him to the place he had appointed
for our encampment. I left him seated, waiting until all
his troops were collected, and till intelligence came in re-
garding the enemy, who were encamped close to Arsuf.

God alone knows the depth of grief which filled his
heart after this battle; all our men were wounded, some in
their bodies, some in their spirits.

II
LAST STANDS

THERMOPYLAE
MASADA

Thermopylae (480 B.C.)

Herodotus

The great Persian Empire stretched over most of southern Asia, from the borders of India westward to the Mediterranean, and around the eastern and southern coasts of that sea. In the early years of the fifth century B.C., revolts against the Persians broke out in the Greek cities of Asia Minor (the coasts and nearby islands of modern Turkey).

The Persians subdued the revolt, and then proceeded against mainland Greece, since the Greek cities had aided the rebels in Asia Minor. The first Persian invasion ended in defeat at Marathon, in 490 B.C.; the Athenians, almost alone, defeated a much larger army of Persians on the plain near their own city of Athens.

Ten years later the Persian fleet and army returned. This time they moved overland, and this time it was the city of Sparta that led the defense. The small band of Spartans and their allies held off the invaders in the pass of Thermopylae. Though ultimately defeated, they delayed the Persian movement, and permitted other Greek forces to gather. The delay, and the great strengthening of Greek purpose from the glory of Thermopylae, contributed to the defeats of the Persians on land at Plataea and at sea at Salamis. These defeats ended the Persian invasions and left Greece free for the great developments of the fifth century.

The account following is by Herodotus (who died about 425 B.C.), a Greek from Halicarnassus, resident in later life at Athens. He was a great traveler

*and collector of stories. He probably obtained his
information from veterans of the campaigns he wrote
about.*

King Xerxes pitched his camp in the region of Malis
called Trachinia, while on their side the Greeks occupied
the straits. These straits the Greeks in general call
Thermopylae (the Hot Gates), but the natives and those
who dwell in the neighbourhood call the Pylae (the Gates).
Here then the two armies took their stand; the one master
of all the region lying north of Trachis, the other of the
country extending southward of that place to the verge of
the continent.

The Greeks who at this spot awaited the coming of
Xerxes were the following: From Sparta, 300 men-at-
arms: from Arcadia, 1,000 Tegeans and Manthineans, 500
of each people; 120 Orchomenians, from the Arcadian
Orchomenus; and 1,000 from other cities: from Corinth,
400 men: from Phlius, 200: and from Mycenae, 800.
Such was the number from the Peloponnese. There
were also present, from Boetia, 700 Thespians and 400
Thebans.

Besides these troops, the Locrians of Opus and the Phocians had obeyed the call of their countrymen, and sent,
the former all the force they had, the latter 1,000 men.

The various nations had each captains of their own under
whom they served; but the one to whom all especially
looked up, and who had the command of the entire force,
was the Lacedaemonian, Leonidas. He had come to
Thermopylae, accompanied by the 300 men which the law
assigned him, whom he had himself chosen from among
the citizens, and who were all of them fathers with sons
living. On his way he had taken the troops from Thebes,
whose number I have already mentioned, and who were
under the command of Leontiades. The reason why he
made a point of taking troops from Thebes and Thebes
only was, that the Thebans were strongly suspected of
being well inclined to the Medes. Leonidas therefore called
on them to come with him to the war, wishing to see
whether they would comply with his demand, or openly
refuse, and disclaim the Greek alliance. They, however,
though their wishes leant the other way, nevertheless sent
the men.

The force with Leonidas was sent forward by the Spartans in advance of their main body, that the sight of them might encourage the allies to fight, and hinder them from going over to the Medes, as it was likely they might have done had they seen Sparta backward. They intended presently, when they had celebrated the Carneian festival, which was what now kept them at home, to leave a garrison in Sparta, and hasten in full force to join the army. The rest of the allies also intended to act similarly; for it happened that the Olympic festival fell exactly at this same period. None of them looked to see the contest at Thermopylae so speedily; wherefore they were content to send forward a mere advanced guard. Such accordingly were the intentions of the allies.

The Greek forces at Thermopylae, when the Persian army drew near to the entrance of the pass, were seized with fear, and a council was held to consider about a retreat. It was the wish of the Peloponnesians generally that the army should fall back upon the Peloponnese, and there guard the Isthmus. But Leonidas, who saw with what indignation the Phocians and Locrians heard of this plan, gave his voice for remaining where they were, while they sent envoys to the several cities to ask for help, since they were too few to make a stand against an army like that of the Medes.

While this debate was going on, Xerxes sent a mounted spy to observe the Greeks, and note how many they were, and what they were doing. He had heard, before he came out of Thessaly, that a few men were assembled at this place, and that at their head were certain Lacedaemonians, under Leonidas, a descendent of Heracles. The horseman rode up to the camp, and looked about him, but did not see the whole army; for such as were on the further side of the wall, it was not possible for him to behold; but he observed those on the outside, who were encamped in front of the rampart. It chanced that at this time the Lacedaemonians held the outer guard, and were seen by the spy, some of them engaged in gymnastic excercises, others combing their long hair. At this the spy greatly marvelled, but he counted their number, and when he had taken accurate note of everything, he rode back quietly; for no one pursued him, or paid any heed to his visit. So he returned, and told Xerxes all that he had seen.

Upon this, Xerxes, who had no means of surmising the truth—namely, that the Spartans were preparing to do or die manfully—but thought it laughable that they should be engaged in such employments, sent and called to his presence Demaratus, the son of Ariston, who still remained with the army. When he appeared, Xerxes told him all that he had heard, and questioned him concerning the news, since he was anxious to understand the meaning of such behavior on the part of the Spartans. Then Demaratus said, "I spoke to you, O king, concerning these men long since, when we had but just begun our march upon Greece; you, however, only laughed at my words, when I told you of all this which I saw would come to pass. Earnestly do I struggle at all times to speak truth to you, sire; and now listen to it once more. These men have come to dispute the pass with us, and it is for this that they are now making ready. It is their custom, when they are about to hazard their lives, to adorn their heads with care. Be assured, however, that if you can subdue the men who are here and the Lacedaemonians who remain in Sparta, there is no other nation in all the world which will venture to lift a hand in their defence. You have now to deal with the first kingdom and town in Greece, and with the bravest men."

Then Xerxes, to whom what Demaratus said seemed altogether to surpass belief, asked further, "How is it possible for so small an army to contend with mine?"

"O king," Demaratus answered, "let me be treated as a liar, if matters fall not out as I say."

But Xerxes was not persuaded any the more. Four whole days he suffered to go by, expecting that the Greeks would run away. When, however, he found on the fifth that they were not gone, thinking that their firm stand was mere impudence and recklessness, he grew wroth, and sent them the Medes and Cissians, with orders to take them alive and bring them into his presence. Then the Medes rushed forwards and charged the Greeks, but fell in vast numbers: others, however, took the places of the slain, and would not be beaten off, though they suffered terrible losses. In this way it became clear to all, and especially to the king, that though he had plenty of combatants, he had but very few warriors. The struggle, however, continued during the whole day.

Then the Medes, having met so rough a reception, withdrew from the fight; and their place was taken by the band of Persians under Hydarnes, whom the king called his Immortals: they, it was thought, would soon finish the business. But when they joined battle with the Greeks, it was with no better success than the Median detachment—things went much as before—the two armies fighting in a narrow space, and the barbarians using shorter spears than the Greeks, and having no advantage from their numbers. The Lacedaemonians fought in a way worthy of note, and showed themselves far more skillful in fight than their adversaries, often turning their backs, and making as though they were all flying away, on which the barbarians would rush after them with much noise and shouting, when the Spartans at their approach would wheel round and face their pursuers, in this way destroying vast numbers of the enemy. Some Spartans likewise fell in these encounters, but only a very few. At last the Persians, finding that all their efforts to gain the pass availed nothing, and that whether they attacked by divisions or in any other way, it was to no purpose, withdrew to their own quarters.

During these assaults, it is said that Xerxes, who was watching the battle, thrice leaped from the throne on which he sat, in terror for his army.

Next day the combat was renewed, but with no better success on the part of the barbarians. The Greeks were so few that the barbarians hoped to find them disabled, by reason of their wounds, from offering any further resistance; and so they once more attacked them. But the Greeks were drawn up in detachments according to their cities, and bore the brunt of the battle in turns, all except the Phocians, who had been stationed on the mountain to guard the pathway. So when the Persians found no difference between that day and the preceding, they again retired to their quarters.

Now, as the king was at a loss, and knew not how he should deal with the emergency, Ephialtes, the son of Eurydemus, a man of Malis, came to him and was admitted to a conference. Stirred by the hope of receiving a rich reward at the king's hands, he had come to tell him of the pathway which led across the mountain to Thermopylae; by which disclosure he brought destruction on the band of Greeks who had there withstood the barbarians.

Great was the joy of Xerxes on this occasion; and as he approved highly of the enterprise which Ephialtes undertook to accomplish, he forthwith sent upon the errand Hydarnes, and the Persians under him.

The Persians took the path, and crossing the Asopus, continued their march through the whole of the night, having the mountains of Oeta on their right hand, and on their left those of Trachis. At dawn of day, they found themselves close to the summit. Now the hill was guarded, as I have already said, by 1,000 Phocian men-at-arms, who were placed there to defend the pathway, and at the same time to secure their own country.

The ascent of the Persians became known to the Phocians in the following manner: During all the time that they were making their way up, the Greeks remained unconscious of it, inasmuch as the whole mountain was covered with groves of oak; but it happened that the air was very still, and the leaves which the Persians stirred with their feet made, as it was likely they would, a loud rustling, whereupon the Phocians jumped up and flew to seize their arms. In a moment the barbarians came in sight, and perceiving men arming themselves, were greatly amazed; for they had fallen in with an enemy when they expected no opposition. Hydarnes, alarmed at the sight, and fearing lest the Phocians might be Lacedaemonians, inquired of Ephialtes to what nation these troops belonged. Ephialtes told him the exact truth, whereupon he arrayed his Persians for battle. The Phocians, galled by the showers of arrows to which they were exposed, and imagining themselves the special object of the Persian attack, fled hastily to the crest of the mountain, and there made ready to meet death; but while their mistake continued, the Persians, with Ephialtes and Hydarnes, not thinking it worth their while to delay on account of Phocians, passed on and descended the mountain with all possible speed.

The Greeks at Thermopylae received the first warning of the destruction which the dawn would bring on them from the seer Megistias, who read their fate in the victims as he was sacrificing. After this deserters came in, and brought the news that the Persians were marching round by the hills: it was still night when these men arrived. Last of all, the scouts came running down from the heights, and brought in the same accounts, when the day was just beginning to break. Then the Greeks held a council to consider what they should do, and here opinions were divided: some were strong against quitting their post, while others contended to the contrary. So when the council had broken up, part of the troops departed and went their ways homeward to their several states; part, however, resolved to remain, and to stand by Leonidas to the last.

It is said that Leonidas himself sent away the troops who departed, because he tendered their safety, but thought it unseemly that either he or his Spartans should quit the post which they had been especially sent to guard. For my own part, I incline to think that Leonidas gave the order, because he perceived the allies to be out of heart and unwilling to encounter the danger to which his own mind was made up. He therefore commanded them to retreat, but said that he himself could not draw back with honour; knowing that, if he stayed, glory awaited him, and that Sparta in that case would not lose her prosperity. For when the Spartans, at the very beginning of the war, sent to consult the oracle concerning it, the answer which they received from the priestess was that either Sparta must be overthrown by the barbarians, or one of her kings must perish.

So the allies, when Leonidas ordered them to retire, obeyed him and forthwith departed. Only the Thespians and the Thebans remained with the Spartans; and of these the Thebans were kept back by Leonidas as hostages, very much against their will. The Thespians, on the contrary, stayed entirely of their own accord, refusing to retreat, and declaring that they would not forsake Leonidas and his followers. So they abode with the Spartans, and died with them. Their leader was Demophilus, the son of Diadromes.

At sunrise Xerxes made libations, after which he waited until the time when the market-place is wont to fill, and then began his advance. Ephialtes had instructed him thus, as the descent of the mountain is much quicker, and the distance much shorter, than the way round the hills, and the ascent. So the barbarians under Xerxes began to draw nigh; and the Greeks under Leonidas, as they now went forth determined to die, advanced much further than on previous days, until they reached the more open portion of the pass. Hitherto they had held their station within the wall, and from this had gone forth to fight at the point where the

pass was the narrowest. Now they joined battle beyond the
defile, and carried slaughter among the barbarians, who
fell in heaps. Behind them the captains of the squadrons,
armed with whips, urged their men forward with continual
blows. Many were thrust into the sea, and there perished;
a still greater number were trampled to death by their own
soldiers; no one heeded the dying. For the Greeks, reckless
of their own safety and desperate, since they knew that,
as the mountain had been crossed, their destruction was
nigh at hand, exerted themselves with the most furious
valour against the barbarians.

By this time the spears of the greater number were all
shivered, and with their swords they hewed down the ranks
of the Persians; and here, as they strove, Leonidas, fell
fighting bravely, together with many other famous Spartans, whose names I have taken care to learn on account of
their great worthiness, as indeed I have those of all the
300. There fell, too, at the same time very many famous
Persians.

And now there arose a fierce struggle between the Persians and the Lacedaemonians over the body of Leonidas,
in which the Greeks four times drove back the enemy, and
at last by their great bravery succeeded in bearing off the
body. This combat was scarcely ended when the Persians
with Ephialtes approached; and the Greeks, informed that
they drew nigh, made a change in the manner of their
fighting. Drawing back into the narrowest part of the pass,
and retreating even behind the cross wall, they posted
themselves upon a hillock, where they stood all drawn up
together in one close body, except only the Thebans. The
hillock whereof I speak is at the entrance of the straits,
where the stone lion stands which was set up in honour of
Leonidas. Here they defended themselves to the last, such
as still had swords using them, and the others resisting with
their hands and teeth; till the barbarians, who in part had
pulled down the wall and attacked them in front, in part
had gone round and now encircled them upon every side,
overwhelmed and buried the remnant left beneath showers
of missile weapons.

Thus nobly did the whole body of Lacedaemonians and
Thespians behave, but nevertheless one man is said to have
distinguished himself above all the rest, to wit, Dieneces
the Spartan. A speech which he made before the Greeks

engaged the Medes, remains on record. One of the Trachinians told him, "Such was the number of the barbarians, that when they shot forth their arrows the sun would be darkened by their multitude." Dieneces, not at all frightened at these words, but making light of the Median numbers, answered, "Our Trachinian friend brings us excellent tidings. If the Medes darken the sun, we shall have our fight in the shade." Other sayings, too, of a like nature are said to have been left on record by this same person.

Next to him two brothers, Lacedaemonians, are reputed to have made themselves conspicuous: they were named Alpheus and Maro, and were the sons of Orsiphantus. There was also a Thespian who gained greater glory than any of his countrymen: he was a man called Dithyrambus, the son of Harmatidas.

The slain were buried where they fell; and in their honour, nor less in honour of those who died before Leonidas sent the allies away, an inscription was set up, which said:

> Here did four thousand men from Pelops' land
> Against three hundred myriads bravely stand.

This was in honour of all. Another was for the Spartans alone:

> Go, stranger, and to Lacedaemon tell
> That here, obeying her behests, we fell.

Masada (72 A.D.)

Flavius Josephus

*Masada is a plateau in the south of Palestine,
fortified by Herod early in the first century. When
the Roman armies put down the rising of the Hebrews
in the 70s A.D., a band of Hebrews made their last
stand at Masada.*

*The account of the stand is by Flavius Josephus,
himself a Hebrew leader who surrendered to Rome.
He wrote the principal remaining account of the
Hebrews under the Roman Empire.*

*Archaeologists of Israel in the 1960s have investi-
gated Masada, and have uncovered much of the
fort and evidences of the last stand of Eleazar and
his group.*

The Roman general advanced at the head of his forces
against Eleazar and his band of Sicarii who held Masada,
and promptly making himself master of the whole district,
established garrisons at the most suitable points, threw up
a wall all round the fortress, to make it difficult for any of
the besieged to escape, and posted sentinels to guard it. He
himself encamped at a spot which he selected as most convenient for siege operations, where the rocks of the fortress
abutted on the adjacent mountain, although ill situated
for commissariat purposes. For not only were supplies
conveyed from a distance, entailing hard labour for the
Jews told off for this duty, but even water had to be brought
into the camp, there being no spring in the neighbourhood.
Having completed these preliminary arrangements Silva
turned his attention to the siege, which demanded great
skill and severe exertion, owing to the strength of the fortress, the nature of which was as follows.

A rock of no slight circumference and lofty from end to end is abruptly terminated on every side by deep ravines, the precipices rising sheer from an invisible base and being inaccessible to the foot of any living creature, save in two places where the rock permits of no easy ascent. On this plateau the high priest Jonathan first erected a fortress and called it Masada; the subsequent planning of the place engaged the serious attention of King Herod. For first he enclosed the entire summit, a circuit measuring seven furlongs, with a wall of white stone, twelve cubits high and eight broad; on it stood thirty-seven towers, fifty cubits high, from which access was obtained to apartments constructed round the whole interior of the wall. For the actual top, being of rich soil and softer than any plain, was given up by the king to cultivation in order that, should there ever be a dearth of provisions from outside, those who had committed their lives to the protection of the fortress might not suffer from it. There, too, he built a palace on the western slope, beneath the ramparts on the crest and inclining towards the north. The palace wall was strong and of great height, and had four towers, sixty cubits high, at the corners. The fittings of the interior—apartments, colonnades, and baths—were of manifold variety and sumptuous: columns, each formed of a single block, supporting the building throughout, and the walls and floors of the apartments being laid with variegated stones. Moreover, at each spot used for habitation, both on the summit and about the palace, as also before the wall, he had cut in the rock numerous large tanks as reservoirs for water, thus procuring a supply as ample as where springs are available. A sunk road led up from the palace to the summit of the hill, imperceptible from without. But even of the open approaches it was not easy for an enemy to make use; Herod barred at its narrowest point by a great tower, distant no less than a thousand cubits from the crest. This tower it was neither possible to pass nor easy to capture, exit being rendered difficult even for passengers who had no cause for alarm. So strongly had this fortress been intrenched against an enemy's attack, both by nature and the hand of man.

But the stores laid up within would have excited still more amazement, alike for their lavish splendour and their durability. For here had been stored a mass of corn, amply sufficient to last for years, abundance of wine and oil, besides every variety of pulse and piles of dates. Indeed, the Romans found what remained of the fruits undecayed. It would not be erroneous to attribute such durability to the atmosphere, which at the altitude of the citadel is untainted by all earth-born and foul alloy. There was also found a mass of arms of every description, hoarded up by the king and sufficient for ten thousand men, besides unwrought iron, brass, and lead; these preparations having, in fact, been made for grave reasons. For it is said that Herod furnished this fortress as a refuge for himself, suspecting a twofold danger: peril on the one hand from the Jewish people, lest they should depose him and restore their former dynasty to power; the greater and more serious from Cleopatra, Queen of Egypt. For she never concealed her intention, but was constantly importuning Antony, urging him to slay Herod, and praying him to confer on her the throne of Judaea. And, far from expecting him to refuse to gratify her, one might rather be surprised that Antony should never have obeyed her behests, basely enslaved as he was by his passion for her. It was such fears that drove Herod to fortify Masada, which he was destined to leave to the Romans as a final task in their war with the Jews.

The Roman general, having now completed his wall surrounding the whole exterior of the palace, and taken the strictest precautions that none should escape, applied himself to the siege. He had discovered only one spot capable of supporting earthworks. For in rear of the tower which barred the road leading from the west to the palace and the ridge, was a projection of rock, of considerable breadth and jutting far out, but still three hundred cubits below the elevation of Masada; it was called Leuce. Silva, having accordingly ascended and occupied this eminence, ordered his troops to throw up an embankment. Working with a will and a multitude of hands, they raised a solid bank to the height of two hundred cubits. This, however, being still considered of insufficient stability and extent as an emplacement for the engines, on top of it was constructed a platform of great stones fitted closely together, fifty cubits broad and as many high. The engines in general were similarly constructed to those first devised by Vespasian and afterwards by Titus for their siege operations; in addition a sixty-cubit tower was constructed entirely cased in iron, from which the Romans by volleys of missiles from numerous quick-firers and *ballistae* quickly beat off the defenders on the ramparts and prevented them from showing themselves. Simultaneously, Silva, having further provided himself with a great battering-ram, ordered it to be directed without intermission against the wall, and having, though with difficulty, succeeded in effecting a breach, brought it down in ruins. The Sicarii, however, had already hastily built up another wall inside, which was not likely to meet with a similar fate from the engines; for it was pliable and calculated to break the force of the impact, having been constructed as follows. Great beams were laid lengthwise and contiguous and joined at the extremities; of these there were two parallel rows a wall's breadth apart, and the intermediate space was filled with earth. Further, to prevent the soil from dispersing as the mound rose, they clamped, by other transverse beams, those laid longitudinally. The work thus presented to the enemy the appearance of masonry, but the blows of the engines were weakened, battering upon a yielding material which, as it settled down under the concussion, they merely served to solidify. Observing this, Silva, thinking it easier to destroy this wall by fire, ordered his soldiers to hurl at it showers of burning torches. Being mainly made of wood, it quickly caught fire, and, from its hollow nature becoming ignited right through, blazed up in a volume of flame. At the first outbreak of the fire, a north wind which blew in the faces of the Romans caused them alarm; for, diverting the flame from above, it drove it against them, and the fear that all their engines would be burnt up had almost reduced them to despair. Then suddenly the wind veering, as if by divine providence, to the south and blowing with full force in the opposite direction, wafted and flung the flames against the wall, which now through and through was all ablaze. The Romans, thus blessed by God's aid, returned rejoicing to their camp, with the determination of attacking the enemy on the morrow; and throughout that night they kept stricter watch lest any of them should secretly escape.

However, neither did Eleazar himself contemplate flight, nor did he intend to permit any other to do so. Seeing the wall consuming in the flames, unable to devise any further means of deliverance or gallant endeavor, and setting before his eyes what the Romans, if victorious, would inflict on them, their children and their wives, he deliberated on the death of all. And, judging, as matters stood, this course the best, he assembled the most doughty of his comrades and incited them to the deed by such words as these:

"Long since, my brave men, we determined neither to serve the Romans nor any other save God, for He alone is man's true and righteous Lord; and now the time is come which bids us verify that resolution by our actions. At this crisis let us not disgrace ourselves; we who in the past refused to submit even to a slavery involving no peril, let us not now, along with slavery, deliberately accept the irreparable penalties awaiting us if we are to fall alive into Roman hands. For as we were the first of all to revolt, so are we the last in arms against them. Moreover, I believe that it is God who has granted us this favour, that we have it in our power to die nobly and in freedom—a privilege denied to others who have met with unexpected defeat. Our fate at break of day is certain capture, but there is still the free choice of a noble death with those we hold most dear. Let our wives thus die undishonoured, our children unacquainted with slavery; and, when they are gone, let us render a generous service to each other, preserving our liberty as a noble winding-sheet. But first let us destroy our chattels and the fortress by fire; for the Romans, well I know, will be grieved to lose at once our persons and the lucre. Our provisions only let us spare; for they will testify, when we are dead, that it was not want which subdued us, but that, in keeping with our initial resolve, we preferred death to slavery."

Thus spoke Eleazar; but his words did not touch the hearts of all hearers alike. Some, indeed, were eager to respond and all but filled with delight at the thought of a death so noble; but others, softer-hearted, were moved with compassion for their wives and families, and doubtless also by the vivid prospect of their own end, and their tears as they looked upon one another revealed their unwillingness of heart. Eleazar, seeing them flinching and their courage breaking down in face of so vast a scheme, feared that their whimpers and tears might unman even those who had listened to his speech with fortitude. Far, therefore, from slackening in his exhortation, he roused himself and, fired with mighty fervour, essayed a higher flight of oratory on the immortality of the soul. Indignantly protesting and with eyes intently fixed on those in tears, he exclaimed:

"Deeply, indeed, was I deceived in thinking that I should have brave men as associates in our struggles for freedom—men determined to live with honour or to die. But you, it seems, were no better than the common herd in valour or in courage, you who are afraid even of that death that will deliver you from the direst ills, when in such a cause you ought neither to hesitate an instant nor wait for a counsellor. For from of old, since the first dawn of intelligence, we have been continually taught by those precepts, ancestral and divine—confirmed by the deeds and noble spirit of our forefathers—that life, not death, is man's misfortune. For it is death which gives liberty to the soul and permits it to depart to its own pure abode, there to be free from all calamity. Nay, I would that we had all been dead ere ever we saw that holy city razed by an enemy's hands, that sacred sanctuary so profanely uprooted! But seeing that we have been beguiled by a not ignoble hope, that we might perchance find means of avenging her of her foes, and now that hope has vanished and left us alone in our distress, let us hasten to die honourably; let us have pity on ourselves, our children and our wives, while it is still in our power to find pity from ourselves. Unenslaved by the foe let us die, as free men with our children and wives let us quit this life together!"

He would have pursued his exhortation but was cut short by his hearers, who, overpowered by some uncontrollable impulse, were all in haste to do the deed. Like men possessed they went their way, each eager to outstrip his neighbour and deeming it a signal proof of courage and sound judgement not to be seen among the last: so ardent the passion that had seized them to slaughter their wives, their little ones and themselves. Nor, as might have been expected, did their ardour cool when they approached the task: inflexibly they held to the resolution, which they had formed while listening to the address, and though personal emotion and affection were alive in all, reason which they knew had consulted best for their loved ones, was paramount. For, while they caressed and embraced their wives and took their children in their arms, clinging in tears to those parting kisses, at that same instant, as though served by hands other than their own, they accomplished their purpose, having the thought of the ills they would endure under the enemy's hands to console them for their constraint in killing them. And in the end not one was found a truant in so daring a deed: all carried through their task with their dearest one. Wretched victims of necessity, to whom to slay with their own hands their own wives and children seemed the lightest of evils! Unable, indeed, any longer to endure their anguish at what they had done, and feeling that they wronged the slain by surviving them if it were but for a moment, they quickly piled together all the stores and set them on fire; then, having chosen by lot ten of their number to dispatch the rest, they laid themselves down each beside his prostrate wife and children, and, flinging their arms around them, offered their throats in readiness for the executants of the melancholy office. These, having unswervingly slaughtered all, ordained the same rule of the lot for one another, that he on whom it fell should slay first the nine and then himself last of all; such mutual confidence had they all that neither in acting nor in suffering would one differ from another. Finally, then, the nine bared their throats, and the last solitary survivor, after surveying the prostrate multitude, to see whether haply amid the shambles there were yet one left who needed his hand, and finding that all were slain, set the palace ablaze, and then collecting his strength drove his sword clean through his body and fell beside his family. They had died in the belief that they had left not a soul of them alive to fall into Roman hands; but an old woman and another, a relative of Eleazar, superior in sagacity and training to most of her sex, with five children, escaped by concealing themselves in the subterranean aqueducts, while the rest were absorbed in the slaughter. The victims numbered nine hundred and sixty, including women and children; and the tragedy occurred on the fifteenth of the month Xanthicus.

The Romans, expecting further opposition were by daybreak under arms and, having with gangways formed bridges of approach from the earthworks, advanced to the assault. Seeing none of the enemy but on all sides an awful solitude, and flames within and silence, they were at a loss to conjecture what had happened. At length, as if for a signal to shoot, they shouted to call forth haply any of those within. The shout was heard by the women-folk, who, emerging from the caverns, informed the Romans how matters stood, one of the two lucidly reporting both the speech and how the deed was done. But it was with difficulty that they listened to her, incredulous of such amazing fortitude; meanwhile they endeavored to extinguish the flames and soon cutting a passage through them entered the palace. Here encountering the mass of slain, instead of exulting as over enemies, they admired the nobility of their resolve and the contempt of death displayed by so many in carrying it, unwavering, into execution.

The fortress being thus taken, the general left a garrison on the spot and himself departed with his army to Caesarea.

III
"SOMEBODY
BLUNDERED"

BALAKLAVA
MEXICO CITY

Balaklava (1854)

William H. Russell

*"The Charge of the Light Brigade", familiar to
almost every reader of English verse, from Alfred
Lord Tennyson's poem, actually took place at Balaklava, October 25, 1854. Balaklava is a small town
in the Crimean peninsula, near Sebastopol. The battle
was part of the war between the Russian and Ottoman Turkish empires, in which Great Britain and
France joined as allies of the Turks. The war maintained the shaky Turkish empire; it also served to
make the reputation of Florence Nightingale for her
services to the wounded and sick, and to demonstrate
the general ineptitude of military command, and its
failure to advance since Napoleonic wars. The charge
of the "six hundred" is only the most dramatic and
best known of the episodes.*

*The account of the charge and battle is from the
correspondence of William H. Russell (1821–1909)
for the London Times. Russell was probably the most
famous war correspondent of the period. He made
a reputation in the Crimean War which he enhanced
with his reports of the early campaigns of the American Civil War and the Austro-Prussian and Franco-
Prussian Wars.*

At half-past seven o'clock on the morning of the 25th,
an orderly came galloping into the headquarters camp with
the news that at dawn a strong corps of Russian horsemen,
supported by guns and battalions of infantry, had marched
into the valley and had nearly dispossessed the Turks of the
redoubt No. 1, and had opened fire on the redoubts Nos. 2,
3 and 4. Lord Lucan, who was in one of the redoubts

when they were discovered, had brought up his guns and some of his heavy cavalry, but they were obliged to retire owing to the superior weight of the enemy's metal.

Orders were despatched to Sir George Cathcart and to H.R.H. the Duke of Cambridge, to put their respective divisions, the Fourth and the First, in motion for the scene of action; and intelligence of the advance of the Russians was also furnished to General Canrobert. Immediately on receipt of the news, the General commanded General Bosquet to get the Third Division under arms, and sent a strong body of artillery and some 200 Chasseurs d'Afrique to assist us in holding the valley. Sir Colin Campbell, who was in command of Balaklava had drawn up the 93rd Highlanders a little in front of the road to the town, at the first news of the advance of the enemy. The marines on the heights got under arms; the seamen's batteries and marines' batteries on the heights close to the town were manned, and the French artillerymen and the Zouaves prepared for action along their lines. Lord Lucan's little camp was the scene of great excitement. The men had not had time to water their horses; they had not broken their fast from the evening of the day before and had barely saddled at the first blast of the trumpet when they were drawn up on the slope behind the redoubts in front of their camp to operate on the enemy's squadrons.

It was soon evident that no reliance was to be placed on the Turkish infantry or artillerymen. All the stories we had heard about their bravery behind stone walls and earthworks proved how differently the same or similar people fight under different circumstances. When the Russians advanced, the Turks fired a few rounds at them, got frightened at the distance of their supports in the rear, looked round, received a few shots and shell, then 'bolted' with an agility quite at variance with the common-place notions of Oriental deportment on the battle field.

Soon after eight o'clock, Lord Raglan and his staff turned out and cantered towards the rear of our position. The booming of artillery, the spattering roll of musketry, were heard rising from the valley, drowning the roar of the siege guns before Sebastopol. As I rode in the direction of the firing, over the thistles and large stones which cover the undulating plain that stretched away towards Balaklava, I observed a French light infantry regiment advancing from our right towards the ridge near the telegraph-house, which was already lined by companies of French infantry, while mounted officers scampered along its broken outline in every direction.

Looking to the left towards the gorge, we beheld six compact masses of Russian infantry, which had just debouched from the mountain passes near the Tchernaya, and were slowly advancing with solemn stateliness up the valley. Immediately in their front was a regular line of artillery at least twenty pieces strong. Two batteries of light guns were already a mile in advance of them and were playing with energy on the redoubts, from which feeble puffs of smoke came at long intervals. Behind these guns, in front of the infantry, were enormous bodies of cavalry. They were in six compact squares, three on each flank, moving down *en echelon* towards us, and the valley was lit up with the blaze of their sabres and lance points and gay accoutrements. In their front, and extending along the intervals between each battery of guns, were clouds of mounted skirmishers, wheeling and whirling in the front of their march, like autumn leaves tossed by the wind. The Zouaves close to us were lying like tigers at the spring, with ready rifles in hand, hidden chin deep by the earthworks which ran along the line of these ridges on our rear; but the quick-eyed Russians were manoeuvring on the other side of the valley, and did not expose their columns to attack. Below the Zouaves we could see the Turkish gunners in the redoubts, all in confusion as the shells burst over them. Just as I came up, the Russians had carried No. 1 redoubt, the farthest and most elevated of all, and their horsemen were chasing the Turks across the interval which lay between it and redoubt No. 2.

At that moment the cavalry, under Lord Lucan, were formed in glittering masses—the Light Brigade, under Lord Cardigan in advance; the Heavy Brigade, under Brigadier-General Scarlett, in reserve. They were drawn up just in front of their encampment, and were concealed from the view of the enemy by a slight 'wave' in the plain. Considerably to the rear of their right the 93rd Highlanders were drawn up in line, in front of the approach to Balaklava. Above and behind them, on the heights, the marines were visible through the glass, drawn up under arms, and the gunners could be seen ready in the earthworks, in

which were placed the ships' heavy guns. The 93rd had originally been advanced somewhat more into the plain, but
the instant the Russians got possession of the first redoubt
they opened fire on them from our own guns, which inflicted some injury, and Sir Colin Campbell 'retired' his
men to a better position.

Meanwhile the enemy advanced his cavalry rapidly. To
our inexpressible disgust, we saw the Turks in redoubt No.
2 fly at their approach. They ran in scattered groups across
towards redoubt No. 3 and towards Balaklava; but the
horse-hoof of the Cossack was too quick for them, and
sword and lance were busily plied among the retreating
herd. The yells of the pursuers and pursued were plainly
audible. As the Lancers and Light Cavalry of the Russians
advanced they gathered up their skirmishers with great
speed and in excellent order. Then up came their guns, in
rushed their gunners to the abandoned redoubts, and the
guns of No. 2 redoubt soon played with deadly effect upon
the dispirited defenders of No. 3. Two or three shots in return and all was silent. The Turks swarmed over the earthworks, and ran in confusion towards the town, firing their
muskets at the enemy as they ran. Again the solid column
of cavalry opened like a fan and resolved itself into a 'long
spray' of skirmishers. It lapped the flying Turks, steel
flashed in the air, and down went the poor Moslem, quivering on the plain split through fez and musket-guard to the
chin and breast-belt. It was evident the Russians had been
too quick for us. The Turks had been too quick also, for
they had not held their redoubts long enough to enable us
to bring them help. In vain the naval guns on the heights
fired on the Russian cavalry; the distance was too great for
shot or shell to reach. In vain the Turkish gunners in the
earthern batteries which were placed along the French entrenchments endeavoured to protect their flying countrymen; their shot flew wide and short of the swarming
masses.

The Turks betook themselves towards the Highlanders,
where they checked their flight and formed into companies
on the flanks of the Highlanders. As the Russian cavalry on
the left of their line crowned the hill across the valley, they
perceived the Highlanders drawn up at the distance of
some half mile, calmly waiting their approach. They halted,
and squadron after squadron came up from the rear, till

they had a body of some 3,500 men along the ridge—
Lancers, and Dragoons, and Hussars. Then they moved
en echelon, in two bodies, with another in reserve. The
cavalry who had been pursuing the Turks on the right were
coming up to the ridge beneath us, which concealed our
cavalry from view. The Heavy Brigade in advance was
drawn up in two lines. The first line consisted of the Scots
Greys, and of their old companions in glory, the Enniskilleners; the second, of the 4th Royal Irish, of the 5th
Dragoon Guards, and of the 1st Royal Dragoons. The
Light Cavalry Brigade was on their left, in two lines also.

The silence was oppressive; between the cannon bursts
one could hear the champing of bits and the clink of sabres in the valley below. The Russians on their left drew
breath for a moment, and then in one grand line charged
in towards Balaklava. The ground flew beneath their
horses' feet; gathering speed at every stride, they dashed on
towards that thin red streak * tipped with a line of steel.
The Turks fired a volley at eight hundred yards and ran.
As the Russians came within six hundred yards, down went
that line of steel in front, and out rang a rolling volley of
Minie musketry. The distance was too great; the Russians
were not checked, but still swept onwards through the
smoke, with the whole force of horse and man, here and
there knocked over by the shot of our batteries above. With
breathless suspense every one awaited the bursting of
the wave upon the line of Gaelic rock; but ere they came
within two hundred and fifty yards, another deadly volley
flashed from the levelled rifle and carried terror among the
Russians. They wheeled about, opened files right and left
and fled faster than they came. 'Bravo, Highlanders! well
done!' shouted the excited spectators. But events thickened;
the Highlanders and their splendid front were soon forgotten—men scarcely had a moment to think of this fact,
that the 93rd never altered their formation to receive that
tide of horsemen. 'No,' said Sir Colin Campbell, 'I did not
think it worth while to form them even four deep!' The
ordinary British line, two deep, was quite sufficient to repel
the attack of these Muscovite cavaliers.

Lord Raglan perceived that the intention of the Russians

*This description of the 93rd Highlanders' stand, later misquoted
as a 'thin red line,' provided the origin of that famous phrase.

was to attack Balaklava, and sent orders to Lord Lucan to
move down his Heavy Horse to cover the approaches,
and they were just moving from their position near the
vineyard and orchard, when his lordship, seeing that a large
body of the enemy's cavalry were coming after him over
the ridge, rode after them, wheeled them round, and advanced to meet them. We saw Brigadier-General Scarlett
ride along in front of his massive squadrons. The Russians
—evidently *corps d'élite*—their light blue jackets embroi-
dered with silver lace, were advancing on their left at an
easy gallop towards the brow of the hill. A forest of lances
glistened in their rear and several squadrons of grey-coated
dragoons moved up quickly to support them as they
reached the summit. The instant they came in sight, the
trumpets of our cavalry gave out the warning blast which
told us all that in another moment we should see the shock
of battle beneath our very eyes. Lord Raglan, all his staff
and escort, and groups of officers, the Zouaves, French
generals and officers, and bodies of French infantry on the
height, were spectators of the scene as though they were
looking on the stage from the boxes of a theatre. Nearly
everyone dismounted and sat down, and not a word was
said. The Russians advanced down the hill at a slow canter,
which they changed into a trot, and at last nearly halted.
Their first line was at least double the length of ours—it
was three times as deep. Behind them was a similar line,
equally strong and compact.

The trumpets rang out again through the valley, and the
Greys and Enniskilleners went right at the centre of the
Russian cavalry. The space between them was only a few
hundred yards; it was scarce enough to let the horses
'gather way,' nor had the men quite space sufficient for
the full play of their sword arms. The Russian line brought
forward each wing as our cavalry advanced, and threatened
to annihilate them as they passed on. Turning a little to
their left, so as to meet the Russian right, the Greys rushed
on with a cheer that thrilled to every heart—the wild shout
of the Enniskilleners rose through the air at the same instant. As lightning flashed through cloud, the Greys and
Enniskilleners pierced through the dark masses of Russians. The shock was but for a moment. There was a clash
of steel and a light play of sword-blades in the air, and then
the Greys and the redcoats disappeared in the midst of the

shaken and quivering columns. In another moment we saw them emerging with diminished numbers and in broken order, charging against the second line. It was a terrible moment. The first line of Russians, which had been utterly smashed by our charge, and had fled off at one flank and towards the centre, were coming back to swallow up our handful of men. By sheer steel and sheer courage Enniskillener and Scot were winning their desperate way right through the enemy's squadrons, and already grey horses and redcoats had appeared right at the rear of the second mass, when, with irresistible force, like one bolt from a bow, the 4th Dragoon Guards, riding straight at the right flank of the Russians, and the 5th Dragoon Guards, following close after the Enniskilleners, rushed at the remnants of the first line of the enemy, went through it as though it were made of pasteboard and put them to utter rout.

The Russian horse in less than five minutes after it met our dragoons was flying with all its speed before a force certainly not half its strength. A cheer burst from every lip—in the enthusiasm, officers and men took off their caps and shouted with delight; and thus keeping up the scenic character of their position they clapped their hands again and again. Lord Raglan at once despatched Lieutenant Curzon, aide-de-camp, to convey his congratulations to Brigadier-General Scarlett, and to say 'Well done!' The gallant old officer's face beamed with pleasure when he received the message. 'I beg to thank his lordship very sincerely,' was his reply.

The cavalry did not long pursue their enemy. Their loss was very slight, about thirty-five killed and wounded in both affairs. Our most material loss was from the cannon playing on our Heavy Dragoons and afterwards, when covering the retreat of our Light Cavalry.

Soon after, it appeared that the Quartermaster-General, Brigadier Airey, thinking that the Light Cavalry had not gone far enough in front when the enemy's horse had fled, gave an order in writing to Captain Nolan, 15th Hussars, to take to Lord Lucan, directing his lordship 'to advance' his cavalry nearer to the enemy. A braver soldier than Captain Nolan the army did not possess. A matchless horseman and a first-rate swordsman, God forbid I should cast a shade on the brightness of his honour, but I am bound to state what I am told occurred.

When Lord Lucan received the order from Captain Nolan, and had read it, he asked, we are told, 'Where are we
to advance to?' Captain Nolan pointed with his finger to
the line of the Russians, and said, 'There are the enemy,
and there are the guns,' or words to that effect, according to
the statements made after his death.

Lord Lucan, with reluctance, gave the order to Lord
Cardigan to advance upon the guns, conceiving that his
orders compelled him to do so. The noble Earl, though he
did not shrink, also saw the fearful odds against him. It
is a maxim of war, that 'cavalry never act without a support,' that 'infantry should be close at hand when cavalry
carry guns, as the effect is only instantaneous,' and that it
is necessary to have on the flank of a line of cavalry some
squadrons in column, the attack on the flank being most
dangerous. The only support our Light Cavalry had was the
reserve of Heavy Cavalry at a great distance behind them,
the infantry and guns being far in the rear. There were no
squadrons in column at all, and there was a plain to charge
over before the enemy's guns could be reached, of a mile
and a half in length.

At ten minutes past eleven, our Light Cavalry Brigade
advanced. As they rushed towards the front, the Russians
opened on them from the guns in the redoubt on the right
with volleys of musketry and rifles. They swept proudly
past, glittering in the morning sun in all the pride and
splendour of war. We could scarcely believe the evidence
of our senses. Surely that handful of men were not going
to charge an army in position? Alas! it was but too true—
their desperate valour knew no bounds, and far indeed was
it removed from its so-called better part—discretion. They
advanced in two lines, quickening their pace as they closed
towards the enemy. A more fearful spectacle was never
witnessed than by those who, without the power to aid,
beheld their heroic countrymen rushing to the arms of
death. At the distance of 1,200 yards the whole line of the
enemy belched forth, from thirty iron mouths, a flood of
smoke and flame, through which hissed the deadly balls.
Their flight was marked by instant gaps in our ranks, by
dead men and horses, by steeds flying wounded or riderless across the plain. The first line was broken—it was
joined by the second; they never halted or checked their
speed an instant. With diminished ranks, thinned by those

thirty guns, which the Russians had laid with the most deadly accuracy, with a halo of flashing steel above their heads, and with a cheer which was many a noble fellow's death-cry, they flew into the smoke of the batteries; but ere they were lost from view, the plain was strewed with their bodies and with the carcasses of horses. They were exposed to an oblique fire from the batteries on the hills on both sides, as well as to a direct fire of musketry.

Through the clouds of smoke we could see their sabres flashing as they rode up to the guns and dashed between them, cutting down the gunners as they stood. To our delight we saw them returning, after breaking through a column of Russian infantry and scattering them like chaff, when the flank fire of the battery on the hill swept them down, scattered and broken as they were. At the very moment when they were about to retreat a regiment of Lancers was hurled upon their flank. Colonel Shewell of the 8th Hussars, saw the danger, and rode his few men straight at them, cutting his way through with fearful loss. The other regiments turned and engaged in a desperate encounter. With courage too great almost for credence they were breaking their way through the columns which enveloped them, when there took place an act of atrocity without parallel in the modern warfare of civilized nations. The Russian gunners, when the storm of cavalry passed, returned to their guns, and poured murderous volleys of grape and canister on the mass of struggling men and horses. It was as much as our Heavy Cavalry Brigade could do to cover the retreat of the miserable remnants of that band of heroes as they returned to the place they had so lately quitted in all the pride of life. At thirty-five minutes past eleven not a British soldier except the dead and dying, was left in front of these bloody Muscovite guns.

Captain Nolan, as he rode in advance of the first line, cheering them on, was killed by the first shot fired. Lord Lucan was slightly wounded. Lord Cardigan received a lance thrust through his clothes.

While our affair was going on, the French cavalry made a most brilliant charge at the battery on our left, which was firing on our men, and cut down the gunners; but they could not get off the guns without support and had to retreat. The ground was left covered with our men and with hundreds of Russians and we could see the Cossacks busy

searching the dead. Our infantry made a forward movement towards the redoubts after the cavalry came in, and
the Russian infantry in advance slowly retired towards the
gorge; at the same time the French cavalry pushed forward on their right, and held them in check, pushing out a
line of skirmishers, and forcing them to withdraw their
guns. The Russians, feeling alarmed at our steady advance
and at the symptoms of our intention to turn or cut off
their right, retired from No. 1 redoubt, which was taken
possession of by the allies. At fifteen minutes past eleven,
they abandoned redoubt No. 2, blowing up the magazine;
and, as we still continued to advance, they blew up and
abandoned No. 3, but to our great regret, we were not in
time nor in force to prevent their taking off seven out of
nine guns in these earthworks.

Lord Raglan continued on the hill-side all day, watching
the enemy. It was dark ere he returned to his quarters.
With the last gleam of day we could see the sheen of the
enemy's lances in their old position in the valley; and their
infantry gradually crowned the heights on their left.

On the night of the 25th, when our guns were taken into
Sebastopol, there was joy throughout the city, and it was
announced that the Russians had gained a great victory. A
salvo of artillery was fired, and at nine o'clock P.M., a
tremendous cannonade was opened against all our lines by
the enemy. It did no injury.

Mexico City (1847)

Ulysses S. Grant

*The expansion of the United States to the south-
west in the 1830s and 1840s brought on conflict with
Mexico, which broke into open war when President
James K. Polk ordered General Zachary Taylor and
his troops into disputed territory on the Texas border.
Taylor moved southward into Mexico with considerable success, but in 1847 the United States shifted
its main offensive to a movement from Vera Cruz on
the coast inland to the capital. General Winfield
Scott commanded this invading army.*

*Scott's forces made a remarkable march—several
times defeating Mexican troops—to the outskirts of
the capital itself. There, in September, 1847, the
final battles took place. Accompanying Scott's army
was a peace commissioner, Nicholas P. Trist, who
undertook negotiations with the Mexicans while the
campaign halted. Ultimately, despite difficulties with
General Scott, Trist negotiated the Treaty of
Guadalupe Hidalgo, which brought the war to a
close and gave the United States possession of California and the Southwest.*

*Among Scott's officers and men were many who
later achieved fame in the Civil War, notably Robert
E. Lee and a young lieutenant named Ulysses S.
Grant. Grant recorded his experiences and opinions
in his* Personal Memoirs *almost forty years after
the campaign in Mexico.*

Negotiations were commenced at once and were kept
up vigorously, between Mr. Trist and the commissioners
appointed on the part of Mexico, until the 2d of Septem-

ber. At that time Mr. Trist handed in his ultimatum. Texas
was to be given up absolutely by Mexico, and New Mexico
and California ceded to the United States for a stipulated
sum to be afterwards determined. I do not suppose Mr.
Trist had any discretion whatever in regard to boundaries.
The war was one of conquest, in the interest of an institution, and the probabilities are that private instructions
were for the acquisition of territory out of which new
States might be carved. At all events the Mexicans felt so
outraged at the terms proposed that they commenced preparations for defence, without giving notice of the termina-
tion of the armistice. The terms of the truce had been
violated before, when teams had been sent into the city to
bring out supplies for the army. The first train entering the
city was very severely threatened by a mob. This, however,
was apologized for by the authorities and all responsibility
for it denied; and thereafter, to avoid exciting the Mexican
people and soldiery, our teams with their escorts were sent
in at night, when the troops were in barracks and the citizens in bed. The circumstance was overlooked and negotiations continued. As soon as the news reached General
Scott of the second violation of the armistice, about the
4th of September, he wrote a vigorous note to President
Santa Anna, calling his attention to it, and, receiving an
unsatisfactory reply, declared the armistice at an end.

General Scott, with Worth's division, was now occupying Tacubaya, a village some four miles south-west of the
City of Mexico, and extending from the base up the moun-
tain-side for the distance of half a mile. More than a mile
west, and also a little above the plain, stands Molino del
Rey. The mill is a long stone structure, one story high and
several hundred feet in length. At the period of which I
speak General Scott supposed a portion of the mill to be
used as a foundry for the casting of guns. This, however,
proved to be a mistake. It was valuable to the Mexicans
because of the quantity of grain it contained. The building
is flat roofed, and a line of sand-bags over the outer walls
rendered the top quite a formidable defence for infantry.
Chapultepec is a mound springing up from the plain to the
height of probably three hundred feet, and almost in a
direct line between Molino del Rey and the western part of
the city. It was fortified both on the top and on the rocky
and precipitous sides.

The City of Mexico is supplied with water by two aqueducts, resting on strong stone arches. One of these aqueducts draws its supply of water from a mountain stream coming into it at or near Molino del Rey, and runs north close to the west base of Chapultepec; thence along the centre of a wide road, until it reaches the road running east into the city by the Garita San Cosme; from which point the aqueduct and road both run east to the city. The second aqueduct starts from the east base of Chapultepec, where it is fed by a spring, and runs northeast to the city. This aqueduct, like the other, runs in the middle of a broad road-way, thus leaving a space on each side. The arches supporting the aqueduct afforded protection for advancing troops as well as to those engaged defensively. At points on the San Cosme road parapets were thrown across, with an embrasure for a single piece of artillery in each. At the point where both road and aqueduct turn at right angles from north to east, there was not only one of these parapets supplied by one gun and infantry supports, but the houses to the north of the San Cosme road, facing south and commanding a view of the road back to Chapultepec, were covered with infantry, protected by parapets made of sand-bags. The roads leading to garitas (the gates) San Cosme and Belen, by which these aqueducts enter the city, were strongly intrenched. Deep, wide ditches, filled with water, lined the sides of both roads. Such were the defences of the City of Mexico in September, 1847, on the routes over which General Scott entered.

Prior to the Mexican war General Scott had been very partial to General Worth—indeed he continued so up to the close of hostilities—but, for some reason, Worth had become estranged from his chief. Scott evidently took this coldness somewhat to heart. He did not retaliate, however, but on the contrary showed every disposition to appease his subordinate. It was understood at the time that he gave Worth authority to plan and execute the battle of Molino del Rey without dictation or interference from any one, for the very purpose of restoring their former relations. The effort failed, and the two generals remained ever after cold and indifferent towards each other, if not actually hostile.

The battle of Molino del Rey was fought on the 8th of

September. The night of the 7th, Worth sent for his brigade and regimental commanders, with their staffs, to come to his quarters to receive instructions for the morrow. These orders contemplated a movement up to within striking distance of the Mills before daylight. The engineers had reconnoitred the ground as well as possible, and had acquired all the information necessary to base proper orders both for approach and attack.

By daylight on the morning of the 8th, the troops to be engaged at Molino were all at the places designated. The ground in front of the Mills, to the south was commanded by the artillery from the summit of Chapultepec as well as by the lighter batteries at hand; but a charge was made, and soon all was over. Worth's troops entered the Mills by every door, and the enemy beat a hasty retreat back to Chapultepec. Had this victory been followed up promptly, no doubt Americans and Mexicans would have gone over the defences of Chapultepec so near together that the place would have fallen into our hands without further loss. The defenders of the works could not have fired upon us without endangering their own men. This was not done, and five days later more valuable lives were sacrificed to carry works which had been so nearly in our possession on the 8th. I do not criticise the failure to capture Chapultepec at this time. The result that followed the first assault could not possibly have been foreseen, and to profit by the unexpected advantage, the commanding general must have been on the spot and given the necessary instructions at the moment, or the troops must have kept on without orders. It is always, however, in order to follow a retreating foe, unless stopped or otherwise directed. The loss on our side at Molino del Rey was severe for the numbers engaged. It was especially so among commissioned officers.

I was with the earliest of the troops to enter the Mills. In passing through to the north side, looking towards Chapultepec, I happened to notice that there were armed Mexicans still on top of the building, only a few feet from many of our men. Not seeing any stairway or ladder reaching to the top of the building, I took a few soldiers, and had a cart that happened to be standing near brought up, and, placing the shafts against the wall and chocking the wheels so that the cart could not back, used the shafts as a sort of ladder extending to within three or four feet of the top. By this I climbed to the roof of the building, followed by a few men, but found a private soldier had preceded me by some other way. There were still quite a number of Mexicans on the roof, among them a major and five or six officers of lower grades, who had not succeeded in getting away before our troops occupied the building. They still had their arms, while the soldier before mentioned was walking as sentry, guarding the prisoners he had *surrounded*, all by himself. I halted the sentinel, received the swords from the commissioned officers, and proceeded, with the assistance of the soldiers now with me, to disable the muskets by striking them against the edge of the wall, and throw them to the ground below.

Molino del Rey was now captured, and the troops engaged, with the exception of an appropriate guard over the captured position and property, were marched back to their quarters in Tacubaya. The engagement did not last many minutes, but the killed and wounded were numerous for the number of troops engaged.

During the night of the 11th batteries were established which could play upon the fortifications of Chapultepec. The bombardment commenced early on the morning of the 12th, but there was no further engagement during this day than that of the artillery. General Scott assigned the capture of Chapultepec to General Pillow, but did not leave the details to his judgment. Two assaulting columns, two hundred and fifty men each, composed of volunteers for the occasion, were formed. They were commanded by Captains McKinzie and Casey respectively. The assault was successful, but bloody.

In later years, if not at the time, the battles of Molino del Rey and Chapultepec have seemed to me to have been wholly unnecessary. When the assaults upon the garitas of San Cosme and Belen were determined upon, the road running east to the former gate could have been reached easily, without an engagement, by moving along south of the Mills until west of them sufficiently far to be out of range, thence north to the road above mentioned; or, if desirable to keep the two attacking columns nearer together, the troops could have been turned east so as to come on the aqueduct road out of range of the guns from Chapultepec. In like manner, the troops designated to act against Belen could have kept east of Chapultepec, out of range, and come on to the aqueduct, also out of range of Chapultepec. Molino del Rey and Chapultepec would both have been necessarily evacuated if this course had been pursued, for they would have been turned.

General Quitman, a volunteer from the State of Mississippi, who stood well with the army both as a soldier and as a man, commanded the column acting against Belen. General Worth commanded the column against San Cosme. When Chapultepec fell the advance commenced along the two aqueduct roads. I was on the road to San Cosme, and witnessed most that took place on that route. When opposition was encountered our troops sheltered themselves by keeping under the arches supporting the aqueduct, advancing an arch at a time. We encountered no serious obstruction until within gun-shot of the point where the road we were on intersects that running east to the city, the point where the aqueduct turns at a right angle. I have described the defences of this position before. There were but three commissioned officers besides myself, that I can now call to mind, with the advance when the above position was reached. One of these officers was a Lieutenant Semmes, of the Marine Corps. I think Captain Gore, and Lieutenant Judah, of the 4th Infantry, were the others. Our progress was stopped for the time by the single piece of artillery at the angle of the roads and the infantry occupying the house-tops back from it.

West of the road from where we were, stood a house occupying the south-west angle made by the San Cosme road and the road we were moving upon. A stone wall ran from the house along each of these roads for a considerable distance and thence back until it joined, enclosing quite a yard about the house. I watched my opportunity and skipped across the road and behind the south wall. Proceeding cautiously to the west corner of the enclosure, I peeped around and seeing nobody, continued, still cautiously, until the road running east and west was reached. I then returned to the troops, and called for volunteers. All that were close to me, or that heard me, about a dozen, offered their services. Commanding them to carry their arms at a trail, I watched our opportunity and got them across the road and under cover of the wall beyond, before the enemy had a shot at us. Our men under cover of the arches kept a close watch on the intrenchments that crossed our path and the house-tops beyond, and whenever a head showed itself above the parapets they would fire at it. Our crossing was thus made practicable without loss.

When we reached a safe position I instructed my little command again to carry their arms at a trail, not to fire at the enemy until they were ordered, and to move very cautiously following me until the San Cosme road was reached; we would then be on the flank of the men serving the gun on the road, and with no obstruction between us and them. When we reached the south-west corner of the enclosure before described, I saw some United States troops pushing north through a shallow ditch near by, who had come up since my reconnaissance. This was the company of Captain Horace Brooks, of the artillery, acting as infantry. I explained to Brooks briefly what I had discovered and what I was about to do. He said, as I knew the ground and he did not, I might go on and he would follow. As soon as we got on the road leading to the city the troops serving the gun on the parapet retreated, and those on the house-tops near by followed; our men went after them in such close pursuit—the troops we had left under the arches joining—that a second line across the road, about half-way between the first and the garita, was carried. No reinforcements had yet come up except Brooks's company, and the position we had taken was too advanced to be held by so small a force. It was given up, but retaken later in the day, with some loss.

Worth's command gradually advanced to the front now open to it. Later in the day in reconnoitring I found a church off to the south of the road, which looked to me as if the belfry would command the ground back of the garita San Cosme. I got an officer of the voltigeurs, with a mountain howitzer and men to work it, to go with me. The road being in possession of the enemy, we had to take the field to the south to reach the church. This took us over several ditches breast deep in water and grown up with water plants. These ditches, however, were not over eight or ten feet in width. The howitzer was taken to pieces and carried by the men to its destination. When I knocked for admission a priest came to the door, who, while extremely polite, declined to admit us. With the little Spanish then at my command, I explained to him that he might save property by opening the door, and he certainly would save

himself from becoming a prisoner, for a time at least; and
besides, I intended to go in whether he consented or not.
He began to see his duty in the same light that I did, and
opened the door, though he did not look as if it gave him
special pleasure to do so. The gun was carried to the belfry
and put together. We were not more than two or three
hundred yards from San Cosme. The shots from our little
gun dropped in upon the enemy and created great confusion. Why they did not send out a small party and capture
us, I do not know. We had no infantry or other defences
besides our one gun.

The effect of this gun upon the troops about the gate of
the city was so marked that General Worth saw it from his
position. He was so pleased that he sent a staff officer,
Lieutenant Pemberton—later Lieutenant-General commanding the defences of Vicksburg—to bring me to him.
He expressed his gratification at the services the howitzer in the church steeple was doing, saying that every shot
was effective, and ordered a captain of voltigeurs to report
to me with another howitzer to be placed along with the
one already rendering so much service. I could not tell the
General that there was not room enough in the steeple for
another gun, because he probably would have looked
upon such a statement as a contradiction from a second
lieutenant. I took the captain with me, but did not use his
gun.

The night of the 13th of September was spent by the
troops under General Worth in the houses near San
Cosme, and in line confronting the general line of the
enemy across to Belen. The troops that I was with were in
the houses north of the road leading into the city, and were
engaged during the night in cutting passage-ways from one
house to another towards the town. During the night Santa
Anna, with his army—except the deserters—left the city.
He liberated all the convicts confined in the town, hoping,
no doubt, that they would inflict upon us some injury before daylight; but several hours after Santa Anna was out
of the way, the city authorities sent a delegation to General Scott to ask—if not demand—an armistice, respecting
church property, the rights of citizens and the supremacy
of the city government in the management of municipal
affairs. General Scott declined to trammel himself with
conditions, but gave assurances that those who chose to

remain within our lines would be protected so long as they behaved themselves properly.

General Quitman had advanced along his line very successfully on the 13th, so that at night his command occupied nearly the same position at Belen that Worth's troops did about San Cosme. After the interview above related between General Scott and the city council, orders were issued for the cautious entry of both columns in the morning. The troops under Worth were to stop at the Alameda, a park near the west end of the city. Quitman was to go directly to the Plaza, and take possession of the Palace—a mass of buildings on the east side in which Congress has its sessions, the national courts are held, the public offices are all located, the President resides, and much room is left for museums, receptions, etc. This is the building generally designated as the "Halls of the Montezumas."

IV
FIGHTS FOR FREEDOM

AYACUCHO
NEW ORLEANS

Ayacucho (1824)

William Miller

The great Spanish Empire in the New World,
founded by men like Columbus, Cortes, and Pizarro,
spread over most of South America and the southern
part of North America. By the early nineteenth century, it had been weakened, and the American and
French revolutions, followed by the Napoleonic wars
(which included occupation of Spain by French
armies), broke it down. Sections of the empire declared their independence and organized republican
governments.

After the defeat of Napoleon, the Spanish king-
dom attempted to restore its control in America. The
revolutionary forces resisted under leaders such as
José de San Martín of Argentina, who crossed the
Andes to help secure Chile and Peru, Bernardo
O'Higgins in Chile, and Simón Bolívar in northern
South America. The struggle was long, and the
battle of Ayacucho, December 9, 1824, is usually
regarded as the final blow. Ayacucho is on a plateau
in southern Peru. The revolutionary forces, politically
Bolívar's, were under the command of Antonio
José de Sucre; the Spanish, or royalist, army, under
the viceroy Antonio de la Serna.

A number of foreigners, especially Englishmen and
Irishmen, served with the revolutionary armies and
navies, either for pay or for the cause of liberty.
Among them was William Miller, from whose
memoirs, as recorded by his brother, this account of
the battle is taken.

Quinua, an Indian village, is on the western extremity of

the plain of Ayacucho, the shape of which is nearly square, about a league in circumference, and flanked right and left by deep, rugged ravines. In the rear of the plain, or towards the west, is a gradual descent of two leagues to the main road from Guamanga to Guanta, which runs along the base of a mountain range, that rises like a wall with no apparent outlet. The eastern boundary of the plain is formed by the abrupt and rugged ridge of Condorkanki, which gigantic bulwark, running north and south, overlooks the field of Ayacucho. A little below the summit of this ridge was perched the royalist army.

The liberating army was drawn up on the plain, in front of the Spaniards, at an interval of about a mile, having Quinua in the rear, each corps being formed in close column, to await the attack of the royalists.

During the night of the 8th, a brisk fire was maintained between the royalist and patriot outposts. It was the object of Sucre to prevent the royalists descending in the night. For this purpose the bands of two battalions were sent with a company near to the foot of the ridge, and continued playing for some time whilst a sharp fire was kept up. This feint had the desired effect, for the royalists did not stir from their lines.

The viceroy's position on the night of the 8th was very much exposed; his infantry, occupying the front of the ridge of Condorkanki, was within musket range of the foot of the hill. The fire from two or three battalions, deployed into line, might have obliged the royalists to abandon their position. As it was, a lieutenant-colonel and two or three men, within the Spanish encampment, were killed, as they sat round their fires, by chance balls from the patriot company at the foot of the hill.

The night of the 8th was one of deep and anxious unrest. A battle was inevitable on the following day, and that battle was to decide the destinies of South America. The patriots were aware that they had to contend with twice their own numbers; and that nothing but a decisive victory could save them and their country from ignominious servitude. The patriot soldier might indeed expect to escape with life, reduced to the condition of a slave; but with the patriot generals and officers, it was only a choice between death and victory. They knew full well what would be the cruel policy of the Spaniards if they proved victorious. The viceroy was, it is true, a man of humane disposition, but the individual who counselled Monet to shoot two patriot officers in the pass of San Mateo, and the other man (if such he may be called) who ran his sword through the wounded and defenceless Major Gumer, on the field at Ica, were, with others, of a character equally sanguinary, amongst the advisers of La Serna; and it is extremely probable that unsparing execution would have been resorted to in the hope of destroying the very germ of future insurrection. Every one felt that the approaching battle was to have no common result.

The morning of the 9th dawned particularly fine. At first there was a chillness in the air which seemed to influence the minds of the men, but when the sun rose above the mountain, the effects of its genial warmth became manifest in the renovated spirits of the soldiers. The men on both sides were observed rubbing their hands, and exhibiting every token of content and satisfaction. At nine A.M. the division Villalobos began to descend. The viceroy, on foot, placed himself at its head; and the files wound down the craggy side of Condorkanki, obliquing a little to their left. The division Monet, forming the royalist right, commenced at the same time to defile directly into the plain. The cavalry, leading their horses, made the same movement, though with greater difficulty, between the infantry of each division. As the files arrived on the plain, they formed into column. This was a moment of extraordinary interest. It appeared as though respiration were suspended by feelings of anxiety, mingled with doubts and hope.

It was during this operation, which had an imposing effect, that Sucre rode along his own line, and, addressing a few emphatic words to each corps, recalled to memory its former achievements. He then placed himself in a central point, and, in an inspiring tone of voice, said that upon the efforts of that day depended the fate of South America; then pointing to the descending columns, he assured his men that another day of glory was about to crown their admirable constancy. This animating address of the general produced an electric effect, and was answered by enthusiastic "*vivas*."

By the time that rather more than half the royalist division, Monet and Villalobos, had reached and formed upon the arena, Sucre ordered the division Cordova and two regiments of cavalry to advance to the charge. The gallant Cordova placed himself about fifteen yards in front of his division, formed into four parallel columns with the cavalry in the intervals. Having dismounted, he plunged his sword into the heart of his charger, and turning to the troops, exclaimed, "There lies my last horse; I have now no means of escape, and we must fight it out together!" Then waving his hat above his head, he continued, *"Adelante, con paso de vencedores"* (onwards with the step of conquerors). These words were heard distinctly throughout the columns, which, inspired by the gallant bearing of their leader, moved to the attack in the finest possible order. The Spaniards stood firmly and full of apparent confidence. The viceroy was seen, as were also Monet and Villalobos, at the head of their divisions, superintending the formation of their columns as they reached the plain. The hostile bayonets crossed, and for three or four minutes the two parties struggled together, so as to leave it doubtful which would give way. At this moment the Colombian cavalry, headed by Colonel Silva, charged. This brave officer fell covered with wounds, but the intrepidity of the onset was irresistible. The royalists lost ground, and were driven back with great slaughter. The vice-king climbed the sides of Condorkanki, the patriots, who had deployed, kept up a well-directed fire, and numbers of the enemy were seen to drop and roll down, till their progress was arrested by the brush-wood, or some jutting crag.

Miller, who had followed up Cordova's division, perceiving its complete success, returned to the regiment of Usares de Junin, which fortunately had been left in reserve.

At dawn of day, the royalist division Valdez commenced a detour of nearly a league. Descending the sides of Condorkanki on the north, Valdez had placed himself on the left of the patriots at musket-shot distance, separated by a ravine. At the important moment of the battle, just described, he opened a heavy fire from four field-pieces and a battalion in extended files. By this, he obliged two battalions of the Peruvian division La Mar to fall back. The Colombian battalion Bargas, sent to support the Peruvian division, also began to give way. Two royalist battalions crossed the deep ravine, already spoken of, on the left, and advanced in double quick time in pursuit of the retiring patriots. At this critical juncture, Miller took upon himself to lead the hussars of Junin against the victorious Spaniards, and by a timely charge drove them back, and followed them across the ravine, by which time he was supported by the granaderos a caballo and by the division La Mar, which had rallied. The brave Colonel Plaza crossed the ravine at the head of the legion on the left. Lieutenant-Colonel Moran, at the head of the battalion Bargas, made a similar movement on the right of the cavalry. These two battalions and the cavalry, mutually supporting and rivalling each other in valour, repeated their charges with such resolution, that the division Valdez was broken; its artillery taken; its cavalry obliged to fly in disorder; and its infantry dispersed.

The royalists had now lost the battle, and fled to the ridge from which they had descended, in the morning, with so much confidence.

The action lasted an hour. Fourteen hundred royalists were killed, and seven hundred wounded, and they lost fifteen pieces of artillery.

The loss on the part of the patriots was three hundred and seventy killed, and six hundred and nine wounded.

The single piece of artillery belonging to the patriots did considerable execution on the royalist columns, and was of service also in attracting a heavy fire from their artillery, which if it had been directed upon the patriot columns, would have occasioned the loss to be more considerable.

The plan of the royalists was to wait until Valdez had outflanked the left of Sucre's position, from which having driven him, the whole army was to advance and complete the victory. The mistake of the viceroy in attacking at all, originated in suffering himself to be impelled to it by the eagerness of his troops. Their patience had been worn out by the terrible marches, which appeared to them to be endless. It may be fairly said that they were goaded by their own soldiers into a general action contrary to their own judgment.

The royalists, upon regaining the heights of Condorkanki, rallied as many of their defeated troops as they possibly could. The patriot divisions La Mar and Lara gained the summit of the heights at about one P.M. Before sunset Canterac sued for terms, and an hour afterward rode down to the tent of Sucre, where a capitulation was agreed upon.

The battle of Ayacucho was the most brilliant ever fought in South America. The troops on both sides were in a state of discipline which would have been creditable to the best European armies. The ablest generals and chiefs of either party were present, and it is difficult to say which army most panted for an appeal to the sword, as every man fought with undaunted bravery. What the patriots wanted in numbers was made up by enthusiasm, and by a perfect knowledge that, if beaten, retreat was utterly impracticable. It was not a victory of mere chance, but the result of the most determined valour, and of an irresistible onset, conceived and executed at the proper moment.

New Orleans (1815)

James Roberts

A variety of forces—tensions arising out of the war between Britain and Napoleon, and the difficulties for United States' neutral trade, Indian troubles on the frontier, ambitions for Canada—together with the difficulties of communication across the Atlantic, helped bring on war between the United States and Great Britain in 1812. More than two years of fighting, marked by both serious blunders and heroic feats, resulted in the Treaty of Ghent, December 24, 1814. Practically speaking, the treaty returned the two countries to the situation before the war.

Before the news of the treaty reached the United States, British forces in the Gulf of Mexico attacked New Orleans and were defeated by United States forces, largely militia, under General Andrew Jackson, January 8, 1815. The victory had no effect, therefore, on the settlement; it did, however, strengthen American patriotism and confidence, and helped make Jackson President thirteen years later.

The account is by a Negro slave, James Roberts, conscripted into the American forces. It is quite obviously the recollection of an old man long after the events—and events he may not have altogether understood. The editors do not offer it as an accurate reconstruction of the battle, but as a remarkable human view.

General Jackson, in order to prepare to meet Packenham, the British General, in the contest at New Orleans, came into our section of the country, enlisting soldiers. He came to Calvin Smith's, and made a bargain with him to enlist five hundred negroes. Jackson came into the field, chose out the ones he wanted, and then addressed us thus: "Had you not as soon go into the battle and fight, as to stay here in the cotton-field, dying and never die? If you will go, and the battle is fought and the victory gained on Israel's side, you shall be free." This short speech seemed to us like divine revelation, and it filled our souls with buoyant expectations. Hardships, of whatever kind or however severe, vanished into vapor at the sound of freedom, and I made Jackson this reply: that, in hope of freedom we would "run through a troop and leap over a wall"; that I had as well go there and die for an old sheep as for a lamb. We were taken to Washington, in Louisiana, and drilled. Jackson again told us that we should be free after the battle. Calvin Smith said to Jackson, "encourage your soldiers by telling them they shall be free; then they will fight the more valiantly for freedom." He said to Jackson: "If there are not enough of blacks in place of my sons, go to the Springfield plantation and get as many more. If the negroes should get killed, they are paid for; but if my children should go and get killed, they cannot be replaced." For what man will not think more of his child than he will of a negro? and a negro has got more ambition to fight than a white man. Captain Brown, of Tennessee, said to Smith: "I glory in your spunk; let us have as many negroes as you can spare, for we are sure that those negroes you give us will gain the victory."

Captain Brown mustered and drilled us, taking us through the evolutions: how to wheel to the right and left, from a single file to a double platoon; to march and wheel with the left foot foremost; to charge, cock and fire, ease arms, &c. Being satisfied as to our proficiency in military tactics, we prepared to start to New Orleans.

We took up our march from Natchez, and traveled the whole distance, three hundred miles by land, on foot. Every man had a sack and musket. When we came to the swamps in Louisiana, the water in some places was knee deep, with thick green scum over it, which we had to remove before we could get to the stinking water. At night we made little piles of brush, wood and grass for our beds. Here the mosquitos, gallinippers and the red-belly snakes, at night when we laid down, contested with one another, over our bodies, which should get the greatest share of blood before morning. We had to sleep with one eye, keep awake with the other, in order to keep off the snakes, which we would thrust away a dozen times a night, when they would be crawling over us.

A number of the white Kentuckians died in the swamps from drinking the poisonous water. Jackson addressed them to this effect: It is a pity that you white devils did not stay at your homes. The negroes are no trouble at all. It would have been far better for us to have had no whites, for there is not a day or night passes that we do not have to dig a hole and bury five or six of you. It will be better for us to discharge you all and take you no farther.

In one week after leaving Natchez, we arrived in sight of New Orleans. We marched forward till we came in sight of the British army, and the first view of it was very impressive indeed. The British soldiers wore large, brilliant steel breast-plates, steel caps and steel covers on their arms up to the shoulders. The sun shining on these plates, and on their bright swords and spears, gave an appearance that inspired in me a dread and fear that is not easily described. Jackson said to us: "Don't be discouraged. Take the second look at them; they are but men like yourselves. Courage will overcome your fears and dread." We then marched next to the marsh and formed a single file. Then Jackson and Packenham the British general met and held a consultation. Then each general counted the number of the other's army. Packenham had ten to Jackson's one. Packenham asked Jackson if he was ready for operations. Jackson replied, he had not consulted his mind. Packenham said, I will give you two days to make up your mind.

Now Jackson consulted what was best to be done. In the meantime Packenham drew up his army along the water side, and remained there two days. There was in Jackson's army a colored soldier named Pompey, who gave Jackson the first idea about the *cotton-bag fort,* and superintended the construction of it. We engaged in making it, and it was completed in the latter part of the second day. The cotton-bags were so placed as to leave port holes for three muskets to point through each.

On the third day, Packenham, buoyant with hope and flush with ambition, came towards our camp and demanded an interview with Jackson. The two generals met,

in full view of the two armies, and held a consultation
again. Packenham asked Jackson if he was ready for operations now, who replied that he was, and then asked Packenham how he liked his wooly-headed boys. Packenham
said he had rather fight ten white men to their one, for,
when they begin, there is no rule with them to stop but
death. Then, said Jackson, say the word, and the wool flies.
This day, said the exulting Packenham, I will either eat my
dinner in the city of New Orleans, or in h—l! Poor, ill-
fated man! little did he know that, within two hours from
that moment, he was to fall by the hand of one of the
wooly-headed boys.

Each general returned to his respective army, and in
twenty minutes the British fired. They fired three rounds,
and the fourth we opened up on them. Here they began to
throw shells into our fort, and had they continued to do so
for some time, there is no doubt but victory would have
been easy to them. But Packenham, who headed his army,
impatient to carry everything by main force, doubting
nothing as to his ability to take the fort in a short period,
rushed forward in quick evolutions; and, as they came, we
felled them like grass before the scythe. Platoon after
platoon lay like scattered hail upon the ground. Packenham
seeing this, and observing the rapid loss of his men,
marched them single file up to our fort. He himself
mounted the wall, encouraging his men in the most ener-
getic manner. And here, at this point of the battle he might
have succeeded, had he exercised some discretion. Instead
of ordering the bags to be pushed inside next to us, he
ordered them to be pulled outside, which entangled his
men, and while in that entanglement we slew them by
scores, and piled them by hundreds upon the bags as
they endeavored to climb over them. While this was going
on in the main body of our fort, the left wing of the fort
gave way, which brought us and the British in immediate
contact with the broad-sword, and they fell before us like
grass before the scythe. At this point I lost the forefinger
of my left hand, and received a deep wound on my head
from a British sword. After that I took the fellow's head off,
and five more of his fellow soldiers'. Packenham at that
moment was shot from the wall, and in two minutes the red
flag was hauled down and the white one hoisted, the battle
ceased and victory declared on our side. Jackson, who,

during the battle, had taken a stand at some distance, ordering his men by an aid-de-camp, came up to the line and gave us three cheers, and observing me to be all over bloody, asked me what was the matter with me. I told him not anything, for I had not yet discovered the loss of my finger, nor the wound upon my head. He said, "you have lost one of your fingers and received a deep wound upon your head; go to the hospital and have your wounds dressed." I did so, and returned to him, and asked him to let me go on the side of the British and see the slain. He said, "go where you please; the ground is free to you all, and all yours." I went and saw the slain lying, for one quarter of a mile, as thick as they could lie upon the ground, and I walked shoe deep in blood that distance and back. Some of the poor fellows were dead, some dying, some half dead, some cut in half and still living, and, as I passed by them, they grated their teeth at me, and made efforts to come at me. We were ordered to bury the slain of the British. We dug trenches and pulled them in with our grab-hooks, whether they were dead or still breathing. We were ordered to cover up the devils whether dead or alive, which we did, and tramped them down with our feet, into the blood and water knee deep. We then buried our own dead, putting them into coffins and burying them in the city.

In that battle some sixty or seventy or more of the colored men were killed, of whom no account whatever was ever taken in the details of the war, although they were, without doubt, as Jackson himself acknowledged, the instrumental cause of the victory. Such black ingratitude deserves the deepest reprehension. A savage would have been more grateful. Had we thus fought in the army of the cruel Turks, we should have received that applause which such merit deserved. But this inhuman neglect was left for Jackson's reprehensible duplicity.

Having buried our dead, we returned back to the fort. The British had by this time got a pipe of rum from the city, to preserve the body of Packenham, into which the body was put and headed up.

We formed a line, took our arms, and serenaded the battle-ground. Gabriel Winton, with his two colored boys, conducted the music. One played the fife, and the other the bass drum. One was named Spot, and the other Wot. These

boys excelled, in this department of necessary warfare, any
that were upon that battle-ground. The battle was now
fully closed. Next day morning, we put all our guns away
in the ammunition house, and Jackson ordered them to be
unloaded, to serve a wicked end he had in view, which I
shall presently notice. The next day morning, being the
second day after the battle, we came to get our guns, to
march. We had power to put our guns away, but none to
take them out of the ammunition house. A white man
handed them out to us. We formed a line and marched
down Fourth street, up Porass street, where the ladies
through the windows waved their handkerchiefs and com-
plimented Jackson on his success and victory. Here we
formed a line in the presence of thousands. Jackson came
riding along and said, "Well done, my brave boys, I will
give you the praise; you have fought like bull-dogs, and
wallowed in your blood"; then, addressing the crowd, he
said, "if you ever want a battle fought, get the negro's
ebenezer up, he will run through a troop and leap over a
wall. They are the best nation to fight in existence." Again
turning to his colored soldiers, he said, "Now, behave yourselves well, and go home to your masters." I then said, A
word to you, General, if you please: have you time to
speak a word to me? "What is the word you wish to speak
to me?" I asked him if he did not promise me my freedom,
if that battle was fought and victory gained? He replied, "I
did, but I took your master's word, as he told me. You are
not my property, and I cannot take another man's property and set it free." My answer was, You can use your
influence with our master, and have us set free. He replied
thus: "If I were to hire you my horse, could you sell it
without my leave? You are another man's property, and I
have not money sufficient to buy all of you, and set you
free." At that moment I cocked my gun; but there being
no priming in it, I bit off a piece of cartridge, and, going to
prime it, I for the first time discovered it was not loaded.
Had my gun been loaded, doubtless Jackson would have
been a dead man in a moment. There was no fear in my
soul, at that time, of anything, neither man, death, nor
mortal. The war-blood was up. I had just two days before
cut off the heads of six brave Englishmen, and Jackson's
life, at that moment, appeared no more to me than theirs.
It was well for him that he took the precaution to have our

guns unloaded when in the ammunition house. His guilty
conscience smote him, and told him he was doing us a
great piece of injustice, in promising us, by the most
solemn protestation, that we should be free if the victory
were gained. I would then have shot him dead a thousand
times, if that could have been done. My soul was stirred
in me, and maddened to desperation, to think that we had
placed our lives in such imminent peril, through the per-
suasions of such false-heartedness, and now told to go
back home to our masters!

Jackson asked me if I contended for freedom. I said I
did. He said, "I think you are very presumptuous." I told
him, the time had come for us to claim our rights. He said,
"You promised me that you would fight manfully." I did,
sir, and now is the time for me to claim the benefit of the
promise you made me. I did fight manfully and gained the
victory, now where is my freedom? He replied, as he had
nothing else to reply, "You are a day too late; and if you
are not willing to go home, I will put you in confinement,
and send for your master; he will take you home; you seem
to be the hardest among the whole crew." Some of the
whites standing round said, "He ought to be shot." Now,
just think of that! Two days before, I had, with my fellow
soldiers, saved their city from fire and massacre, and their
wives and children from blood and burning; now, "he
ought to be shot!" simply for contending for my freedom,
which, both my master and Jackson had solemnly before
high heaven promised, before I left home.

Captain Brown, however, who knew something at least
of the value of our services, or in some degree appreciated
them, said, "No, he shall not be shot. You should not have
promised him his liberty," addressing Jackson, "if you did
not intend to fulfil your word. All negroes are not fools,"
said he; "some of them have as good sense as you or I."

I said, as for my part, I have sense enough to know there
has been great falsehood practiced in this whole transac-
tion; and had I had the least anticipation of it, I would
never have come here to put my life in peril for such a
cause.

Captain Brown said, pointing significantly at me, "That
Jim, who is contending for his rights, is no fool. Some of
the negroes you can scare; but there is no scare in him."

Then Jackson said, "We will march to the Kentucky

Tavern, on Water street." Having arrived there, he told the landlord to give us as much liquor as we could drink. The most of them drank heartily and freely, while others drank nothing at all, being sorely oppressed with grief, and saying that they would rather die than go back to the plantation, where misery only awaited them on their return from the glorious battle-field of the country's defence. I told Jackson, when he insisted on my drinking, I was now going back to die in the cotton-field, and that I would not drink a drop. I told him I did not like such base falsehood as was now to be practiced upon us. I was not such a fool as to be paid with a glass of liquor for such meritorious services.

Now Jackson commenced his speech about the negroes. "Never," said he, "suffer negroes to have arms; if you do, they will take the country. Suffer them to have no kind of weapons over ten inches long. Never allow them to have a piece of paper with any writing on it whatever. You must examine your slaves very closely, for the time is coming when the slave will get light; and if ever his mind is enlightened on the subject of freedom, you cannot keep him. One slave bought from the East will ruin a multitude of those raised here. Before a slave of mine should go free, I would put him in a barn and burn him alive. Gentlemen, take me at my word; for if you do not, you will be sorry for it before many years. Never arm another set of colored people. We have fooled them now, but never trust them again; they will not be fooled again with this example before them. If you do, you will repent of it but once. Look," said he, "at Pompey, whom we ordered to be shot on the battle-ground, because he would not stop fighting, even after the battle had ended, till he was shot down. Look, I entreat you, at his indomitable spirit; he had the disposition of the bull-dog."

Such was Jackson's speech in our presence. Why was not this speech published in the history of that war? No mention is made of it whatever. Such monstrous deception and villainy could not, of course, be allowed to disgrace the pages of history, and blacken the character of a man who wanted the applause and approbation of his country. But we here drag it to light, that it may be held up to universal execration by all lovers of right, justice and freedom.

Night now drew on, when we were ordered back to the calaboose, for safe-keeping till morning. Mr. Seymour

Johnson, the keeper of the calaboose, said, "Not so; they have done no crime. My order is, to take them back to the tavern, and board them there till the morning."

Here was another act of intolerable injustice to soldiers just from the field of victory and glory, but now to be incarcerated in a criminal jail!

The next morning the steamer *Walk-in-the-Water* was to leave New Orleans for Natchez, and our passage was engaged on her. We marched down to the boat, followed by an immense crowd of pedestrians, and ladies and gentlemen in carriages. Having arrived at the river, and halted, the ladies made this speech to Jackson:

"GENERAL: It is wrong, decidedly wrong, to treat these men so. You took the martial law into your own hands, for which you was fined a large sum, and which sum we ladies paid for you; and now, we wish for our remuneration—nothing more than the freedom of these men, by your interceding with their masters for them. Will you promise us to do it?"

Jackson replied, "I cannot,"—and the boat started.

When we reached Natchez, Calvin Smith was there ready to receive his hands.

"Well, Jim," said he; "you did not get killed."

"No, sir, I did not."

"Then you can raise more cotton and sugar yet."

I said, "I think I ought to be free."

"I'll give you freedom on your back."

"I am only contending, master, for what you promised me. You ought never to have promised to set me free, if you had no mind to do it. You promised me if I would go down and fight, in the place of your children, I should be free."

"When I get you home I'll give you freedom."

He took me home and delivered me to the overseer, and gave him a letter from Jackson, stating how I had contended with him in New Orleans for my freedom. "Now, therefore, scourge him severely." The overseer asked how many lashes he should give me. "Give one hundred; it will bring him to his feeling." His oldest son Stephen came up and said: "Father, it is wrong; you ought never to have promised it to him. It is wrong to whip him for what you promised to do for him." By that means I got clear of my whipping. Stephen ordered the overseer not to whip me.

The overseer then took my clothes from me, and clothed me, who had just saved the country from destruction, in a breech-clout, and sent me into the field to work.

The next that was sent to the field was Simon, and he would not work at all. "You promised me freedom," said he, "and freedom I'll have or die." The overseer, James Randum, and Simon began to fight. He whipped the overseer, who went to the house and brought the master out. But Simon still cried, "Give me freedom or give me death." They conquered him and killed him dead in the field, and cut joint from joint, and threw the body over into the wood.

V
THE KING GOES
TO WAR

KADESH
AGINCOURT
LÜTZEN

Kadesh (1288 B.C.)

Author Unknown

Ramses II, the Egyptian pharaoh, about 1300 B.C., enlarged his empire, both military and commercial, around the curve of the Mediterranean Sea to the coasts of present-day Israel, Syria, and Lebanon. Egyptians there came in contact with the Hittites, advancing from the north. The two kingdoms came to battle at Kadesh on the Orontes (in northern Syria), about 1280 B.C. Though Ramses' reports treat it as a victory, many later historians are inclined to treat it as a drawn battle, in the sense that expansion of both powers was halted.

The accounts that follow are translations of the hieroglyphic writings on the temple walls at Karnak and Abydos. One is a poetic version, the other an official record, in all probability the work of scribes and priests.

INTRODUCTION

Beginning of the victory of King Usermare-Setepnere (Ramses II), who is given life forever, which he achieved in the land of Kheta and Naharin, in the land of Arvad, in Pedes, in the Derden, in the land of Mesa, in the land of Kelekesh, Carchemish, Kode, the land of Kadesh, in the land of Ekereth and Mesheneth.

PREPARATIONS AND MARCH TO
THE FRONTIER AT THARU

Behold, his majesty prepared his infantry and his chariotry. His majesty proceeded northward, his infantry and

his chariotry being with him. He began the goodly way, to
march. Year 5, the second month of the third season, on
the ninth day, his majesty passed the fortress of Tharu.
Every country trembled before him, fear was in their
hearts; all the rebels came bowing down for fear of the
fame of his majesty, when his [army] came upon the narrow road.

MARCH FROM THARU TO
THE REGION OF KADESH

His majesty proceeded northward, and he then arrived at
the highland of Kadesh. Then his majesty marched before,
like his father, Montu, lord of Thebes, and crossed over the
channel of the Orontes.

THE COALITION OF
THE PRINCE OF KHETA

When his majesty reached the city, behold, the wretched,
vanquished chief of Kheta had come, having gathered together all countries from the ends of the sea to the land of
Kheta, which came entire: the Naharin, likewise, and
Arvad, Mesa, Keshkesh, Kelekesh, Luka, Kezweden, Carchemish, Ekereth, Kode, the entire land of Nuges, Mesheneth and Kadesh. He left not a country which was not
brought, together with their chiefs who were with him,
every man bringing his chariotry, an exceeding great multitude, without its like. They covered the mountains and
the valleys; they were like grasshoppers with their multitudes. He left not silver nor gold in his land but he plundered it of all its possessions and gave to every country, in
order to bring with him to battle.

THE POSITIONS OF THE TWO ARMIES

Behold, the wretched, vanquished chief of Kheta, together with the numerous allied countries, were stationed
in battle array, concealed on the northwest of the city of
Kadesh while his majesty was alone by himself, with his
bodyguard, and the division of Amon was marching behind
him. The division of Re crossed over the river-bed on the
south side of the town of Shabtuna at the distance of an

iter from the division of Amon. The division of Ptah was on the south of the city of Aranami and the division of Sutekh was marching upon the road. His majesty had formed the first rank of all the leaders of his army, while they were on the shore in the land of the Amor. Behold, the wretched vanquished chief of Kheta was stationed in the midst of the infantry which was with him, and he came not out to fight, for fear of his majesty. Then he made to go the people of the chariotry, an exceedingly numerous multitude like the sand, being three people to each chariot. Now, they had made their combinations [thus]: among every three youths was one man of the vanquished of Kheta, equipped with all the weapons of battle. Lo, they had stationed them in battle array, concealed on the northwest, the city of Kadesh.

THE ATTACK OF THE ASIATICS

They came forth from the southern side of Kadesh, and they cut through the division of Re in its middle, while they were marching without knowing and without being drawn up for battle. The infantry and chariotry of his majesty retreated before them. Now, his majesty had halted on the north of the city of Kadesh, on the western side of the Orontes. Then came one to tell it to his majesty.

RAMSES' ATTACK

His majesty shone like his father Montu, when he took the adornments of war; as he seized his coat of mail, he was like Baal in his hour. The great chariot which bore his majesty, called "Victory-in-Thebes," from the great stables of Ramses, was in the midst of the leaders. His majesty halted in the rout, then he charged into the foe, the vanquished of Kheta, being alone by himself and none other with him. When his majesty went to look behind him, he found 2,500 chariotry surrounding him, in his way out, being all the youth of the wretched Kheta, together with its numerous allied countries: from Arvad, from Mesa, from Pedes, from Keshkesh, from Erwenet, from Kezweden, from Aleppo, Eketeri, Kadesh, and Kuka being three men to a chariot acting in unison.

DATE

Year 5, third month of the third season, day 9, under the majesty of Horus: Mighty Bull, Beloved of Truth; King of Upper and Lower Egypt: Usermare-Setepnere; Son of Re; Ramses-Meriamon, given life forever.

CAMP SOUTH OF KADESH

Lo, his majesty was in Zahi on his second victorious campaign. The goodly watch in life, prosperity and health, in the tent of his majesty, was on the highland south of Kadesh.

FALSE MESSAGE OF THE SHASU NEAR SHABTUNA

When his majesty appeared like the rising of Re, he assumed the adornments of his father, Montu. When the king proceeded northward, and his majesty had arrived at the locality south of the town of Shabtuna, there came two Shasu, to speak to his majesty as follows: "Our brethren, who belong to the greatest of the families with the vanquished chief of Kheta, have made us come to his majesty, to say: 'We will be subjects of Pharaoh and we will flee from the vanquished chief of Kheta; for the vanquished chief of Kheta sits in the land Aleppo, on the north of Tunip. He fears because of Pharaoh to come southward.'" Now, these Shasu spake these words, which they spake to his majesty, falsely, for the vanquished chief of Kheta made them come to spy where his majesty was, in order to cause the army of his majesty not to draw up for fighting him, to battle with the vanquished chief of Kheta.

POSITIONS OF THE TWO ARMIES

Lo, the vanquished chief of Kheta came with every chief of every country, their infantry and their chariotry, which he had brought with him by force, and stood, equipped, drawn up in line of battle behind Kadesh the Deceitful, while his majesty knew it not. Then his majesty proceeded northward and arrived on the northwest of Kadesh; and the army of his majesty made camp there.

EXAMINATION OF HITTITE SCOUTS

Then, as his majesty sat upon a throne of gold, there arrived a scout who was in the following of his majesty, and he brought two scouts of the vanquished chief of Kheta. They were conducted into the presence, and his majesty said to them: "What are ye?" They said: "As for us, the vanquished chief of the Kheta has caused that we should come to spy out where his majesty is." Said his majesty to them: "He! Where is he, the vanquished chief of Kheta? Behold, I have heard, saying: 'He is in the land of Aleppo.'" Said they: "See, the vanquished chief of Kheta is stationed, together with many countries, which he has brought with him by force, being every country which is in the districts of the land of Kheta, the land of Naharin, and all Kode. They are equipped with infantry and chariotry, bearing their weapons; more numerous are they than the sand of the shore. See, they are standing, drawn up for battle, behind Kadesh the Deceitful."

THE COUNCIL OF WAR

Then his majesty had the princes called into the presence, and had them hear every word which the two scouts of the vanquished chief of Kheta, who were in the presence, had spoken. Said his majesty to them: "See ye the manner wherewith the chiefs of the peasantry and the officials under whom is the land of Pharaoh have stood, daily, saying to the Pharaoh: 'The vanquished chief of Kheta is in the land of Aleppo, he has fled before his majesty, since hearing that, behold, he came.' So spake they to his majesty daily. But see, I have held a hearing in this very hour, with the two scouts of the vanquished chief of Kheta, to the effect that the vanquished chief of Kheta is coming, together with the numerous countries that are with him, being people and horses, like the multitudes of the sand. They are stationed behind Kadesh the Deceitful. But the governors of the countries and the officials under whose authority is the land of Pharaoh were not able to tell it to us."

Said the princes who were in the presence of his majesty: "It is a great fault, which the governors of the countries and the officials of Pharaoh have committed in not informing that the vanquished chief of Kheta was near the king; and in that they told his report to his majesty daily."

THE DIVISIONS IN THE SOUTH ARE ORDERED UP

Then the vizier was ordered to hasten the army of his majesty, while they were marching on the south of Shabtuna, in order to bring them to the place where his majesty was.

THE ATTACK OF THE ASIATICS

Lo, while his majesty sat talking with the princes, the vanquished chief of Kheta came, and the numerous countries, which were with him, crossed over the channel on the south of Kadesh, and charged into the army of his majesty while they were marching, and not expecting it. Then the infantry and chariotry of his majesty retreated before them, northward to the place where his majesty was. Lo, the foes of the vanquished chief of Kheta surrounded the bodyguard of his majesty, who were by his side.

RAMSES' PERSONAL ATTACK

When his majesty saw them, he was enraged against them, like his father, Montu, lord of Thebes. He seized the adornments of battle, and arrayed himself in his coat of mail. He was like Baal in his hour. Then he betook himself to his horses, and led quickly on being alone by himself. He charged into the foes of the vanquished chief of Kheta, and the numerous countries which were with him. His majesty was like Sutekh, the great in strength, smiting and slaying among them; his majesty hurled them headlong, one upon another into the water of the Orontes.

RAMSES' OWN STATEMENT

"I charged all countries, while I was alone, my infantry and my chariotry having forsaken me. Not one among them stood to turn about. I swear, as Re loves me, as my father, Atum, favors me, that as for every matter which his majesty has stated, I did it in truth, in the presence of my infantry and my chariotry."

Agincourt (1415)

Author Unknown

Henry V of England, in alliance with the French Duke of Burgundy and his supporters, renewed the Hundred Years' War * with France. The two armies met October 25, 1415, near Agincourt. The French had great superiority in numbers, but English tactics and archery won the victory. Later, but as a consequence of the victory, the French king recognized Henry as his heir, and the English and the Burgundians took control of most of France.

The battle forms one of Shakespeare's most stirring episodes in the play Henry V. *The account here is from the narrative originally written in Latin by a priest, who accompanied the English army.*

On the morrow, viz. Friday, the feast of Saints Crispin and Crispinian [*sic*], the XXVth of October, the French at break of day arrayed themselves in battalions, troops and squadrons, and took their position in terrific numbers before us in the said plain named Agincourt, through which lay our road to Calais; and they placed many companies of horse in hundreds, at each side of their van-guard, to break up the line and strength of our archers. The van being a line of infantry, all selected from the nobles and choicest of them, forming a forest of lances, with a great multitude of helmets shining among them, and the horse in the flanks, making a number, by computation, thirty times greater than all ours. But the troops and squadrons composing their rear-guard and wings were all on horse-back, as if prepared for flight rather than for battle, and compared with us were an innumerable multitude. Our King in the

*See the introduction to Crécy.

mean time, after giving praises to God and hearing mass,
disposed himself on the plain not far from his quarters, and
had formed one line of battle, placing the van-guard commanded by the Duke of York, as a wing on the right, and
his rear-guard commanded by the Lord de Camoys, as a
wing on the left, with the archers in the form of a wedge
between the lines, making them fix their poles before
them, as had been before determined, to prevent them
being broken through by the horse; and when the enemy
learnt this by their scouts, either on that account, or from
other fears, God knows, they kept at a distance opposite to
us without approaching. And when a great part of the day
had been spent in delay of this sort, and both armies stood
without moving a foot one against the other, the King determined to advance towards them, seeing that the opposing multitude deferred the charge which he had expected
from them, and stood so across our route as either to break
up our array, or terrify us by their number; or else intended to impede our route, or were expecting more
auxiliaries who might be on their way, or at least knowing
our want of provisions, would conquer by famine those
whom with the sword they dare not attack.

And he ordered the baggage of the army to the rear of
the battle, for fear it should fall into the enemy's hands,
it having been placed, together with the priests who were
about to officiate and pray earnestly for the King and his
men in the before-mentioned villages and closes, with
directions to wait till the end of the battle; for the French
plunderers had already on every side their eyes upon it,
with an intention of attacking it as soon as they saw both
armies engage; and upon the rear of which, where by the
inactivity of the royal vassals the baggage of the King was,
they did fall as soon as the battle began, carry off the royal
treasures, the sword and the crown, with other jewels, and
all the household staff. And when the King thought that
almost all the baggage had arrived in the rear, he moved
towards the enemy, who then advanced; but I who write
this, sitting on horseback among the baggage in the rear of
the battle, and the other priests who were there, did then
and whilst the conflict lasted, humble our souls before
God; and remembering which at that time the Church was
reading, we said in our hearts, 'Remember us, Oh Lord!
Our enemies are gathered together and boast in their

might; shatter their strength, and disperse them, that they may know that there is none other that fighteth for us but only thou our God.' Also with fear and trembling in our eyes, we cried unto heaven, beseeching God to have compassion upon us and the crown of England, and not to suffer the prayers and tears which the English churchmen had poured out, and probably at that hour were pouring out for us in their accustomed processions, to become fruitless; but that he would admit them to the bosom of his graciousness, and not permit our King, devoted to the worship of God, the welfare of the Church, and peace of the realm, to be destroyed by the enemy; but rather in the declared munificence of his mercy, would now and hereafter exalt and mercifully deliver us from these perilous events as from others.

And now coming within reach of the enemy, the horsemen of the French posted along the flanks, began to attack our archers on both sides of the army. But by the will of God, they were quickly compelled amidst showers of darts to retreat, and to fly to the hindermost ranks; with the exception of a very few who ran between the archers and the woods, yet not without slaughter and wounds: yea, with the exception also of a great many, both horses and horsemen, who were arrested in their flight by the stakes and the sharp arrows, so that they could not escape far. But the enemy's cross-bow-men, behind the men-at-arms and on the flanks, after the first but too hasty discharge, in which they hurt very few, retreated, from the fear of our bows. And when the men-at-arms on both sides had nearly reached each other, the flanks of both armies (viz. ours and the adversary's) immerged into the woods on each side. But when the French nobility, who at first approached in full front, had nearly joined battle, either from fear of the arrows, which by their impetuosity pierced through the sides and beavers of their bacinets, or that they might more speedily penetrate our ranks to the banners, they divided themselves into three troops, charging our lines in the three places where the banners were: and intermingling their spears closely, they assaulted our men with so ferocious an impetuosity, that they compelled them to retreat almost at spear's length; and then we who were assigned to clerical warfare, upon beholding it, fell upon our faces in veneration before the throne of God, crying out in bitterness of spirit for God still to remember us and the crown of England, and by the grace of his supreme bounty, to deliver us from this iron furnace and dire death which we had hitherto escaped. Nor did God forget the multitude of the many prayers and supplications offered up in England, through which, it is piously believed, our men quickly regaining strength, and making a brave resistance, repulsed the enemy, until they recovered the lost ground. Then the battle raged very fiercely, and our archers pierced the flanks with their arrows and continually renewed the conflict; and when the arrows were exhausted, seizing up axes, poles, swords, and sharp spears which were lying about, they prostrated, dispersed, and stabbed the enemy. For the mighty and merciful God, who is always wonderful in his works, who would show his mercy to us, and who was pleased that the crown of England should, under our gracious King his soldier and that handful, continue invincible as of old, as soon as the armies were thus joined, and the battle began, increased our strength, which had before been debilitated and wasted for want of victuals, took away our terrors, and gave us a fearless heart. Never had our elders seen the English more daringly and intrepidly, or voluntarily charge their enemies; and the very same just judge who would smite the haughty multitude of the enemy with the bolt of vengeance, cast them away from his face, broke up their power, their bow, buckler, sword, and battle. Nor was it ever seen in former times, or mentioned in chronicles or history, that so many very choice and robust soldiers made so sluggish, so disorderly, so cowardly, or so unmanly a resistance. For they were seized with fear and panic; there were some, even of the more noble of them, as it was reported in the army, who on that day surrendered themselves more than ten times. But no one had leisure to make prisoners of them, and all without distinction of persons, as they were cast down to the ground, were put to death without intermission, either by those who threw them down, or by others that followed after, by what secret judgment of God is not known. For God had smitten them also with another irrecoverable affliction, thus, when some of them in the engagement had been killed, and fell in the front, so great was the undisciplined violence and pressure of the multitude behind, that the living fell over the dead, and others also falling on the living, were slain; so that in three places, where the force and host of our standards were, so great grew the heap of the slain, and of those who were overthrown among them, that our people ascended the heaps, which had increased higher than a man, and butchered the adversaries below with swords, axes, and other weapons. And when at length, in two or three hours, that front battle was perforated and broken up, and the rest were driven to flight, our men began to pull down the heaps, and to separate the living from the dead, proposing to keep the living as slaves, to be ransomed. But behold, immediately (in what wrath of God is not known) there arose a clamour, that the hinder battle of the enemy's cavalry, in incomparable and fresh numbers, was repairing its ranks and array, to come upon us who were so few in numbers, and so wearied. And immediately the prisoners, without regard to persons, excepting the Dukes of Orléans and certain other illustrious individuals who were in the King's retinue, and a very few others, either of his own prisoners, or of others who were following him, fell by the sword, lest they should be ruin to us in the coming battle. But after a little while the adversary's ranks, by the will of God, having felt the sharpness of the arrows, as our King was approaching towards them, left us a field of blood, with waggons and many other carriages filled with victuals, arrows, spears, and bows. And when, it being so ordered by God, their forces had been routed, and the severity of war was at an end, we returned victorious through the heaps and piles of slain: nor could several refrain from grief and tears, that so many soldiers of such distinction and power, should in such a manner on our account, entirely against our will, have sought their own deaths, destroying and spoiling the glory and honor of their own population to no purpose. And if that sight caused compunction and compassion in us who were strangers passing through the country, how much more did it excite mourning and distress in the native inhabitants, as they waited and saw the soldiery of the country destroyed and disarmed in such a manner. And firmly I believe there is not a heart of flesh nor of stone, if it had seen and contemplated the dreadful destruction and bitter wounds of so many Christians, but would have dissolved and melted into tears from grief. Not even had the illustrious or distinguished on our return, any covering whatever, save only in the secret parts of nature, beyond what they received at their very birth.

Oh! that the French nation would come to peace and unity with the English, and turn back from their iniquities and their wicked ways, in which they are led on, having been seduced and bewildered, lest that saying of the prophet should hasten upon them: 'God is a just judge, strong and forbearing. Is he angry every day? unless ye be converted he will brandish his sword; he hath bent his bow and made it ready, and in it he hath prepared vessels of death. And unless they quickly repent, let them feel that which follows: behold he bringeth forth unrighteousness, he hath conceived grief, and hath produced iniquity: he hath opened a pool and dug it, and hath fallen into the pit which he hath made. Let his grief be turned upon his head, and let his iniquity descend upon his own head: for God is a merciful and long-suffering judge; but when he hath exhausted the remedies and mercy of long suffering, he is a severe avenger, and he oftentimes takes away the powers of strong men, who are not righteous.' This is manifest from the multitude of our enemies, all of whom, without distinction, he hath given over to flight, captivity, or the sword, by means of us who struggled for justice in such few numbers. For they had, according to their own reckoning, more than sixty thousand that drew the sword, when our fighting men did not exceed six thousand: and out of their numbers fell the Dukes of Brabant, Barre and Alençon, five Counts, upwards of ninety Barons and standard bearers, whose names are written in the Book of Records; and more than one thousand five hundred Knights, according to their own computation, and between four and five thousand other nobles, being nearly all the nobility of the French chivalry. And there were taken of the remaining number, the Dukes of Orléans and Bourbon; the Counts of Richmond, of Vendosme, and Ewe; also the most mighty soldier Lord Bucicald, Marshal of France, and but few other noblemen. And there was great joy and wonder among our army; for of our numbers, which were so few, there were found slain in the field not more than nine or ten persons, besides the illustrious and most wise Prince, Lord Edward Duke of York, and Lord Michael Earl of Suffolk, a valiant youth, and two lately created Knights, who fell in the battle. But our Duke of Gloucester, Humphrey, the King's younger brother, a valiant Prince, as he dealt out to others, so he received himself, and was grievously wounded in the King's battalion; and no wonder among so many swords, spears, and axes, brandished with such violence; yet soon after his arrival at Calais he recovered, God be praised. England has therefore cause both of joy and grief; reason to rejoice at the victory gained, and the preservation of her men; reason also to grieve from compassion at the destruction and death of Christians.

And after the battle, our King returned where he had rested the night before, and took his march on the morrow towards Calais, through those heaps of patriotism and blood where sunk the power of the French.

Lützen (1632)

Author Unknown

From 1618 to 1648 sporadic war in Bohemia (modern Czechoslovakia) and Germany, with repercussions elsewhere in Europe, destroyed much of those lands and altered the political and religious scene. Together, the struggles are known as the Thirty Years' War. In part they resulted from the division of European Christianity into Catholic and Protestant, in part from the tension between the Hapsburg emperor and the lesser princes of the Holy Roman Empire. The conflicts were encouraged by the national and religious aspirations of France, Denmark, Sweden, and even some forces in Great Britain.

In the 1630s the direct intervention of Sweden, led by King Gustavus Adolphus, began to change the character of the war. Gustavus was the hero of the Lutheran and Protestant parties in Europe, and one of the military geniuses of history. At Lützen in 1632 he met the Imperial forces under Wallenstein (or Waldstein), and lost his life in the battle.

The account that follows is anonymous, printed in London the year after the battle, obviously from an observer and an admirer of the Swedish king.

The King, having mustered his troops, and those of Duke Bernard of Saxon-Weimar about Erfurt, the army received command to advance towards Naumburg.

The King came thither in person on St. Martin's day, and cut in pieces two regiments of Merode that opposed him by the way. He was no sooner arrived at Naumburg, but he received intelligence, that the enemy's forces lay encamped at Leipsick, and Noerspurg, and stretched thence in length, as far as Weissenfels, and that they were intrenched in a place advantageous. Which proceeding of theirs obliged the King to do the like, at Naumburg, and to seek the means to join his army with the Electoral, which then lay about Torgau, consisting of fifteen thousand men, and reinforced with two thousand horse belonging to the Duke of Lüneburg. He sent divers posts to inform them of his coming, and of the courses that were to be taken for their uniting. Walstein and Pappenheim, being lodged between them, and had an eye on them both, and made it their only study to hinder their conjunction. On the fourteenth of November, the scouts of the King brought him word, the enemy had sacked and abandoned the city and castle of Weissenfels, laid plain his trenches, and retired himself towards Lützen, two German miles from Leipsick. The King, hearing this news, resolved no longer to delay the fight; his courage not permitting him to temporize any further, nor to attend the return of his posts sent to the Elector.

That, which confirmed him in this his resolution, was the assurance of certain prisoners brought him by Relinguen, that Pappenheim was gone to Hall, with six regiments. Wherefore, his army had order to march towards the enemy, the fifteenth, three hours before day, and to dare him to a battle. The diligence of the van was such, that it reached the enemy by the second hour after noon, and began the assault. The Imperialists failed not to make head, and a strong resistance. Many charges were given, with advantage, and loss equal, the victory inclining now to this side, then to that, till at length the Swedes gave fire to their small field-pieces, which pierced and broke sundry Imperial companies and forced them to a retreat. The Swedes became masters of the field, and brought to the King a standard taken from the enemy, with this device: *La fortune et l'aigle Romain,* "Fortune and the Roman eagle." Hence some drew this prognostick, that the enemy should, before long, part with the one and the other. A thick mist and the night coming upon them, the Swedes were hindered in the pursuit of the enemy, and the victory.

The King remained in the field, and stood in order of battle all night; having no other shelter than his caroach, resolved to follow close his design, and engage the enemy to a general combat. He communicated his intention to the Dukes of Saxon-Weimar, and other remarkable commanders, who passed away that night near his caroach, having nothing over their heads, but the heavenly arch, nor any thing under them, but trusses of straw laid upon the earth. Their field-furniture they left behind, believing they should return to lodge in Naumburg; but the patience of their General made them with ease pass over these inconveniences. Some of the principal officers endeavored to dissuade the King from giving battle, alleging, that the forces of the enemy were great, his seats advantageous; their own army feeble and wearied with continual marches; and that it was far safer to wait for the arrival of the Saxon, and make so strong an union, as may promise success in the equality of their armies. Their reasons were not received, but crossed by the King with many more solid, derived from the experience of the times past, and the present astonishment of the enemy; from the courage of his soldiers, and his advantages obtained; from the justice of his arms, from the benediction from above, from the absence of Pappenheim, and the discommodities he should be subject to, in that season now waxing bitter, in case he should suffer the enemy to perfect his trenches, which he had already begun in many places: to which he added his reputation, and how important it was to hasten the combat, saying aloud that he would not suffer Walstein to beard him, without calling him to an account, and letting him see, by proof, that he was not to be faulted; that before this he had not seen him with his sword in his hand; that he desired to make trial of his ability in the field, and ferret him out of his burrows.

The commanders, perceiving by the language and tone of the King, that his decree to fight was inevitable, and their opposition fruitless, confirmed their wills by an humble obedience to his, not without reiterated protestations to subscribe themselves his in their own blood, and seal it with the loss of their lives: whereat the King rejoiced extremely; nor could he contain his joy from appearing in his face, but, by his cheerful looks, expressed his inward content, and forthwith called for a new suit of chamois, which he presently put on. Then they presented to him his arms, and the Duke Bernard of Saxon-Weimar, and sundry other princes and officers conjured him, by all things dear and holy, to wear his helmet and cuirass; but they could not win him to it, he objecting the incumbrance, and laying his hand on the musket-bullet still remaining in his shoulder, which to him, made the least weight unsupportable.

The King's design was to begin the combat by the peep of day; but so thick and dark a mist arose, that it confined the eye to a small distance, and rendered any enterprise not only difficult, but dangerous; wherefore the King was constrained to expect till the sun had chased it away, which, till then, had deprived of all sight of the enemy. The interim, according to his custom, he employed in his devotions, and in making the round of his army, to mark the disposition and countenance of his soldiers, and encourage them to fight manfully. Coming to the quarter of the Swedes and Finlanders, he put them in battle-array; and, with a voice and countenance alike cheerful, he thus bespoke them: "My friends and comrades, this is the day that invites you to demonstrate what you are: shew yourselves men of valour, keep your ranks, and fight courageously for yourselves and your King. If this day the bravery of your spirits shine forth, you shall find the heavenly benediction perched on the points of your swords, honour, and a recompence of your valour: on the contrary, if you turn back, and basely and foolishly commit the armed band to the protection of the unarmed foot, you shall find infamy, my disgrace, and your own ruin; and I protest to you, on the word of a king, that not the least piece of you, or of your bones, shall return again into Swedenland."

This exhortation, delivered in a high and piercing tone, won from the Swedes and Finlanders only these general acclamations: That they would approve themselves men of honour; that they had lives only for him, which they were ambitious to preserve in the obtaining of victory and his good graces.

The Swedes being placed in rank and file, the King embattled the Alman regiments, and thus, in a few words, exhorts them: "My friends, officers, and soldiers, I conjure you, by your love to Heaven and me, this day to manifest whose you are: you shall fight not only under me, but with me; my blood and life shall mark you out the way to honour; break not your ranks, but second me with courage.

If you perform this, victory is ours with all her glories, you and your posterity shall enjoy it; if you give back, your lives and liberties have one period."

This speech was answered with an universal shout, and vows reciprocal, that they would make it appear they knew the way to victory, or to death; that the King should receive all satisfaction in their service, and the enemy should acknowledge he had to do with men of honour.

Walstein and his principal officers discovered quickly by his scouts the resolution of the King, and the countenance of his; and thereupon grounded this resolution: That "they must needs come to blows." Walstein was infinitely desirous to avoid the combat; but he was wisely admonished, by some about him, that every step his men made in a retreat would take from their courage, and give it to the enemy, and bring upon his army a panic fear and an utter confusion. He spent that whole night in digging and intrenching, in embattling his army, and planting his artillery in divers places advantageous, the better to sustain the shock of the enemy. Pappenheim was sent for back in post-haste, who was gone to Hall, being very desirous to invest it, not believing that the King would give, or accept of battle, before the forces of Saxony were arrived. In the meantime, the utmost endeavors of Walstein were not wanting to hearten his men; and he laid before them honour, reward, their advantages, their forces, the justice of their cause, which God, the Catholic Church, the Emperor, and the whole empire justified against the violence and usurpation of a stranger: and all this, and more, he uttered in a litter, which his gout would not permit him to forsake.

This was subject to divers interpretation; some believing, that indeed he felt some symptoms of that sickness very familar to him; others maintained this posture to have no good grace on a day of battle, and judged that Walstein was very willing to preserve himself safe and sound, that he might hereafter serve his master and his party: others averred he was much indebted to his gout, which did warrant his retreat without his reproach, necessity commanding the stoutest courage to yield to such an enemy.

On the other side, the King being ready at all points, and his army embattled, he would take no reflection, because he would be an example to his men, and lose no time. Being placed in the head of Steinbock's regiment, he thus spoke with a voice audible: "Now, now is the time, comrades, we must go on undaunted; let us charge, let us charge in the name of God. Jesus, Jesus, Jesus, aid me in fighting this day, and favour my right!"

These words were no sooner pronounced, but he gave spurs to his horse, and, with his head inclined, gave a charge to a battalion of twenty-four companies of cuirassiers, which were esteemed the flower of the Imperial army. Two Swedish regiments had order to second him. The artillery of the King was advanced, and five cannonshot discharged upon the enemy, who answered them with two hundred, which went off with a horrid noise, and lightning, but with small loss to the Swedes, the cannoneers of Walstein not having well taken their aim. But the first shock was fatal to the King, and all the enemy; for though the squadrons, led by so brave a chief, with an unheard-of resolution, gave on, like thunder, on the enemy, and made him recoil; yet one shot, from a pistol, gave him new courage, which pierced the King's arm, and broke the bone. When those next the King saw him bleed, they were amazed, and cried out, "The King is wounded." Which words the King heard with much distaste and repining, fearing it would abate the valour of his men; wherefore, dissembling his grief, with a joyful and undaunted look, he sought to qualify the fear of his soldiers, with these masculine words: "The hurt is slight; comrades, take courage, let us make use of our odds, and return to the charge." The commanders that were about him, with hands lifted up, earnestly besought him to retire; but the apprehension of frightening his men, and his ambition to overcome, prevailed.

The assault being re-begun with vigour and fervour, and the King fighting again in the head of his troops, once more to break those ranks, that were again made up, the loss of blood, and the grief which he felt in the agitation of his body, enfeebled much his spirits and voice, which caused him to whisper these words in the ear of the Duke of Saxon-Lavenburgh: "Convey me hence, for I am dangerously wounded." He had scarcely ended his speech, and turned head to retire, when a cuirassier (marking this retreat) advanced, upon the gallop, from the battalion of the enemy, and discharged his carbine full in the shoulder of the King, with this insulting speech: "And art thou there then? Long it is that I have sought thee." Some imagined, that it was Pappenheim that gave the blow, by reason he had often vaunted, that an ancient prediction was found amongst the records of his family: That a stranger king should die by the hand of a Pappenheim, with divers scars in his body, and mounted on a white horse. And, for this cause (having many scars in his face, and divers other parts of his body stiched up), he reflected on himself, and believed the prophecy should be accomplished by his hand. But this needs no other confutation, than the absence of Pappenheim at the time when the King received his hurt, which was in the very beginning of the assault, before Pappenheim could make one of the adverse party. I may add, that the discretion of this worthy Count would not have suffered him to run into an error so uncivil, as to speak so undecently to a Prince of that eminency.

When the King had received this mortal wound, which pierced him through and through, he fell from his horse, and gave up the ghost, with nothing but "My God," in his mouth. He that made this accursed shot was beaten down with a storm of harquebusados, and sacrificed to the indignation of the Swedes. But while the groom of the King's chamber, and divers others lighted, to raise the body, the charge began again, more furiously than ever: the enemy having taken notice of this blow; and concluding that all was now finished, and that he should have Swedes good cheap. This hindered the King's servants from bearing of his body, and summoned every man to regain the stirrup, and withstand the foe; so that the King could not be defended from receiving another pistol-shot in the head, and being twice run through with a sword: the Imperialists fearing him, even after death, and cowardly suspecting his speedy resurrection. The poor groom of his chamber never forsook him, but breathed his last upon his master's carcase, after the receipt of an infinity of wounds.

But neither the King's death, nor the great odds that the enemy had, being strongly intrenched in divers places, could let the Swedes (maddened with their inestimable loss) from assaulting the Imperialists with an unspeakable fury; insomuch that they compelled the battalion of cuirassiers, which made the left wing, to retire into their trenches, whom they dislodged about noon, and gained seven of their cannon, together with many colours and cornets.

Lieutenant-Colonel Relinguen received command to advance, and, with three hundred horse, to charge four regiments of Crabbats, commanded by Isolani, which made the right wing of the enemy; which he performed with so much bravery and courage, that he twice pierced through them, and brought back three standards, leaving behind one of his own. All his officers were wounded, and he himself, in the second onset, had his arm shot through with a pistol-bullet, which forced him to retire. Isolani, general of the Crabbats, lost his life, with a great number of his men. Eighteen of his companies charged some German regiments that guarded the baggage; but they were stoutly opposed, the combat fierce, the assaults reiterated, the earth dyed crimson, and burthened with carcases; the Crabbats driven back, though not without some disorder of the German horse, recoiled amongst the carts; but this disadvantage the enemy could not espy, by reason of a thick cloud which then arose, and gave the Germans opportunity to rank themselves.

The Imperial commanders, Galas, Merode, and Holok (longing to recover their seat, and cannon lost), took selected bands, fired the four corners of Lützen to blind the Swedes, and keep them from piercing that side, to the succour of their friends. This essay was followed by success, the trench forced by the Imperialists, the seven pieces of cannon lost regained, and some Swedish regiments disordered.

The Duke Bernard of Saxon-Weimar seeing the confusion of his men, and being advertised, by Kinphausen, of the King's death, was extremely incensed; and protesting he had not so base a wish as to survive him, he ran, with his head couched, on the enemy, seconded by the regiments of the Prince of Anhalt and Count Lowenstein. Then the fight became obstinate on both sides, the charges redoubled, the carcases piled up, the pikes broken, and the difference came to be decided by dint of sword. The eye of man, nor that Greater of the world, ever beheld a joust more furious. The Imperialists strove to hold their advantage recovered, and the Swedes to dispossess them of it. The Duke Bernard did wonders that day; thrice, like lightning, shot he through the forces of the enemy; nor could a wound, received on the left arm, cause him to leave the field, before he had constrained the enemy to abandon the cannon and his post.

The winning of this, opened him the way to the conquest of another; for this valiant Prince pressed the Imperialists so hard, that he again disranked them, and compelled them to quit another post, guarded with thirteen cannon. His dexterity in the drilling of his men, in the opening and shutting of his ranks, was such, that they received little or no hurt from the enemy's cannon. The Duke, undaunted, pierced through the clouds of smoke, displaced the enemy, and made himself master likewise of this place, and of the cannon, and drove the enemy to a confused retreat. The slaughter was great, and the Swedes, well blooded, made good use of their advantage, and the disorder of their foes; passing over their bellies, killing all that came in their way, and stopping their ears against all motives for quarter.

The Duke, possessed of this place, and master of the field, between two and three in the afternoon; thinking there was but one post to force, seated by a windmill, and guarded by three Imperial regiments, endeavored to remove them; sending, in the meantime, sundry squadrons to chase the fugitives. But then the fight grew more cruel than ever; for Pappenheim was returned from Hall, and came upon the gallop with certain fresh regiments. His reputation, and his encouragement, gave new spirits to the runaways, and called them to the combat. The Duke, having notice of this, quits this place, new-ranks and encourages his men, and gives Pappenheim a meeting in the midway. All the charges past were nothing, in respect of these latter; Pappenheim employed his utmost cunning and diligence, and shewed himself, in all places, in the head of his troops, to embolden them. On the other side, the Duke Bernard fixed a resolution, either to die or overcome; and the Swedes and Finlanders, enraged for the death of their King, fought like lions, and desperately ran upon the enemy. The artillery advanced, and began to thunder, and to enter divers battalions, and to make legs and arms to fly from one place to another. The smaller shot was also so violent, that the squadrons encountered in the palpable darkness, caused by the smoke, without knowledge of their parties. This furious shock continued two hours, with equal loss to both; victory opening her arms to embrace now one side, then another. Galas, Merode, and Holok, were wounded to death, and a cannon-shot cut off Pappenheim by the middle.

His death, and the loss of divers other commanders, staggered the Imperialists, as much as that of the King's incensed the Swedes. Then the enemy (upon the receipt of a new salute from twenty-four cannon, which pierced their thickest troops) began to fly; and the Swedes pressed and pursued them far within night, which favoured the retreat of the fugitives, and hindered the Swedes from ranging further in the chase. Indeed, they were so tired, that they had neither breath nor force further to follow them. The Imperialists (giving fire to their camp, and part of their baggage) took some the way of Leipsick; others that of Leutmeritz, towards the frontiers of Bohemia; whither it was thought Walstein was gone, having heard of the loss of the battle, to find a safe place of retreat, and to gather together his dispersed troops.

VI
WOMEN AT WAR

ORLÉANS
SARATOGA

Orléans (1429)

Author Unknown

After the death of Henry V, and of the French king, his claim to both thrones was inherited by his son, then only a baby, the later Henry VI of England. Control of France remained in English and Burgundian hands, except for a small territory and population under the dauphin—the son of the late French king.

To the dauphin came Joan (Jeanne) of Arc, the peasant from Domrémy, claiming that her "voices" —saints with a message from God—commanded her to free France and place the dauphin on the throne. She persuaded him to let her make the attempt, beginning with an effort to relieve the city of Orléans, which was besieged by the English.

The account of the relief of Orléans is from a contemporary French record known as the "Manuscript of Orléans." This consists chiefly of a record of Joan's trial in 1431, and of the later rehabilitation proceedings, but it opens with an account of Joan's life and achievements.

A few terms may need explanation. "Pucelle"— maiden—was the name frequently applied to Joan. "Boulevard" was a wide rampart or fortification; our meaning derives from the fact that much later, when the walls of some French cities were torn down, wide avenues were laid out in the open spaces thus provided.

The king, recognizing that she told the truth, put faith in her words and believed that she came from God; and had great hope that she would aid him to recover his kingdom;

and decided to accept her help and to believe her counsel
in all his affairs. . . .

The king, seeing that it was very necessary to send
prompt assistance to those who were besieged in the town
of Orléans, called his Council together, to which he had
also called the said Jeanne, to consider how they could best
help and victual the besieged citizens. This she undertook
to do, if she were given forces. The king took counsel
with his captains, who, seeing the great necessity of the
besieged, the great fortune of the English, who had so far
always succeeded in all their enterprises, and the extremity
in which the affairs of the king and the kingdom then were,
were of opinion that the king should follow the advice of
the Pucelle; this they decided to do. The Sire de Rais and
the Sire de Lore who were appointed to take her there
and accompany her, brought her to Blois, where were
Messires Regnault de Chartres, Archbishop of Rheims and
Chancellor of France, the Bastard of Orléans, La Hire,
Potin, and several other captains, by whom Jeanne and her
company were honourably received; and these advised her
to provide with all diligence whatever was necessary to
victual the town of Orlèans, that is to say, food, waggons,
carts, horses, and such other things as would be necessary.
And while these were being gathered together, the Pucelle
wrote a letter to the King of England, the Duke of Bedford, and other lords and captains of that country, as
follows:

JESUS MARIA

King of England, and you, Duke of Bedford, who
call yourself Regent of the kingdom of France; you,
Guillaume de la Pole, Earl of Suffolk, John, Sire de
Talbot, and you, Thomas, Lord Scales, who call yourself lieutenant of the said Bedford, do right before the
King of Heaven. Hand over to the Pucelle, who is sent
from God the King of Heaven, the keys of all the
towns which you have taken and ravaged in France.
She is come here on God's behalf to restore the blood
royal. She is quite ready to make peace, if you are
willing to do right, that is, to leave France, and to
make amends for the injuries you have done, and to
hand back the monies you have received all the time
that you have been here.

And you, archers, soldiers, gentlemen and others who are now besieging the town of Orléans, get you back in God's Name into your own country. And if you will not do so, then expect to hear from the Pucelle, who will shortly encounter you, to your very great hurt.

King of England, if you do not do so, I am a chieftain of war, and assure you that wherever I find your people in France, I shall fight them and drive them out; and shall make them go, whether they will or no; and if they will not obey, I shall have them put to death. I am sent here by God the King of Heaven to fight them and to drive them out of France. And if they will obey, I will have mercy on them. And do not think that you will stay here any longer, for you do not hold the realm of France from God the King of Heaven, Son of the Virgin Mary. For he who will thus hold it is Charles, the true heir, for God the King of Heaven so desires. And it is revealed to him by the Pucelle that very shortly he will enter Paris with a good company. And if you do not believe the message of God and the Pucelle, I inform you that wherever we find you, we will fight you, and will make so great a to-do (*hay-hay*) there that not for a thousand years has France had one so great. And firmly believe that the King of Heaven will send such strength to the Pucelle that neither you nor your soldiers will be able to repel either her or her forces. And when it comes to blows we shall see who has the better right.

And you, Duke of Bedford, who now besiege Orléans, the Pucelle begs that you will not compel her to destroy you. And if you will do right, you may yet see the French doing the greatest deed which has ever been done for Christendom.

And I beg you, if you desire to make peace, to answer me in the city of Orléans, where we hope to be very shortly; and if you do not do so, you will remember it by reason of your great sufferings.

Written this Tuesday in Holy Week. The preparations being made for the revictualling of the town of Orléans, Jeanne the Pucelle, accompanied by the Bastard of Orléans, the Seigneurs de Rais and de Lore, La Hire, Messire de Baudricourt, who was newly come from Vaucoleurs, and other captains, together with a number of men-at-arms, left Blois in order to bring the food which was ready. She took the road on the side of the Sologne, making her company travel with all speed. When the English, who were in a strong boulevard that they had made at Saint Jean le Blanc, were warned of the arrival of the French, they left the boulevard and took up their positions inside the Augustins, which they had greatly strengthened. The Pucelle, seeing that the enemy had retired, sent all the foodstuffs on ahead, and with all speed had them loaded into boats to cross the river. When this was done, she and all her company also crossed over, and bringing the foodstuffs with them, entered the town, where they were welcomed.

The next day, when Jeanne and the lord and captains saw that the foodstuffs which they had brought would suffice but a very short while, they decided to send again to Blois to my lord the Chancellor, to procure more food and revictual the town. For this purpose they sent the Bastard of Orléans and the Seigneurs de Rais and de Lore together with their men-at-arms, to explain the necessity of the inhabitants of the town, and to say that if it was not succoured immediately they would be compelled to surrender to the enemy. And Jeanne the Pucelle stayed in the town with the rest of the captains and the men-at-arms, to give courage to the citizens and to help them defend the town if the enemy tried to take it by assault.

After this explanation had been made by the Bastard, de Rais and de Lore, to my lord the Chancellor and other members of the king's Council who were present there, they ordered a great quantity of food to be gathered, which was done with all speed, and decided that it should be taken by the La Beauce route.

And as soon as everything was ready, the Bastard and the Seigneurs de Rais and de Lore, together with as many men-at-arms as they could gather together, left Blois and took the road on the side of La Beauce, as had been decided. Bringing the food with them, they spent the night at a point half way between Blois and Orléans; and the next morning early they marched towards a little place near Orléans. The Pucelle, warned of their approach, made ready all the captains and soldiers in the town, and immediately left, and ordered her forces so cleverly that she and they passed in front of the enemy, who did not leave their forts. Thus they passed by without any interference, and joined those who were bringing in the foodstuffs. And when they had joined forces, and it seemed to them that they were sufficiently strong, they marched towards the town with the food, [again] passing in front of the forts, and entered the town without any interference.

Here one must understand that on the La Beauce side the English had constructed two strong forts, one of which they had named London, because it was the biggest and strongest; the other was smaller, which they had called Saint Leu. And on the Sologne side they had built two others, one at the end of the bridge and the other at the Augustins, together with a boulevard which they had constructed at Saint Jean le Blanc.

The next morning Jeanne the Pucelle put on her armour and had the lords, captains, and men-at-arms do the same, and was the first to leave the town to assault the fort Saint Leu; and when the English who were in the big fort saw the heavy assault made against their men, they sallied from their fort to help them, but were so strongly driven back by the French that they were forced to retire into the fort. Whereupon the French assaulted again so fiercely that the fort was very soon taken, and all those who were in it killed or taken. The Pucelle immediately had the fort demolished, and with her troops returned to the town.

Both the following day and several days afterwards the lords and captains assembled on various occasions, and took secret counsel as to whether they should assault the other fort called London. The Pucelle was not invited to these meetings. And in the end they decided that they should make an assault on the fort, thinking that those on the Sologne side would cross the river to go to the help of those in the London fort and leave their own forts undefended, and that a very small number of men could easily take the forts on the Sologne side. Having taken this decision, they asked the Pucelle if it seemed wise to her to assault the fort.

She answered: 'It seems to you, my lords and captains, that since I am a woman I cannot know how to keep a secret. I tell you that I am aware of all you have decided, and assure you that I shall never tell what ought to be kept secret.'

When they heard this, they came to the conclusion that

the Bastard of Orléans, who was most in her confidence,
should tell her what they had decided on. This he did. And
when the Pucelle had heard their decision she said that she
thought it praiseworthy, if matters came to pass as they
anticipated, but that as she thought they probably would
not turn out so, she was not of their opinion. The lords and
captains did not dare to carry out their plan contrary to her
wish, considering that she had always brought to a successful conclusion everything that she had undertaken. Wherefore they asked her what they ought to do, to which she
replied that it seemed to her that they should attack the
forts which were on the other side of the river in the fau-
bourg of Saint Laurent, and it was decided to do so.

Beside the town walls were a large number of boats,
which she filled with all the men-at-arms, and she and they
together crossed over to the other side of the river. As
quickly as possible she arrayed them in order, to attack one
of the forts, and marched them against the one which was
at the bridgehead. Then, trusting in God, she made a fierce
assault upon it. The enemy defended it very strongly, and
the assault lasted until about an hour before sunset.

The Pucelle, seeing the great resistance made by the
enemy, ordered the retreat, and made them retire towards the boats in which they had crossed. The English,
seeing the French retreat, sallied out of the fort to attack
them. Seeing this, the Pucelle set her forces in order of
battle, and gave them such heart that they compelled the
enemy to draw back into the fort of the Augustins, which
she attacked so fiercely that although it was very strong
and well furnished with both artillery and men, she took
it by assault. The enemy were forced to flee from the
bridgehead, where there was a very strong stone tower.
This done she set a night watch, and with her troops
stayed in the Augustins and the surrounding neighbourhood.

The following morning she set her forces in order,
and told them that it was time to attack the enemy, as-
suring them that the time was come when they should be
defeated and driven out of the kingdom of France. This
instilled great courage into the French, and they attacked
the fort which was very strongly defended by the enemy.
Notwithstanding this, the French did not lessen their

assault, but continued, trusting in the Pucelle's word, she being in the forefront throughout. And although she was wounded in the leg by the bolt from a cross-bow, or as some say in the shoulder, she did not show herself to be wounded nor leave the action, but instilled such courage into her men that they leaped down after her into the moat, and using ladders climbed up onto the walls, forced an entry and took the place by assault. From four to five hundred of the English were killed there, amongst them three of their captains, the Seigneur de Moulins, John de Pommays and William Glasdale, who were in command of the siege on that side; the rest of the English were all taken prisoner. The English who were on the other side of the river saw the assault clearly, but were unable to give any assistance.

The place being taken, the Pucelle and her forces returned to the town by means of the bridge, as she had predicted the previous day when she left the town. After this victory, the inhabitants began to sing *Te Deum Laudamus*, ringing all the church bells, and made merry with much noise throughout the night. And, seeing the great danger they were in, the enemy evacuated the other fort early next morning and set off as fast as possible for Meung. Thus was the siege raised, to the great shame, loss and confusion of the English, and the great honour and glory of the king, his friends and his subjects.

The siege being raised, the Pucelle begged the king to gather together as many soldiers as he could, in order to recover the towns and villages which the enemy held round about Orléans. The king therefore ordered the Duke of Alençon to come to him with all the forces he could muster, which the duke did with all speed. And with him came many lords and men-at-arms, who, although many of them had received no pay from the king, nevertheless came to see the Pucelle who was said to be sent by God, and to make war with her against the enemy.

The troops being assembled, they marched directly upon Jargeau and besieged it. Within a week it was taken by assault through the advice and labours of the Pucelle.

And there the Earl of Suffolk and the Seigneur de la Pole were taken prisoner, and their brother was killed, together with a great number of the English.

Four or five days later, the captains and their men left Jargeau and went to Meung, where they took by assault the bridge and the tower which guarded it. In the tower they left a guard, and as quickly as possible made their way to Beaugency. When the English were apprised of the approach of the French, they abandoned the town, retiring into the castle, and two days later they surrendered it by agreement.

EDITOR'S NOTE

The relief of Orléans was the beginning of Joan's military career. In a series of victories she drove the English and Burgundians back. The coronation of the dauphin at Rheims as Charles VII was the sign of her success. Her tragedy followed. She was wounded, captured, and tried by a Church court on charges of treason. Under pressure, she confessed but later repudiated the confession, was condemned and burnt at Rouen in 1431. This made her a martyr to the French. The spirit she aroused enabled them to drive the English out. A later Church proceeding declared the verdict illegal and unjust. Joan became one of the great heroines of history, the subject of poems, plays, and biographies in many languages, and the inspiration of French patriotism.

Saratoga (1777)

Baroness von Riedesel

Most treatments of the American Revolution have accepted the view that the turning point was the surrender at Saratoga, October 17, 1777, not only for its military significance, but as the main force persuading the French government to sign the alliance with the rebellious British colonies.

Burgoyne's expedition down the Hudson River Valley from Canada was supposed to coordinate with Howe's movements from Philadelphia and divide the colonies north and south. Had the division succeeded, the future of the Revolution would have been slight. In fact the coordination did not take place, and Burgoyne's troops met with Stark and his Vermonters at Bennington and then with the main Continental force under Horatio Gates and Benedict Arnold (then still a loyal, courageous, and most competent general).

This account is by the Baroness von Riedesel, wife of one of the generals of the German troops with Burgoyne—usually called Hessians because many came from the principality of Hesse. The Baroness accompanied her husband on the march, and affords a picture of the battle from behind the lines.

To us today, the presence of wives with an army seems strange, but in those days gentlemen tended to look on the war as little more than a colonial expedition. They would travel with their wives, children, and servants, at a safe distance behind the lines, of course. They never expected to lose battles to the colonial upstarts, but when they did, the wives were

*more involved in the battle than they ever expected
to be.*

We had been warned to keep extremely quiet, fires were
left burning everywhere, and many tents were left standing, so that the enemy would think the camp was still
there. Thus we drove on all through the night. Little
Frederika was very much frightened, often starting to
cry, and I had to hold my handkerchief over her mouth
to prevent our being discovered.

At six o'clock in the morning we stopped, to the amazement of all. General Burgoyne ordered the cannons to be
lined up and counted, which vexed everyone because only
a few more good marches and we would have been in
safety. My husband was completely exhausted and during this halt sat in my calash, where my maids had to
make room for him and where he slept about three
hours with his head on my shoulder. In the meantime
Captain Willoe brought me his wallet with banknotes, and
Captain Geismar brought me his beautiful watch, a ring,
and a well-filled purse and asked me to take care of these
things for them. I promised to do my utmost. Finally the
order was given to march on, but we had hardly gone an
hour when we stopped again, because we caught sight of
the enemy. There were about two hundred men who had
come out to reconnoiter and could easily have been taken
prisoners by our troops if General Burgoyne had not lost
his head. It was pouring; Lady Aciand had had her tent
put up. I urged her again to go to her husband, to whom
she could have been of so much help in his present condition. She finally listened to my reasoning and through General Burgoyne's adjutant, Lord Petersham, requested
permission to go. I told her she had only to insist upon being
allowed to go, and, in the end, the General finally did give
her permission. The English chaplain, Mr. Brudenel, accompanied her, and the two got into a boat with a flag of
truce and sailed across to the enemy (there is a handsome
and well-known etching of this incident). Later on I saw
her again in Albany, where her husband was fully recovered, and they both thanked me for my advice. We spent
the whole of the 9th in a terrible rainstorm, ready to
march on at a moment's notice. The savages had lost courage, and everywhere they were seen retreating. The slightest

setback makes cowards of them, especially if they see no chance of plundering. My maid did nothing but bemoan her plight and tear her hair. I begged her to quiet herself, as otherwise she would be taken for a savage. Hereupon she became still more frantic, and she asked me whether I minded her behavior, and when I answered, "Yes," she tore off her hat, let her hair hang down over her face, and said, "It is easy for you to talk! You have your husband, but we have nothing except the prospect of being killed or of losing all we have." With regard to the latter I consoled her by promising that I would compensate her and the others for anything they might lose. The other maid, my good Lena, although very much afraid, nevertheless said nothing.

Toward evening we finally reached Saratoga, which is only half an hour on the way from the place where we had spent the whole day. I was wet to the skin from the rain and had to remain so throughout the night as there was no place to change into dry clothes. So I sat down before a good fire, took off the children's clothes, and then we lay down together on some straw. I asked General Phillips, who came up to me, why we did not continue our retreat while there was yet time, as my husband had promised to cover our retreat and bring the army through. "Poor woman," he said, "I admire you! Thoroughly drenched as you are, you still have the courage to go on in this weather. If only you were our commanding general! He thinks himself too tired and wants to spend the night here and give us a supper." In fact, Burgoyne liked having a jolly time and spending half the night singing and drinking and amusing himself in the company of the wife of a commissary, who was his mistress and, like him, loved champagne.

On the 10th at seven o'clock in the morning I refreshed myself with a cup of tea, and we now hoped from one moment to the next that we would at last proceed. In order to cover the retreat General Burgoyne ordered fire set to the beautiful houses and mills in Saratoga belonging to General Schuyler. An English officer brought a very good bouillon, which on his urgent entreaties I had to share with him, and after drinking it we continued our march; however, we got only to the next village, not far away. The greatest misery and extreme disorder prevailed in the army. The commissary had forgotten to distribute the food supplies among the troops; there were cattle enough, but not a single one had been slaughtered. More than thirty officers came to me because they could stand the hunger no longer. I had coffee and tea made for them and divided among them all the supplies with which my carriage was always filled; for we had a cook with us who, though an arch-rogue, nevertheless always knew how to get hold of something for us and, as we learned later, often crossed streams at night in order to steal from the farmers sheep, chickens, and pigs, which he sold to us at a good price.

Finally my own supplies were exhausted, and in my desperation at no longer being able to help the others I called to Adjutant-General Petersham, who was just passing by, and, as I was really very much worried, I said to him vehemently: "Come and look at these officers who have been wounded in the common cause and who lack everything they need because they are not getting their due. It is your duty to speak with the General about this." He was very much moved, and, as a result, about a quarter of an hour later General Burgoyne himself came to me and thanked me most pathetically for having reminded him of his duty. He added that a commander is very much to be pitied if he is not properly served and his orders correctly executed. I asked his pardon for having interfered in matters which I well knew were not a woman's business, but said that it had been impossible for me to keep still when I saw how these gallant persons were in need of everything and I, myself, had nothing more to give them. Thereupon he thanked me yet again (although I believe in his heart he never forgave me for this interference) and went to the officers and told them how sorry he was about what had happened; that he had, however, taken care of all by an order; but why, he asked them, had they not come to him for food, as his kitchen was at their disposal at all times? They replied that English officers were not accustomed to visiting the kitchens of their general, and that they had taken each morsel from me with pleasure, being convinced that I had given it to them from the heart. Thereupon he gave strict orders that the provisions be properly distributed. This only delayed us still further and availed us nothing. The General resumed his place at the table, and our calashes were harnessed and made ready for departure. The whole army was in favor of making a retreat, and my husband said it could be done, if only we lost no time. General Burgoyne, however, who had been promised an order if he succeeded in joining General Howe's army, could not make up his mind to leave and lost everything by tarrying.

Toward two o'clock in the afternoon we heard cannon and musketry again, and alarm and confusion prevailed. My husband sent me word to get immediately to a house which was not far away. I got into the calash with my children, and just as we came up to the house I saw five or six men on the other side of the Hudson, who were aiming their guns at us. Almost involuntarily I thrust my children onto the floor of the calash and threw myself over them. The same instant the fellows fired and shattered the arm of a poor English soldier behind me, who had already been wounded and was retiring into the house. Immediately after our arrival a terrifying cannonade began, which was directed principally at the house where we sought shelter, presumably because the enemy, seeing so many people fleeing thither, got the idea that the generals themselves were there. But, alas, the house contained only the wounded and women! We were finally forced to seek refuge in the cellar, where I found a place for myself and the children in a corner near the door. My children lay on the floor with their heads in my lap. And thus we spent the whole night. The horrible smell in the cellar, the weeping of the children, and, even worse, my own fear prevented me from closing my eyes.

Next morning the cannonade went on again, but from the other side. I suggested that everyone leave the cellar for a while so that I could have it cleaned, because otherwise we would all become sick. My suggestion was carried out, and I got many to help, which was highly necessary for this extensive task; the women and children, afraid to go outside, had polluted the entire cellar. When everybody had gone out, I examined our place of refuge; there were three fine cellars with well-vaulted ceilings. I suggested that the most seriously wounded men be put into one cellar, the women in another, and all the others in the third, which was nearest to the door. I had everything swept thoroughly and fumigated with vinegar, when, just as everyone was about to take his place, renewed, terrific cannon fire created another alarm. Many who had no right to enter threw themselves against the door. My children had already gone down the cellar steps, and we would all have been crushed if God had not given me the strength to keep the crowd back by standing in front of the door with outspread arms; otherwise surely someone would have been injured. Eleven cannon balls flew through the house, and we could distinctly hear them rolling about over our heads. One of the poor soldiers who lay on a table, and was just about to have his leg amputated, had the other leg shot off by one of these balls. His comrades had run away from him, and when they returned they found him scarcely breathing, lying in a corner of the room, where he had rolled himself in his agony. I was more dead than alive, not so much on account of our own danger as for the danger that hung over my husband, who kept inquiring how we were and sending me word that he was all right.

Major Harnage's wife, Mrs. Reynell, who had already lost her husband, the wife of the good lieutenant who had been so kind as to share his bouillon with me the previous day, the wife of the commissary, and myself were the only ladies with the army. We were just sitting together and bewailing our fate when someone entered, whispered something to the others, and they all looked at each other sadly. I noticed this and that all eyes were upon me, although nobody said anything. This brought the horrible thought to my mind that my husband had been killed. I screamed; they assured me, however, that such was not the case but indicated with a nod that it was the poor lieutenant's wife to whom this misfortune had befallen. She was called outside a few moments later. Her husband was not yet dead, but a cannon ball had torn his arm away at the shoulder. We heard his moaning all through the night, doubly gruesome as the sound re-echoed through the cellar; the poor fellow died toward morning. However, we spent this night just as we had the previous one. In the meantime my husband visited me, which lightened my anxiety and gave me renewed courage.

Next morning we started putting things in better order. Major Harnage and his wife and Mrs. Reynell made a room for themselves in one corner by partitioning it off with curtains. They wanted to fix up another corner for me just like it, but I preferred staying near the door so that in case of fire I would be able to get out as quickly as possible. I had some straw put down, laid my bedclothes on it, and slept there with the children, with my serving women not far away. Opposite us there were three English officers who had been wounded, but who were determined, in case of retreat, not to stay behind. One of them was a Captain Green, aide to General Phillips, a very estimable and polite man. All three assured me on oath that in case of a hasty retreat they would not forsake me, but that each of them would take one of my children with him on his horse. One of my husband's horses stood saddled and ready for me all the time. My husband often wanted to send me to the Americans, in order to put me out of danger, but I told him it would be worse than anything I had had to bear heretofore to be with people to whom I should have to be polite while my husband was fighting them. He promised me, therefore, that I could continue to follow the army. Many a time in the night, however, I was seized with the fear that he had marched away, and I crept out of my cellar to see; when I saw the troops lying by the fire, as the nights had already grown cold, I was able to sleep more tranquilly again. The things which had been entrusted to me for safekeeping also worried me. I had put them all in the front of my corset because I was constantly afraid of losing part of them, and I made up my mind never again to take such a responsibility upon myself. On the third day I found the first opportunity and a moment to change my underclothing when the courtesy of a small corner was allowed me. Meanwhile, my three above-mentioned officers stood sentry not far off. One of these gentlemen could imitate most realistically the mooing of a cow and the bleating of a calf. Whenever my little daughter Frederika cried at night, he made these sounds for her, and she would become quiet again immediately, at which we all had to laugh.

Our cook brought us food, but we had no water, and I was often obliged to quench my thirst with wine and even had to give the children some. Moreover, it was almost the only drink my husband would take. This finally began to worry our faithful Rockel, who said to me one day, "I fear that the General drinks all this wine because he is afraid of being taken prisoner, and that he is tired of living." The constant danger which surrounded my husband kept me in continuous anxiety. I was the only one among all the women whose husband had not been either killed or at

least wounded, and I often said to myself, "Should I be the
only lucky one?"—particularly as my husband was in such
great danger day and night. He did not spend a single night
in the tent, but lay outside by the sentry's fire all night
long. That, alone, was enough to cause his death, as the
nights were so damp and cold.

Because we were badly in need of water, we finally
found the wife of one of the soldiers who was brave
enough to go to the river to fetch some. This was a thing
nobody wanted to risk doing, because the enemy shot every man in the head who went near the river. However,
they did not hurt the woman out of respect for her sex, as
they told us themselves afterwards.

I tried to divert my mind by busying myself with our
wounded. I made tea and coffee for them, for which I
received a thousand blessings. Often I shared my dinner
with them. One day a Canadian officer came into the cellar, so weak that he could hardly stand up. We finally got
it out of him that he was almost starved to death. I was
very happy to be able to give him my own dinner, which
gave him renewed strength and won me his friendship.
When we returned to Canada later on, I became acquainted
with his family.

One of the worst things we had to bear was the odor
which came from the wounds when they began to fester. At
one time I was nursing a Major Bloomfield, aide to General
Phillips, who had a bullet shot through both cheeks, smash-
ing his teeth and grazing his tongue. He could not keep anything in his mouth; the pus almost choked him, and he
could not take any nourishment at all except a little bouillon or other liquid. We had some Rhine wine. I gave him a
bottle, hoping that the acid would cleanse his wounds. He
took a little of it in his mouth, and this alone had such a
fortunate effect that his wounds healed entirely, and I
gained another friend. Thus even in these hours of suffering
and sorrow I had moments of pleasure which made me
very happy.

On one of these unhappy days General Phillips wanted
to visit me and accompanied my husband, who came to me
once or twice every day at the risk of his life. He saw our
plight and heard me beg my husband not to leave me behind in case of a hasty retreat. He took my part when he
saw how I hated the thought of being left with the Ameri-

cans. When he left me he said to my husband, "No! I would not come here again for ten thousand guineas, for my heart is absolutely broken."

On the other hand, not all the men who were with us deserved pity. Some of them were cowards who had no reason whatever for staying in the cellar, and who later when we were taken prisoners, were well able to stand up in line and march. We were in this dreadful situation six days. Finally there was talk of capitulation, as by delaying too long our retreat was now cut off. A cessation of hostilities took place and my husband, who was completely exhausted, could sleep in bed in the house for the first time in a long while. In order that he would be absolutely undisturbed I had a good bed made for him in a small room and slept with my children and the maids in a large hall close by. At about nine o'clock in the morning someone came and wanted to speak to my husband. With the greatest reluctance I found it necessary to wake him. I noticed that he was not pleased about the message he received and that he immediately sent the man to headquarters and lay down again, much annoyed. Shortly afterwards General Burgoyne sent for all the other generals and staff officers to attend a council of war early in the morning, during which he suggested, on the basis of a false report, that the capitulation which had already been made to the enemy be broken. However, it was finally decided that this would be neither practicable nor advisable, and that was a lucky decision for us, because the Americans told us later that, had we broken the capitulation, we would all have been massacred, which would have been an easy matter, because there were only four to five thousand of us, and we had given them time to get more than twenty thousand of their men together.

On October 16 my husband had to go back on duty, and I had to return to my cellar. That day the officers, who until then had received only salted meat, which was very bad for the wounded, were given a lot of fresh meat. The good woman who always got the water for us cooked a tasty soup with it. I had lost all appetite and had eaten nothing the whole time except a crust of bread dipped in wine. The wounded officers, my companions in misfortune, cut off the best piece of beef and presented it to me with a plate of soup. I told them it was impossible for me to eat anything. Seeing, however, how much in need of nourishment I was, they declared that they would not eat a bite themselves until I had given them the pleasure of joining them. I could no longer resist their friendly pleading, whereupon they assured me that it made them most happy to be able to share with me the first good food they had received.

On October 17 the capitulation went into effect. The generals went to the American Commanding General, General Gates, and the troops laid down their arms and surrendered themselves as prisoners of war. The good woman who had fetched water for us at the risk of her life now got her reward. Everyone threw a handful of money into her apron, and she received altogether more than twenty guineas. In moments like this the heart seems to overflow in gratitude.

At last my husband sent a groom to me with the message that I should come to him with our children. I got into my beloved calash again, and while driving through the American camp I was comforted to notice that nobody glanced at us insultingly, that they all bowed to me, and some of them even looked with pity to see a woman with small children there. I confess that I was afraid to go to the enemy, as it was an entirely new experience for me.

VII

IN THE FACE OF GREAT ODDS

CHÂTEAU-THIERRY AND
BELLEAU WOOD
MALTA

Château-Thierry and Belleau Wood (1918)

Floyd Gibbons

In the spring of 1918, the German army under Hindenburg and Ludendorff launched their last powerful offensive on the Western Front of World War I. Internal troubles and the entrance of the United States into the war made them feel the need for decisive and rapid action, while the Bolshevik revolution and consequent breakdown of Russian war efforts gave them added strength.

The German drive, along the northern French front, but especially in the area of the Aisne and Marne rivers, drove back the Allied forces, and brought into action the first substantial contingents of United States troops, especially Marines. In late May and early June, they held the line, centering at Château-Thierry on the Marne. It was the first full-scale American experience with the developments of modern warfare as 1914–18 knew them—the heavy artillery barrage, the machine gun, and (largely the result of the machine gun) trench warfare.

The account is by Floyd Gibbons, one of the noted newspaper (and later radio) correspondents of the earlier twentieth century. It is from a book, published in 1918, while the war was still in progress, and is based largely on his dispatches from the front.

CHÂTEAU-THIERRY

I have endeavored to show in preceding chapters the development of the young American army in France from a mere handful of new troops up to the creation of units capable of independent action on the front. Only that intense and thorough training made it possible for our overseas forces to play the veteran part they did play in the great Second Battle of the Marne.

The battle developed as a third phase of the enemy's Western Front offensives of the year. The increasing strength of the American forces overseas forced Germany to put forth her utmost efforts in the forlorn hope of gaining a decision on the field before the Allied lines could have the advantage of America's weight.

On March 21st, the Germans launched their first powerful offensive on a front of fifty miles from Arras to Noyon in Picardy.

Some idea of the terrific strength of the enemy offensive may be gained from a recapitulation which would show that in five days the Germans pushed through five successive lines of Allied defence, and penetrated more than twenty-five miles. On the first day, they captured the Chemin des Dames, on the second day, they overcame all resistance on the Aisne, on the third day, their forces, pushing southward, crossed the Vesle River, on the fourth day, they destroyed the lines of resistance along the Ourcq, on the fifth day, they reached the Marne.

It was a crisis. The battle front formed a vast triangle with the apex pointing southward toward Paris. The west side of the triangle extended fifty miles northward from the Marne to the Oise near Noyon. The east side of the triangle ran north-eastward thirty miles to Rheims. The point of this new thrust at Paris rested on the north bank of the Marne at Château-Thierry. The enemy had advanced to within forty miles of the capital of France; the fate of the Allied world hung in the balance.

Undoubtedly I am prejudiced, but I like to feel that I know the real reason why the German hordes stopped at

Château-Thierry on the north bank of the Marne. To me that reason will always be this—because on the south bank of the Marne stood the Americans.

On that day and in that event there materialised the German fears which had urged them on to such great speed and violence. In the eleventh hour, there at the peak of the German thrust, there at the climax of Germany's triumphant advances, there at the point where a military decision for the enemy seemed almost within grasp, there and then the American soldier stepped into the breech to save the democracy of the world.

The Marne River makes a loop at this place and Château-Thierry lies on both banks. The Marne there is called a river, but it would hardly come up to the American understanding of the word. The waterway is more like a canal with banks built up with stone blocks. There are streets on either bank, and these being the principal streets of the town, are bordered with comparatively high buildings.

While the Germans were on the outskirts of the city, American forces had made brilliant counter attacks on both sides. To the west of Château-Thierry the German advance forces had been hurled back by our young troops. To the east of Château-Thierry the enemy had succeeded in crossing the Marne in the vicinity of Jaulgonne.

This operation was carried out by the German 36th Division. On the night of May 30th, at a point where the Marne looped northward eight miles to the east of Château-Thierry, the enemy succeeded in putting a few men across the river.

Almost at the same time, the French defenders at this place received re-enforcements from the Americans. These incompletely trained American units abandoned their bayonet-stabbing of gunny sacks and make-believe warfare to rush forward into the real thing.

On June 2nd, these Americans, under command of French officers, began the counter attack to sweep the Germans back from the south bank. By that time the enemy had succeeded in putting twenty-two light bridges across the Marne and had established a strong bridgehead position with a number of machine guns and a strong force of men in the railway station on the south bank of the river opposite Jaulgonne.

This position was attacked frontally by the Americans and French. Our novices in battle were guilty of numerous so-called strategical blunders, but in the main purpose of killing the enemy, they proved irresistible. The Germans broke and ran. At the same time, the French artillery lowered a terrific barrage on the bridges crossing the river, with the result that many of the fleeing enemy were killed and more drowned. Only thirty or forty escaped by swimming. One hundred of them threw down their arms and surrendered. The remainder of the battalion was wiped out. At the close of the engagement the Americans and the French were in full command of the south bank.

But it was in Château-Thierry itself that the Germans made their most determined effort to cross the river and get a footing on the south bank, and it was there, again, that their efforts were frustrated by our forces. On May 31st, American machine gun units, then in training seventy-five kilometres south of the Marne, were hurriedly bundled into motor lorries and rushed northward into Château-Thierry.

The Germans were advancing their patrols into the north side of the city. They were pouring down the streets in large numbers, with the evident purpose of crossing the bridges and establishing themselves on the south bank.

It was four o'clock in the afternoon of May 31st that those American machine gunners got their first glimpse of real war. That night while the German artillery raked the south bank of the river with high explosive shells, those Americans, shouldering their machine guns, marched into the city and took up defensive positions on the south bank of the river.

During the night many houses were turned into ruins. Shells striking the railroad station had caused it to burn. In the red glare our men saw the houses about them collapse under clouds of dust and debris. Under cover of darkness the Germans filtered through the street on the north side of the river. The American machine gunners went into position in the windows of houses on the south bank and in gardens between the houses, and from these positions it was possible to command all of the bridge approaches and streets leading to the river on the opposite side.

During the night, Lieutenant John T. Bissell, a young

Pittsburgher but recently graduated from West Point, started across one of the bridges and reached the north bank with a squad of a dozen men and two machine guns. This little unit went into position in a place commanding the forked highways which converged not far from the northern approach of the iron bridge crossing the river. It was this unit's function to prevent the enemy advance from this direction. The unit was separated from its comrades on the south bank by the river and about two hundred yards. In spite of the fact that the enemy artillery intensified its shelling of the south bank, the American machine gunners remained at their posts without firing and played a waiting game.

With the coming of dawn the Germans began to make their rushes for the bridges. Small compact forces would dart forward carrying light machine guns and ammunition with them. They encountered a terrific burst of American fire and wilted in front of it. Those that survived crawled back to the shelter of protecting walls, where they were re-enforced with fresh units, and again the massed formations charged down the streets toward the bridges. The slaughter of Germans increased until the approaches were dotted with bodies of the enemy slain.

On June 1st, the Germans having consolidated positions on the hills commanding the city from the north, they directed a terrific artillery and machine gun fire into our exposed positions on the south bank, as well as the small posts held on the north bank by Lieutenant Bissell and his machine gunners. Although the position held by the little American group had long been considered untenable, the members of it stuck it out until nightfall, when they received orders to retire to the south bank. At the same time, French colonials which had held a position throughout the day on the north bank on the edge of the town, withdrew in accordance with the same plan. The retirement of both parties was covered by our machine gunners on the south bank, who poured a hot fire into the evacuated areas as the Germans began occupying them.

By ten thirty that night the completion of the movement was signalised by a terrific explosion, as the French colonials blew up one of the stone bridges over which they had withdrawn. But the destruction of the bridge had cut off the little band of Americans and left them almost surrounded by the enemy on the north bank of the river, which was now becoming strongly populated by the enemy. Through the darkness could be heard the sound of shuffling, hobnailed boots, and even above the crack of the guns there came the weird swish of the grey coats as they pushed forward in mass formations.

The little party of thirteen Americans dismantled their guns and, with each man carrying his allotted piece, they began working their way along the river bank toward the main bridge, where they discovered that the enemy was almost upon them. They immediately went into position behind the stone parapet on the very brink of the river, and although in constant danger from the American fire that poured out from the south bank, they poured streams of lead point-blank into the advancing German ranks.

The Americans on the south bank were not aware of the plight of the little party on the north bank. In spite of their losses, the Germans continued their gruesome rushes toward the approaches of the iron bridge across which our machine gunners were pouring a devastating fire. Lieutenant Bissell and his men made one effort to cross the bridge, but were forced to crawl back to shelter on the north bank, carrying with them three of their wounded. They found themselves between a cross-fire. Then Bissell, alone, approached as near as he dared, and the first intimation that the Americans on the south bank had of the fact that Americans were in front of them was when Lieutenant Cobey heard Bissell's voice calling his name. A cease fire order was immediately given and Bissell and his men rushed across the bridge, carrying their wounded with them.

On the following day the Germans were in occupation of all the houses facing the north bank of the river, and could be seen from time to time darting from one shelter to another. Throughout the day their artillery maintained a terrific downpour of shells on the positions held by our men on the south bank. So intense was the rifle fire and activity of snipers, that it meant death to appear in the open. The Americans manned their guns throughout the day, but refrained from indulging in machine gun fire because it was not desired to reveal the locations of the guns. Nightfall approached with a quiet that was deadly ominous of impending events.

At nine o'clock the enemy formations lunged forward to the attack. Their dense masses charged down the streets leading toward the river. They sang as they advanced. The orders, as revealed in documents captured later, came straight from the high command and demanded the acquisition of a foothold on the south bank at all costs. They paid the costs, but never reached the south bank.

The American machine gun fire was withering. Time after time, in the frequent rushes throughout the night, the remnants of enemy masses would reach sometimes as far as the centre of the big bridge, but none of them succeeded in reaching the south bank. The bridge became carpeted with German dead and wounded. They lay thick in the open streets near the approaches. By morning their dead were piled high on the bridge and subsequent rushes endeavored to advance over the bodies of their fallen comrades. In this battle of the bridges and the streets, our men showed a courage and determination which aroused the admiration of the French officers, who were aware by this time that forty-eight hours before these same American soldiers had seen battle for the first time.

Our machine gunners turned the northern bank of the river into a No Man's Land. Their vigilance was unrelenting and every enemy attempt to elude it met with disaster. There were serious American casualties during that terrific fire, but they were nothing in comparison with the thousand or more German dead that dotted the streets and clogged the runways of the big bridge in piles. The last night of the fight enormous charges of explosive were placed beneath the bridge and discharged.

The bridge was destroyed. High into the air were blown bits of stone, steel, timber, debris, wreckage and the bodies of German dead, all to fall back into the river and go bobbing up and down in the waters of the Marne.

Thus did the Americans save the day at Château-Thierry.

BELLEAU WOOD

It was at five o'clock on the bright afternoon of June 6th that the United States Marines began to carve their way into history in the battle of the Bois de Belleau. Major General Harbord, former Chief of Staff to General Pershing, was in command of the Marine brigade. Orders were received for a general advance on the brigade front. The main objectives were the eastern edge of the Bois de Belleau and the towns of Bussiares, Torcy and Bouresches.

Owing to the difficulty of liaison in the thickets of the wood, and because of the almost impossible task of directing it in conjunction with the advancing lines, the artillery preparation for the attack was necessarily brief. At five o'clock to the dot the Marines moved out from the woods in perfect order, and started across the wheat fields in four long waves. It was a beautiful sight, these men of ours going across those flat fields toward the tree clusters beyond which the Germans poured a murderous machine gun fire.

The woods were impregnated with nests of machine guns, but our advance proved irresistible. Many of our men fell, but those that survived pushed on through the woods, bayoneting right and left and firing as they charged. So sweeping was the advance that in some places small isolated units of our men found themselves with Germans both before and behind them.

The enemy put up a stubborn resistance on the left, and it was not until later in the evening that this part of the line reached the northeast edge of the woods, after it had completely surrounded a most populous machine gun nest which was located on a rocky hill.

In the dense woods the Germans showed their mastery of machine gun manipulation and the method of infiltration by which they would place strong units in our rear and pour in a deadly fire. Many of these guns were located on rocky ridges, from which they could fire to all points. These Marines worked with reckless courage against heavy odds, and the Germans exacted a heavy toll for every machine gun that was captured or disabled, but the Marine advance continued.

Their losses were heavy, but they did the work. The sacrifice was necessary. Paris was in danger. The Marines constituted the thin line between the enemy and Paris. The Marines not only held that line—they pushed it forward.

The fighting was terrific. In one battalion alone the casualties numbered sixty-four per cent. officers and sixty-four per cent. men. Several companies came out of the fighting under command of their first sergeants, all of the officers having been killed or wounded.

I witnessed some of that fighting. I was with the Marines at the opening of the battle. I never saw men charge to their death with finer spirit. I am sorry that wounds prevented me from witnessing the victorious conclusion of the engagement. In view of my subsequent absence from the fight, I wish to give credit and thanks at this place to Major Frank E. Evans, who, as Adjutant of the 6th Regiment of Marines, provided me with much of the foregoing material which occurred while I was in the hospital.

The bravery of that Marine brigade in the Bois de Belleau fight will ever remain a bright chapter in the records of the American Army. For the performance of deeds of exceptional valour, more than a hundred Marines were awarded Distinguished Service Crosses.

Since the days I read Hugo's chapters on the Battle of Waterloo in *Les Miserables,* I always considered as an ideal of fighting capacity and the military spirit of sacrifice the old sergeant of Napoleon's Old Guard. Hugo made me vividly see that old sergeant standing on a field with a meagre remnant of the Old Guard gathered around him. Unable to resist further, but unwilling to accept surrender, he and his followers faced the British cannon. The British, respecting this admirable demonstration of courage, ceased firing and called out to them, "Brave Frenchmen, surrender."

The old sergeant, who was about to die, refused to accept this offer of his life from the enemy. Into the very muzzles of the British cannon the sergeant hurled back the offer of his life with one word, that word was the vilest epithet in the French language. The cannons roared and the old sergeant and his survivors died with the word on their lips. Hugo wisely devoted an entire chapter to that single word.

But I have a new ideal to-day. I found it in the Bois de Belleau. A small platoon line of Marines lay on their faces and bellies under the trees at the edge of a wheat field. Two hundred yards across that flat field the enemy was located in trees. I peered into the trees but could see nothing, yet I knew that every leaf in the foliage screened scores of German machine guns that swept the field with lead. The bullets nipped the tops of the young wheat and ripped the bark from the trunks of the trees three feet from the ground on which the Marines lay. The minute for the Marine advance was approaching. An old gunnery sergeant commanded the platoon in the absence of the lieutenant, who had been shot and was out of the fight. This old sergeant was a Marine veteran. His cheeks were bronzed with the wind and sun of the seven seas. The service bar across his left breast showed that he had fought in the Philippines, in Santo Domingo, at the walls of Peking, and in the streets of Vera Cruz. I make no apologies for his language. Even if Hugo were not my precedent, I would make no apologies. To me his words were classic, if not sacred.

As the minute for the advance arrived, he arose from the trees first and jumped out into the exposed edge of that field that ran with lead, across which he and his men were to charge. Then he turned to give the charge order to the men of his platoon—his mates—the men he loved. He said:

"COME ON, YOU SONS-O'-BITCHES! DO YOU WANT TO LIVE FOREVER?"

Malta (1565)

Francesco Balbi de Correggio

Long after the conclusion of what most people today think of as the Crusades, warfare continued between Moslem and Christian. Particularly in the Mediterranean Sea, the conflict persisted. It was notably bitter between the Ottoman Turkish Empire, which had control of Constantinople (Istanbul) and the eastern Mediterranean after 1453, and the military-religious order known as the Knights of St. John, or Hospitallers, or later the Knights of Rhodes. Driven from the island of Rhodes they took up a new position on the island of Malta, one of the great strategic points of the whole Mediterranean.

Here in 1565 they were besieged by a Turkish fleet and army. The resistance of the Knights on Malta, and the final lifting of the siege, preserved Christian power in the western Mediterranean, and prepared the way for the naval victory of Lepanto in 1571. Though the Turkish Empire retained the eastern Mediterranean and the North African coast, it never again challenged Malta and the powers west of it.

The account of high points of the siege which follow are from the work of Francesco Balbi de Correggio, who fought with the Knights on Malta.

Sunday, 10th June. On Sunday, 10th June, the Grand Master sent munition to Saint Elmo, and, in addition to the usual supplies, sent some missiles which had been recently invented. These consisted of barrel-hoops well covered with caulking tow and well steeped in a cauldron of boiling tar. They were again covered with tow and once more immersed in tar. This process was repeated until they became as thick as a man's leg. During an assault they were set on fire and hurled on the enemy among whom they worked havoc by their flame and smoke.

On this day the Turks bombarded all parts until midday, at which hour they made a reconnoissance in force which amounted to an assault, although not a general one. Both sides fought with great obstinacy. After the reconnoissance the Turks retired with great loss, but, on our side there were some killed and many wounded.

After the Turks had retired the bombardment recommenced and was maintained until the third night watch, at which hour they came on again, but now to assault rather than to reconnoitre because they brought a very large number of ladders. They formed up by the bridge and the Spur of Mas with so much clamour and fury that it was frightful to behold. The darkness of the night was dispelled by the great quantity of fireworks which were hurled from both sides, so much so that we, who were at Saint Michael, could see Saint Elmo most clearly, and the gunners at Saint Angelo and elsewhere could see to lay their guns by the light of the enemy's fire. This assault lasted until dawn, when the Turks retired with the loss of more than one thousand, the greatest number of casualties being caused by our fire-hoops. Our losses were sixty killed, not counting the wounded who were sent over to the Birgu at once. The knights and soldiers of all nationalities had fought with great valour, and not only the knights and soldiers, but even the convicts and hired oarsmen.

Monday, 11th June. On Monday, 11th June, after midday, the enemy, smarting under the heavy losses sustained, commenced to bombard with great fury. Up to now they had been engaged in recovering their dead, and, on our side, we were busy burning ours and sending the wounded to the infirmary, where there were already over two hundred.

Tuesday, 12th June. On Tuesday, 12th June, the enemy confined their offensive to a continuous bombardment of all parts by day and night with their usual fury. Our men in Saint Elmo took cover as best they could but got no rest.

Wednesday, 13th June. On the 13th we were told by a renegade, who had made his escape, that there was great friction between the Pashas and the Janizaries. The Pashas reproached the latter for calling themselves the sons of the sultan, and with their other brave boasts, in spite of which they had not the pluck to take a small fort in ruins against which a bridge had already been placed. The Janizaries replied that, when the customary bombardment had levelled the works they would show that they were worthy of their reputation.

The Turks never ceased from bombarding Saint Elmo day and night, nor to call to arms at all hours, and to reconnoitre in such a manner that their reconnoissances might be called assaults, for, on each occasion, there were many losses on both sides. They did all this to harass the defenders and give them no rest.

Thursday, 14th June. On Thursday, 14th June, the Turks bombarded, day and night, without interruption, and, during the night, they carried a great quantity of earth and brushwood into the ditch; but, much of this brushwood was burnt by our men. Our artillery killed the Aga of the Janizaries who was in their trenches.

Friday, 15th June. On Friday, 15th June, in the morning, the enemy made an assault which lasted four hours, at the end of which they retired with heavy loss, but, not content with this, they made another assault in the afternoon which was kept up until it was dark.

The chiefs in Saint Elmo sent word to the Grand Master to inform him of what had occurred, and to tell him that they were anticipating a general assault on the following day. They also asked him to send re-enforcements of men and supplies of all kinds. His Lordship lost no time in meeting their demands, for, that same night, he sent men to Saint Elmo to replace casualties, and all sorts of munitions for the defence and also provisions.

Saturday, 16th June. On Saturday, 16th June, at dawn, the enemy made a grand assault on all parts. They made so much noise with shouting and the beating of drums, added to the sound of the various musical instruments they use, that it seemed as if the end of the world had come.

The Turks spent the whole of the night preceding this assault collected on the neighbouring high grounds shout-

ing, as they do when they pray, and, two hours before daylight, their priests absolved them from their sins and
exhorted them to fight well and to die for their faith. This
we surmised from what could be heard, because a single
person sang for a while and then all in the camp responded.
This went on until dawn, which was the time they were
waiting for to attack Saint Elmo. There our men were in
readiness to meet the assault which they had anticipated.

When the appointed hour arrived they came to the general assault with fierce determination, but they were met
with no lesser ferocity and determination and with greater
courage and steadiness.

On this occasion both sides experimented with all sorts
of fireworks, with increased destruction to both belliger-
ents.

On this day we suffered more from our own fire than
from the fighting of the Turks. This was due to a fresh
wind from the West, which not only did drive the fire and
smoke of the enemy into the eyes of the defenders so that
they could not see, but also their own fire and smoke, which
made matters worse. This was not the only misfortune
which befell our men, for all the fireworks in the fort
caught fire, and not only were our men deprived of this
means of defence, but many of them were burnt to death.

This assault had lasted seven hours, during which the
enemy attacked many times with fresh men. It then pleased
God that they should retire with a loss of more than one
thousand of their best and most notable men. I was assured by the knights Hernando de Heredia and Juan
Mascon that if the Turks had attacked once more, Saint
Elmo would have been lost on that day, because there was
not one man who could stand from sheer fatigue. The
Christian losses were one hundred and fifty, without counting the wounded, who were many.

Friday, 22nd June. The enemy spent the whole of the night
of the 22nd June in bombarding and in sounding alarms,
all of which indicated that they would assault on the following day. And so it turned out, for, at dawn the Turks
advanced to make their third general assault, and they
came with so great impetus and fury, and they made so
much noise, that it was frightful. This was the most cruel
and most sanguinary assault they had attempted so far.

Not only did the Turks, supported by their guns, attack
by the bridge, but there was not any place in the periphery
of the fort where they did not plant their scaling ladders,
so that, on this day, there was no part where fighting was
not going on with great pertinacity and courage on both
sides, and with heavy loss to each, but, where the contest
was hottest was at the bridge and at the salient of the
bastion of Mas, the Turks trying to penetrate the bul-
warks, and our men to protect our gabions, to which the
enemy had secured ropes in order to pull them down into
the ditch. There were many Turks on this salient on whom
the guns of Saint Angelo fired with great effect.

The attack by the bridge was bravely met with steel,
fire, and stones. That which did most harm on this day
was the fire from the breastwork I have mentioned, because their sharp-shooters killed all our leaders. Our men
took the powder from those who had fallen and reloaded
their guns to fire on the Turks who were at the Post of
Mas.

Finally, to the chagrin of the Turks, they were obliged
to retire after the assault had lasted six hours, with the loss
of about two thousand killed and about twice as many
wounded. They had attacked in full confidence of success,
for it was to have been their final assault.

When the Turks had retired there was not a single officer left in Saint Elmo, and, besides this, five hundred
Christians had been killed. The survivors numbered about
a hundred, mostly wounded, and without munitions or
hope of relief.

That night, the remnants of the garrison, realizing that
relief could not come to them, resigned themselves to their
fate, determined to die in the service of Jesus Christ, and
they comforted each other in their hour of agony. Although half dead from fatigue they never rested that
night, but worked to improve their defences, though they
could not obtain water with which to wet the breastworks.

Saturday, 23rd June. At sunrise, on Saturday, 23rd June,
being the eve of the feast of Saint John the Baptist, the
name-saint and protector of this Order, the Turks began
their last assault. To resist the fury of their attack Saint
Elmo needed a much larger garrison and better defences.
Though few, and without munitions, this handful of heroes

made a brave defence for four hours, at the end of which
the Turks had not entered the fort, nor would they have
done so then had not Medrano, by beat of drum, called a
parley and told the Pasha how few were the men left in
Saint Elmo. The Janizaries were the first to enter the fort
by the high tower. They commenced to throw stones at our
men who were defending their end of the bridge, and they
shouted to the others to enter the fort because there were
none to defend it. At this the Turks rushed in in great
numbers.

Our men being very few, and all wounded and hemmed
in on all sides, could no longer resist, so they retired to the
church in the hope of making a conditional surrender,
but, when they saw that the Turks cut off without pity the
heads of those who surrendered, they rushed to the square
and there sold their lives at a high price. A very few Maltese saved themselves by swimming to the Birgu.

The Turks took Saint Elmo by force in the manner I
have described, after having wasted more than thirty days
in its reduction with the expenditure of eighteen thousand
rounds from their guns and basilisks, and the loss of some
six thousand of their best and most prominent men, including Dragut. At such a price they had not much reason
for rejoicing over their victory.

Saturday, 14th July. On the 14th of July, the enemy bombarded us as usual throughout the day and night, and, on
our side, we did not spare ourselves in doing all we could
to repair our defences, because we had been warned by
renegades that on the following day a general assault
would be made.

Sunday, 15th July. On Sunday, 15th of July, one hour and
a half before daybreak, it became clearly evident that
they were about to assault, because there was a great
commotion in the boats, which numbered over a hundred,
and in which we saw many men embark, and the loading
of fighting material.

When the Turks who had been detailed for the assault
of Saint Michael had assembled at their station, a fire was
lighted at the platform of the Mandra, and this signal was
answered by another fire on the promontory of Saint Elmo.

These must have been the concerted signal to open the attack.

It was now sunrise and the boats could be seen more distinctly. They looked formidable, lined as they were with sacks of wool and cotton, and full of splendid men; a magnificent spectacle were it not so frought with danger.

We afterwards learned that three thousand of the best Turkish troops came in these boats, together with the flower of the men of Dragut and the King of Algiers. There was not a man who did not wear a scarlet tunic; many wore cloth of gold, silver, and crimson damask. They were armed with good muskets of Fez, scimitars of Alexandria and Damascus, fine bows, and they wore rich turbans.

When the Turks saw the fires, which were the signals which sent them to their perdition, their boats got under way, and, when they came nearer, we saw in the leading boats some men who had very long hair, and who wore very large hats, with books in their hands in which they seemed to be reading prayers, but, as is their custom, they were only pretending to consult the augurs which, they said, were good. When they had done this their boats retired, and those advancing to the attack rowed at full speed against the whole front between Bormla and the Post of Don Francisco de Sanoguera, hoping to break the chain. The chain held good, so, in order to land, the attackers were obliged to wade through the water between the chain and the shore, and those who got least wet were waist deep in the water. In spite of this, they advanced to the assault with great spirit and determination, with so much shouting and explosion of firearms as to seem frightful to those not accustomed to their ways.

The first assault of the Turks was against this traverse, where the Spur was very low and levelled by the bombardment, although, at the point of the Spur, there were two earthworks for our protection. Don Jaime went to the traverse with sword and shield, fighting and encouraging his men who, on that day and on all other occasions, behaved like brave men. Although this knight had his face burned by powder he did not retire from his Post.

Meanwhile the Turks mounted the traverse by means of ladders. They had little to climb for it was very low, but a sailor of the galley *Saint Gabriel,* a Provençal called Piron,

defended it valiantly until he was killed. His place was
taken by another Piron, a Genoese of the same galley, and
he also fought most bravely. Here I must mention the
knight Adorno, who not only fought at this traverse but
did wonders at the earthworks as well as on the seashore,
for he was one of the first to go outside.

To add to our disadvantage of small numbers and very
weak defences there came another misfortune. Ciano, one
of our soldiers at this Post was lighting a fireball to throw
on the enemy, when all the others caught fire and Ciano,
together with other soldiers, was burnt. But, to replace the
fireballs of which we had been deprived we had an abundance of stones, and these did more harm to the enemy
than the fireballs could have done.

When Don Francisco de Sanoguera saw that the boats
were making for his Post, fearing that they should enter
by the front, which was very low and greatly damaged by
the bombardment, he mounted the parapet with his sword
and shield. Nicola Rodio, his underclerk, and I followed
Don Francisco and fired our arquebuses at the enemy who
were already at the foot of the battery. The Turks were
already so near, and we so few, that we found it more
expedient to put down our arquebuses and throw stones
because we could thus do the enemy more harm, and more
often.

When the Turks saw Don Francisco, although a small
man, they recognized him as a person of distinction by his
armour and his coloured garments, and, when they were
still in their boats, they aimed at him. He was hit by a
shot from an arquebuse, but, as his breast-piece was bullet-
proof, he was unharmed; unfortunately, soon after, a
Janizary who wore a large black cap with gold ornaments,
and who, kneeling at the foot of the battery, aimed upward
at him and hit him in the left groin. Although the shot
went through steel he fell dead on the very edge of the
parapet. When they saw this knight fall, the Turks shouted
for joy, as they always did when they killed some distinguished person.

When the Turks saw that those in the boats which had
rowed against the chain were obliged to get wet before
landing, ten of their largest boats, which carried their
smartest men, came to the extreme point of the Spur where
they could see no chain. They did not know that the whole

of that stretch of water was commanded by the low battery near the chain of the harbour, which was the Post of Commander Francisco de Guiral, who, on seeing these boats and guessing their intention, ordered all his pieces to be laid on them, and waited for the opportune moment. When he saw the boats approaching and that they were in a position where he could not miss them he ordered a salvo from four or five pieces. Nine of the largest boats were sunk, and all who were in them lost. In these boats there were eight hundred Janizaries and Levantines. Besides being loaded with shot, the pieces which fired on these boats each fired a bag full of stones, pieces of chain, and iron spikes, so that they played havoc, causing those who were not killed or wounded to drown.

It is no wonder that among so many, none should have been saved, because, we heard afterwards, the Pashas sent on this expedition all those who could not swim, so that, not being able to save themselves by swimming, they should fight all the better.

When the enemy saw arrival of reinforcements under the Bailiff of Eagle and of Captain Romegas they commenced to retire, first from Saint Michael and then from the Spur. The assault had lasted five hours.

When the Turks who were on the shore of the Spur saw that their comrades at Saint Michael were retiring, they wished to do likewise, but this they were prevented from doing because the boats from which they had landed had withdrawn and dared not return.

As the fight was going in our favour and victory was within grasp, we decided to go out. The first to do so were five men of the Post, a Maltese named Ramon, a Neapolitan, two Greeks, and myself. We went out by a small gate which led to the seashore, and from behind cover we began to shoot at the enemy who were at the point. Many other soldiers came out from all sides and began to cut off the heads of the Turks, and, of so many who were there, only four were taken alive so that the Grand Master might question them.

The assault lasted five hours, by the end of which the Turks had completed their retirement with an estimated loss of four thousand dead, including those drowned. Our losses were two hundred killed and many wounded.

When the Turks had retired, the Grand Master placed

the captured standards in the church of Saint Lawrence amidst great rejoicings and the solemn singing of a *Te Deum*.

Thursday, 2nd August. On the 2nd of August the enemy bombarded us until near midday, at which time they came to the assault on Saint Michael.

After fully five hours of hard fighting, during which the Turks lost more than six hundred of their boldest and bravest warriors, they began to retire. Forty of our most distinguished soldiers of all nationalities were killed and many were wounded.

Tuesday, 7th August. On the 7th, one hour before daylight, we saw that all the Turks on Cortin had commenced to move on Saint Michael's, and those from the fleet were being conveyed in boats from Marsa-M'xett to Is-Salvatur. This was a sign that the Turks would make an assault that day, as it turned out.

At daybreak a general assault was made on Saint Michael's as well as the Post of Castile, with so much shouting, beating of drums and blaring of trumpets that would have caused wonder had we not experienced it before.

The strength of the assailants on Saint Michael's was eight thousand and those on the Post of Castile four thousand. They attacked simultaneously as was their plan and as we had anticipated. But, when they left their trenches to come to the assault we were already at our posts, the hoops alight, the pitch boiling: in fact, all the materials for our defence were ready for action, and, when they scaled the works they were received like men who were expected.

The assaults on this day were most daring and well fought on both sides with great bitterness and much bloodshed. The greatest effort was made against the Post of Colonel Robles and that of Bormla where Don Bernardo de Cabera commanded. These Posts were the most vulnerable because of being so levelled they seemed easiest to gain. Here most of the fighting of the day took place, the Turks throwing their main force. It was here that the greatest havoc was done amongst them both from the effect of the incendiary missiles and the fire from the traverses of these two Posts which faced each other and supported one another, bringing a deadly cross-fire to bear on the enemy who hoped to enter by this locality.

During the action their artillery did not fire as usual so as not to risk hitting their own men who were in close formation and very exposed. As on all other occasions, we fought behind cover, having been made wiser by our losses in the past.

The assault lasted nine hours, from daybreak until after noon, during which time the Turks were relieved by fresh troops more than a dozen times, while we refreshed ourselves with drinks of well-watered wine and some mouthfuls of bread, for so great was the care which his most illustrious Lordship had for us, that, seeing he could not relieve us by fresh men (like the Turks) because he had so few, he cheered us in this manner.

Victory was ours again but it was due to Divine agency rather than to human effort, for the enemy had intended this to be their final assault and no man who could fight had been left behind in the camp or with the fleet.

As to ourselves, in spite of all the help and encouragement which the Grand Master afforded us, not one could stand on his legs from fatigue or wounds. Many of ours were killed. But the Lord came to our aid in the following manner.

When these assaults had lasted fully nine hours, one might say that our Lord inspired our cavalry who were in the City with their horses. On that day they went out as usual, and, as they did not see a single Turk anywhere, they pushed on as far as the Marsa, where they became aware of the great danger their Order was in. Not knowing how else they could help because they were barely a hundred horse and as many infantry, they made an onslaught on the sick and other non-combatants who were there, killing as many of them as were found, and shouting "Victory and relief" the whole time.

Some Turks from the fleet who were stationed on the promontory of Saint Elmo were the first to notice this commotion going on at the Marsa, and, forming themselves into a squadron, set off in good order to the Marsa. The Turks who were attacking the Post of Castile and Saint Michael's noticed the movement of this squadron, but, seeing that it had not advanced more than a hundred paces when it turned about and made for the fleet with all haste, they halted and abandoned the attack.

At the same time the news reached the Commander of the land forces that those who had been left behind at the Marsa had all been killed and the tents plundered. This news spread to the trenches where it grew until it was said that strong reliefs for us had arrived, and that if they did not retire in time they would all lose their heads. This false rumour had such an effect on the enemy that they all retired from their trenches without waiting for orders from the Pasha or any of their officers.

The Turks soon became aware that a mere handful of men had baulked them of such a great victory, putting them into a state of panic and disorder. They advanced, with their flags unfurled, towards our men; but scouts gave timely warning. Each horseman mounted a footsoldier behind him and in perfect order, without losing a single man, retired to the old City after having killed many of the enemy, and saved the Order and all the besieged.

The humiliation of the Pashas and all the Turks was great when they realised that so few men had done them so much harm and put such a fear into them.

Judging by the haste with which the Turks removed their dead, more than two thousand must have been killed before Saint Michael's, and their wounded (as we ascertained later) were twice that number. Before the Post of Castile more than two hundred of their most distinguished men died; among them being the Greek Ochali. On our side we had sixty killed, but the wounded exceeded that number.

Thursday, 16th August. On the 16th the Turks bombarded us from all parts. They also improved their positions by strengthening their trenches, or by sapping. They made use of ox-hides and goat-skins as a protection against our rain of fire and stones.

From the 16th to the 20th August. From the 16th to the 20th all the enemy did was to bombard us, to no purpose because our works could not be levelled more than they already were, and all that stood between us and the Turks were the retrenchment at the Post of Castile, which measured some ten or twelve feet, and a few barrels at Saint

Michael's, and they continually made attacks and feints so as to wear us out.

Meanwhile the renegades were moved by our perilous condition and took pity on us as they had done on many occasions, speaking to our men from their trenches. It must have appeared to the Turks that they were abusing us but they were really helping us, and, although they spoke in covered terms, we understood their meaning. They called out to us: "Hold on, you dogs, because already you have not many oxen to kill and only sheep are left and they are not fat. There is not much flour and at the next assault you will be free." What they meant by all this was that they had no good soldiers left, nor any powder; they also warned us that one more assault would be made. In addition to this warning the Grand Master had other good reasons for anticipating another general assault.

Monday, 20th August. On the 20th, at dawn, the Turks made a simultaneous attack on Saint Michael's and the Post of Castile. They came with great clamour of voices and musical instruments. Mustapha Pasha, although a man of sixty, was in the front rank and full of pluck. He resorted to a stratagem. The camp followers were told to dress in the clothes of Janizaries and Spahis who had died thus hoping that this dress might infuse them with courage and they were promised that if they fought well they would be made Janizaries. When the Pasha came under the fire of our traverses, a shot from Bormla knocked off his turban and stunned him. Later on, crawling on all fours, he sought shelter in the ditch of Saint Michael's, which he did not leave until dark.

The morning attack lasted a full five hours, during which the assailants were relieved many times while we refreshed ourselves as often in our usual way. This attack was one of the fiercest of the whole siege and the one in which their fire did most harm.

On this day the Illustrious Grand Master had another alarm from the Post of Castile. While he was in the square he was told that the Turks were already inside the Post. Undaunted and with his usual courage he went to the threatened post where his presence worked wonders. Sword in hand, he remained at the most dangerous place until the Turks had retired.

On this day the Turks made four assaults: two on Saint Michael's and two on the Post of Castile. The morning attack lasted about five hours, that in the afternoon three hours. They made all these assaults hoping to wear out our small force.

During these engagements, many convalescents, although not yet fully recovered, used to come to the works and helped as best they could, because, like men of spirit, they preferred to die fighting rather than be cruelly butchered in their quarters if it were our misfortune that the Turks should win.

Tuesday, 21st August. On the morning of the 21st, the Turks made another general assault with the same determination as on the previous day, but, after four hours of very hard fighting, retired with great loss.

Friday, 24th August. From the 24th to the 26th the enemy did nothing but make real and feint attacks, but, thank God, they gained no advantage.

Monday, 27th August. On the 27th the Turks showed signs of their intention to attack. In the morning we saw their men moving from Santa Liena in the direction of the Post of Castile, and from the Marsa towards the trenches opposite Saint Michael's. At a given moment they moved their *manta* towards the "barrels." They were allowed to approach so near that our aim could not miss. When the moment had arrived the gun was fired and the *manta* destroyed with all who were inside it together with some forty others who were following behind.

With the destruction of the *manta* and those who went with it their plan failed and they made no further attack during the day.

Tuesday, 28th August. On the 28th the enemy bombarded the works and houses with great energy during the whole day and night, but, although they kept up such a brave bombardment, we knew that they had embarked many of their pieces because each night we could hear them removing their artillery, although it was done very quietly without the shouting which used to take place when they were moving in their guns.

Wednesday, 29th August. On the 29th the Turks came to the assault although they had to be driven to it by their officers, who used their swords and sticks freely, but although we already regarded them with contempt, we were on our guard. On this day, during the heaviest engagement, it pleased God to send rain which obliged the enemy to retire without having gained any advantage and with the loss of a great many men.

Thursday, 30th August. On the 30th, after midday, the enemy made another attack on Saint Michael's which lasted till nightfall: but they retired after losing more than one hundred. We had one man killed and three wounded.

Friday, 31st August. On the 31st we expected another attack but they did not move, for they were as exhausted as we were.

This same night a Maltese came from the City at no small risk to himself and said publicly that Prince Giovanni Andrea Doria had come in one of his galleys and studied the situation of the besieged and had left behind him a Spanish soldier named Martinez in order to signal the news from the Island to Don Garcia when he should appear with his fleet, as he was on the point of coming to our aid; but that he was acting with great caution in such a grave matter.

Friday, 7th September. During the night some of our men went out of the Post of Castile to the enemy's trenches, but, finding nobody in them, they dismantled them and also those at the mouth of the ditch.

Saturday, 8th September. I do not believe that music ever sounded so sweet to human ears as the peal of our bells did to ours on that 8th day of September—the day of the Nativity of Our Lady. For the last three months they had only been struck to give the alarm signal, but now the Grand Master ordered them to be rung at the hour when the reveille was usually sounded. During the morning they rang for pontifical high mass which was celebrated with great solemnity in thanksgiving to Our Lord God and to His Holy Mother, for the mercy they had shown us.

On this day of the Nativity of Our Lady a renegade came into our lines and said that our reliefs had landed and that he believed the force was a very strong one, although it was spread among the Turks that they were not more than four thousand men.

When the Grand Master saw that there was no more danger from the enemy's artillery he ordered the three galleys which were in shelter in the ditch of Saint Angelo should be brought out and armed at once.

During the whole of this day not a single Turk was to be seen in any of their trenches except in the houses of Bormla where they had more than two thousand men under cover guarding one of their big guns which we had dismounted, and, as it was very heavy, they were unable to remount it and take it away. The circumference of this piece at the breech is nine palms, its length fifteen, and its calibre one.

That night, Commander Antonio Maldonado and the knights Juan Garces and Miquel de Marzilla came from the City and entered the Birgu and told the Grand Master all the details of the relief force which had landed and that Don Garcia had led it in person. They mentioned the names of the illustrious personages who had come with the force and told of the manner in which the landing had been effected, which I shall describe. They further said that His Serene Highness, Don John of Austria, brother of the most powerful and Catholic King our Lord, moved by his great heart although so young, had secretly left the court to join in this memorable expedition and that after His Excellency had waited many days for a passage at Barcelona, seeing that no ships came, returned to the court in obedience to the King's orders. This very brave action is a sure promise of the courage and generosity to be expected of this Prince if it shall please God to preserve him.

VIII
SEA FIGHTS

ARMADA
"BON HOMME RICHARD"
MIDWAY

Armada (1588)

Duke Medina-Sidonia

Religious, dynastic, and colonial rivalry between England and Spain was one of the great features of late sixteenth-century Europe. The Spain of Philip II was wealthy, militarily probably the leading power of the time, and was in control of an empire covering most of the Americas and extending to the Philippines. The seamen and adventurers of the England of Elizabeth I, whom the Spaniards regarded for the most part as pirates, raided and threatened this wealth and might.

Philip, in 1588, organized the "Invincible Armada," which was to join with forces from the Spanish army in the Netherlands to crush England. The fleet of more than 130 vessels was hampered by Sir Francis Drake's destruction of its supplies, but set out. The cooperation with Parma did not work, and the English fleet, under Howard, Hawkins, and Drake, outmaneuvered and outfought the Spanish in the Channel, July 21–29. The remnants of the Spanish suffered greatly from storms to the north of Scotland and Ireland.

Though war continued, and though Spain remained a great power for almost a century, the defeat of the Armada removed the threat of Spanish invasion. It practically ensured the dominance of Protestantism in England, and encouraged, if it did not create, the great mood of confidence, courage, and patriotism which marked the exploits and the literature of Elizabethan England.

The account here is by the Spanish duke Medina-Sidonia, who commanded the Armada.

Journal of the armada in the English expedition under the charge of the Duke of Medina-Sidonia, from the time of their sailing from the Groyne.

July 12. On the 12th of July, 1588, the Duke and all the armada departed from the Groyne with a S.W. wind, which they held for some days and thereby made good progress.

July 19. Friday, the 19th, the wind was West. This same day the coast of England was seen, and was said to be the Lizard.

July 21. Sunday, the 21st, at dawn, the wind had shifted to the W.N.W.; 80 ships were discovered in the weather, and to leeward, near the land, there were 11 others, amongst which were three great galleons, that fought with some of our ships, and continued turning to windward until they joined their fleet. Our armada placed itself in order of battle, and the *capitana* put abroad the royal standard at the foremast. The enemy's fleet passed, firing on our van under the charge of Don Alonso de Leyva, which drove into the rear under the charge of the Admiral Juan Martínez de Recalde, who stood fast and abode the assault of the enemy, although he saw that he was being left unsupported, for that the ships of the rearguard were shrouding themselves in the main body of the armada. The enemy assailed him with great discharging of ordnance, without closing, whereby his ship suffered much in her rigging, her forestay cut, and her foremast had two great shot therein. The *capitana real* struck her fore-topsail and let fly the sheets, and coming to the wind, awaited the rear to gather it into the main body of the fleet. Whereupon the enemy drew off and the Duke collected his fleet, being unable to do anything more, because the enemy having recovered the wind, and their ships being very nimble and of such good steerage, as they did with them whatsoever they desired.

This day in the evening, Don Pedro de Valdes ran foul of the ship Catalina of his squadron, so that he spent his bowsprit and his foresail, and withdrew into the main body of the armada to repair the damage. Our fleet continued until four in the afternoon endeavouring to recover the wind of the enemy. At this hour, on board the vice-

admiral of Oquendo, some of the powder barrels caught
fire, and her two decks and her poop were blown up; in
which was the Paymaster General of this armada with part
of the King's treasure; and the Duke seeing this ship remaining behind, turned the *capitana* towards her, and discharged a piece of ordnance, to the end the fleet should do
the same, and gave order to send boats to her assistance.
The fire was extinguished, and the enemy's fleet, which was
standing towards that ship, desisted when they saw our
capitana bear with her, so as the ship was shrouded and
brought into the main body of the armada.

In this casting about, the foremast of Don Pedro's ship
was broken off by the hatches, and fell on the mainyard.
The Duke turned to succour him, by giving him a hawser;
but though great diligence was used, neither weather nor
sea permitted of it, and so she was left without sails, because it was now night. This night they removed the
wounded and burnt men from the vice-admiral of
Oquendo. The sea and wind increased greatly this night.

July 22. The whole fleet was divided into two squadrons,
Don Alonso de Leyva taking the rear under his charge, and
the Duke having charge of the van. He called to him all the
sergeant majors and commanded them to go in a pinnace,
and range the fleet according to the prescribed order, giving it to each of them in writing that they should put every
ship in her appointed place, and also that any ship which
did not keep that order, or left her appointed place, that
without further stay they should hang the captain of the
said ship; and that for this purpose they should take with
them the provost-marshals and their men; and that three
sergeant majors were to attend to the rear, and the other
three to the van, so as the better to carry out this order.

At eleven this same day the captain of Oquendo advertised the Duke that the ship was sinking, whereupon the
Duke ordered the King's money and the people to be taken
out of her and the ship to be sunk. This day in the evening
the Duke despatched the ensignbearer Juan Gil in a pinnace to the Duke of Parma, to give him advertisement as
to where the fleet was.

July 23. Tuesday, 23rd of July, the day dawned fine, and
the enemy's fleet, being to leeward, was standing towards

the land, endeavouring as much as they could to recover
the wind. The Duke also made a board towards the land in
order to keep the weather. The galleasses went with him in
the van, and the rest of the fleet followed. The enemy, seeing our admiral standing towards the land, and that they
could not in this way recover the wind, cast about to seaward; whereon those of our ships that had the weather of
the enemy, bare room with them and assailed them. Captain Bertendona very gallantly assaulted their admiral,
offering to board her; but as he came near her, she bare
room and stood out to sea. The galleasses of the vanguard
being carried by the current almost within culverin-shot,
the Duke sent them order that by oar and sail they should
endeavor to close with the enemy, to which end also he
turned the *capitana* towards them. The galleasses bore
with the ships of their rear which were in conflict with
some of ours that had closed with them and were endeavouring to board them; but all to little effect, because the
enemy, seeing that we endeavoured to come to hand-stroke
with them, bare room, avoiding our attack by reason of the
lightness of their vessels; and afterwards they returned
with tide and wind in their favour, and assailed Juan Martinez de Recalde, who was in the rear. Don Alonso de
Leyva went to his assistance, during which time our *capitana* was in the hottest of the fight supporting those ships
which were closely engaged with the enemy's rear at a distance from both fleets; and Captain Marolin was ordered to
go in a boat and command those ships which were near at
hand to succour Juan Martinez de Recalde; which they did;
whereupon the enemies left Juan Martinez, and turned
against the *capitana* which was going alone to the assistance of the ships named; and our *capitana,* seeing the
enemy's admiral in the van, turned towards her, and lowered her topsails; and the enemy's admiral and all the fleet
passed her, shot at her, ship by ship, whilst she, on her part,
fired her ordnance very well and fast, so as half the enemy's fleet did not approach, but shot at her from afar.
When the fury of the assault had spent itself, there arrived
to her support Juan Martinez de Recalde, Don Alonso de
Leyva, the Marquis of Penafiel, who was in the San Marcos,
and Oquendo; whereupon the enemy bare room and stood
out to sea; their admiral shortening sail, having, as it
seemed to us, sustained some damage, and collecting

those of his ships which had been in fight with our van. In
this conflict, which lasted more than three hours, the galleon Florencia was one of the foremost ships, and was in
close fight with the enemy.

July 24. Wednesday the 24th, Juan Martinez de Recalde
again took the rear under his charge, Don Alonso de Leyva
remaining with him, reparting between them the 40 or
more ships that were therein. The enemy bore with our
rear, and assaulted the Admiral; the galleasses discharged
their stern pieces, as also did Juan Martinez and Don
Alonso de Leyva, and the other ships of the squadron,
without quitting their station. And so the enemy retired
without any other success, the galleasses having spoiled
their admiral's rigging and shot away his mainyard.

July 25. Thursday the 25th, Feast of St. Dominic, the
Santa Ana and a Portuguese galleon were somewhat
astern, which the enemy assaulted with great fury. The
galleasses, Don Alonso de Leyva and other ships went to
their assistance; and the galleasses did so well, that they
rescued them although they were surrounded by many
of the enemy. At the same time that this conflict was in
the rear, the enemy's admiral and other great ships assailed
our *capitana;* they came nearer than the first day, discharging their large pieces from the lower deck, and cut
the *capitana*'s mainstay, slaying also some soldiers; there
came to his succour the San Luis, Juan Martinez de Recalde, and the San Juan of the squadron of Diego Flores, in
which was Don Diego Enriquez, and Oquendo, which
placed themselves in front of our *capitana,* being by the
currents prevented from keeping together, and the other
ships did the same. Thereupon the enemies retired but their
admiral being much damaged, rested somewhat to leeward
of our fleet, and was now towed by 11 of the enemy's long
boats. Our *capitana,* and the *almiranta,* and the rest of the
ships were gaining on her so much that the enemy stood
towards her, to support her, so as it appeared certain that
we would that day succeed in boarding them, wherein was
the only way to victory. But at this moment the wind
freshened in favour of the enemy's admiral, whereby she
began to slip away from us, and to leave the boats which
were towing her; whereupon the enemy's fleet recovered

the wind, which meantime had fallen somewhat to leeward.

July 26. Friday the 26th dawned calm, the fleets being in
sight of each other; and the Duke despatched a pinnace to
the Duke of Parma with the pilot Domingo Ochoa, to obtain from him shot of four, six and ten lbs., because much
of his munition had been wasted in the several fights; praying him also to send 40 flyboats to join with this armada,
to the end he might be able with them to close with the
enemy, because our ships being very heavy in comparison
with the lightness of those of the enemy it was impossible
to come to hand-stroke with them. He was also to notify
the Duke that it should be well that he would be ready to
come out and join with this armada the day that we should
arrive in sight of Dunkirk.

July 27. Saturday the 27th at daybreak, the two fleets were
very near to each other, though without firing; our armada
sailing with a fair wind, and the rear close up and in very
good order. At ten o'clock, we discovered the coast of
France, being that near to Boulogne. We proceeded towards Calais, where we arrived at four in the afternoon.
At five o'clock in the afternoon, order was given for the
whole fleet to anchor.

This evening 36 ships joined the enemy, whereof five
were large galleons, which were understood to be the
squadron that Juan Acles* had under his charge before
Dunkirk, and they all anchored about a league from our
armada. This night the Duke sent the Secretary Arceo to
the Duke of Parma, to advertise him of the place where he
now was, and that he could not tarry there without endangering the whole fleet.

July 28. Sunday the 28th, at dawn, Captain Don Rodrigo
Tello arrived, which came from Dunkirk. He said that the
Duke (of Parma) was at Bruges, whither he had repaired
to him, and that although he had shown great satisfaction
at the news of the armada being arrived, the Duke had not
yet come thither, and that they were not embarking either

*Acles was Hawkyns. Medina-Sidonia was wrong. Lord Henry Sey-
mour commanded the squadron at the time.

the men or the munition. This day in the morning, the Governor of Calais sent his nephew to visit the Duke and with him a present of refreshments, and to acquaint him that the place wherein he had anchored was very dangerous to remain in, because the currents and countercurrents of that channel were very strong. On Sunday night the Secretary Arceo sent one from Dunkirk to advertise the Duke that Parma had not arrived there, and that the munitions were not embarked, and that it seemed to him unpossible that all things could be prepared within a fortnight. On Sunday at sunset, nine ships joined the enemy, and with them a squadron of 26 ships moved nearer to the land, which the same made us suspect that they had come with some design of fire; whereupon the Duke ordered Captain Serrano to go in a pinnace, taking with him an anchor and cable, so as if any fire-ship should be set forth he might tow it to land. Also he sent to warn all the ships to be on their guard, and to the end to have ready as well boats as soldiers. At midnight two fires were seen kindled in the English fleet, which increased to eight; and suddenly eight ships with sail set, and fair wind and tide, came straight towards our *capitana* and the rest of the fleet, all burning fiercely. The Duke seeing them approach and that our men did not hinder them, fearing that they should be explosion-machines, gave order to weigh, and also for the rest of the armada to do the same, intending when the fires had passed to return and recover the same position. The admiral galleass, in keeping clear of one ship, came entangled with the San Juan de Sicilia, and so damaged herself that she had to remain near the shore. The current was so strong that it drove our armada in such manner as, although our *capitana* and divers of the ships that were near her anchored again, firing a piece of ordnance, the rest did not see her, and were so driven as far as off of Dunkirk.

July 29. Monday the 29th, at daybreak, the Duke seeing that his armada was very far off and that the enemy was coming under a press of sail, weighed anchor to collect his fleet and therewith endeavour to recover the place they had been in. The wind was blowing strong from the N.W., nearly straight on to the coast, and the enemy's fleet, wherein were 136 ships, came on suddenly with wind and tide in their favour, so as the Duke, who was in the rear, seeing that if he bare room with his fleet, it would be to their destruction, for that it was already very near the banks of Dunkirk, as he was assured by his Flemish pilots, chose rather to save it by abiding the enemy's fleet; and so cast about to meet them, discharging his ordnance, and sending off pinnaces to order all the ships to keep a close luff, as otherwise they should drive on to the banks of Dunkirk. The enemy's admiral, with the greater part of their fleet, assaulted our *capitana,* with great shooting of ordnance, approaching within musket-shot, or even harquebus-shot. This continued without ceasing from daybreak; nor did the *capitana* bear room until the fleet was clear of the shoals. And during all this time, the galleon San Marcos, in which was the Marquis of Penafiel, continued hard by the *capitana.*

The admiral galleass, not being able to follow our armada, turned towards Calais, and ran on ground at the entrance of the haven, whither divers of the enemy followed her. It is reported that the French in the castle of Calais supported her with their ordnance, and that her people reached the land.

Several ships sustained the assault of the enemy as stoutly as was possible, so as all these ships were very much spoiled, and almost unable to make further resistance, and the greater part of them without shot for their ordnance. In the rear Don Francisco de Toledo abode the coming of the enemy, and endeavoured to grapple with them; whereupon they assailed him, and by shooting of ordnance brought him to great extremity. Don Diego Pimentel came to relieve him, and both were hard pressed; seeing which, Juan Martinez de Recalde came to their assistance, with Don Agustin Mexia, and rescued them from this strait. Notwithstanding which, these ships returned and again assaulted the enemy; as likewise did Don Alonso de Luzon, and the Santa Maria de Begona, in which went Garibay, and the San Juan de Sicilia, in which went Don Diego Tellez Enriquez. These came near to boarding the enemy, yet they could not grapple with them; they fighting with their great ordnance, and our men defending themselves with harquebus-fire and musketry, the distance being very small.

Whenas the Duke heard the harquebus-fire and the musketry in the rear, but by reason of the smoke was unable to see from the top what it was, except that two of our ships were surrounded by the enemy, and that their whole fleet, having quitted our *capitana,* were assailing them, he gave order to cast about to succour them, although the *capitana* was sorely distressed by great shot between wind and water, so as by no means could the leak be stopped, and her rigging was much spoiled. Nevertheless, when the enemy perceived our *capitana* approach, they left the ships they were assailing. These had been most closely and hotly engaged with the enemy, and had all suffered much damage and were unable for the service, all their people being slain or wounded. The Duke collected his armada and the enemy did the same.

The sea was so high that nothing more could be done, nor could the damage be repaired which the *capitana* had suffered from great shot, whereby she was in danger of being lost.

This day the Duke wished to turn on the enemy with the whole armada, so as he would not leave the Channel; but the pilots told him that it was unpossible, because with the sea and wind from the N.W., setting straight on to the coast, they must by force go into the North Sea, or else that the whole armada would drive on to the banks. Thus in no way could they avoid leaving the Channel; nearly all the best ships being spoiled and unable to resist longer, as well from the damage they had received as from not having shot for their ordnance.

July 30. Tuesday the 30th, eve of San Lorenzo, at two o'clock in the morning, the wind increased, so as our *capitana,* which had stayed in the hope of returning to the Channel, was driven towards the coast of Zealand, although keeping as close a luff as possible. At daybreak the N.W. wind was not so strong, and the enemy's fleet with 109 vessels was discovered astern little more than half a league off. Our *capitana* remained in the rear with Juan Martinez de Recalde and Don Alonso de Leyva, and the galleasses, and the galleons San Marcos and San Juan of Diego Flores, the rest of our fleet being far to leeward. The enemy's ships stood towards our *capitana,* which lay to; the galleasses also abode their coming, as also did the other ships which were in the rear; whereupon the enemy

brought to. The Duke shot off two pieces to collect his
armada, and sent a pinnace with a pilot to order them to
keep a close luff, because they were very near to the banks
of Zealand; for which cause the enemy remained aloof,
seeing that our armada must be lost; for the pilots on board
the *capitana*—men of experience of that coast—told the
Duke at this time that it was not possible to save a single
ship of the armada; for that with the wind as it was, in the
N.W., they must all needs go on the banks of Zealand; that
God alone could prevent it. Being in this peril, without
any sort of remedy, and in six and a half fathoms of water,
God was pleased to change the wind to W.S.W., whereby
the fleet stood towards the North without hurt to any ship,
the Duke sending order to every ship to follow the *capitana*, for that otherwise they would go on the banks of
Zealand.

This evening the Duke summoned the generals and Don
Alonso de Leyva, to consider what was best to be done;
and when the Duke had explained the state of the armada
and the lack of shot—for that all the greatest ships sent
to ask for them—he wished them to say whether it were
best to turn back to the English Channel or to return to
Spain by the North Sea; seeing that the Duke of Parma
had not sent word that he would be presently able to come
out. The Council was wholly of opinion that they should go
back to the Channel if the weather would permit it; but if
not, that then, constrained by the weather, they should
return by the North Sea to Spain, seeing there was such
great lack of provision in the fleet, and that the ships were
spoiled and unable, that hitherto had resisted the enemy.
The wind continued to increase in the S.S.W., and the
Duke stood to seaward, the enemy's fleet following him.

July 31. Wednesday the 31st, our armada pursuing their
course with a strong wind from the S.W. and a high sea,
the enemy's fleet continued to follow us, and in the evening the force of the wind becoming less, they came on
under all sail towards our rear. But when the enemy saw
that our *capitana* had brought to, and that the galleasses of
the rearguard and as many as 12 of our best ships had
done the same, they also brought to and shortened sail,
without shooting of ordnance against us. This night Juan
Acles turned back with his squadron.

August 1. Thursday the 1st, we continued our voyage with the same strong wind, the enemy's fleet keeping a long way off; at evening they came under all sail towards our armada, and we counted the ships of Juan Acles to be missing, and again the galleasses and our *capitana* brought to and abode their coming; whereupon they also brought to, not coming within cannon shot.

August 2. Friday the 2nd, at daybreak, the enemy's fleet was close up with ours, and seeing that we were in good order and our rearguard strengthened, they rested and turned back towards England, until we lost sight of them. Since that time we had always the same wind, until we went out of the channel of the Sea of Norway without it being possible to return to the English Channel though we desired it, until to-day, the 10th of August, when having passed the isles at the north of Scotland we are now sailing towards Spain with the wind at N.E.

"Bon Homme Richard" (1779)

John Paul Jones

British sea power in the 1770s, in contrast to the resources and strength of the revolutionary colonies, was overwhelming. They were able to blockade much of the coast, and to send and transfer troops by sea.

The young United States, however, did have men and ships capable of annoying and injuring the proud mistress of the sea.

Notable among these was John Paul Jones, himself born in Scotland, and with experience as a merchant captain before joining the Continental navy. With a small squadron, he raided the coasts of the British Isles. In 1779, with the French alliance, he could use French ports for refuge and refitting. He was given command of the Bon Homme Richard (*Goodman Richard, from Franklin's* Poor Richard's Almanac) *and several smaller ships.*

The encounter with the Serapis *and* Countess of Scarborough, *September 23, 1779, is one of the most famous ship-to-ship battles. It was marked by skill and great courage on both sides, and gave the infant naval service a magnificent example and a lasting slogan, "I have not yet begun to fight."*

The account that follows is from Jones's own report to Congress through Franklin, then United States Minister to France.

Battle between the *Bon Homme Richard*
and the *Serapis*

Commodore Jones's report to Congress through Dr.
Franklin

on board the ship *Serapis,* at anchor without
the Texel, in Holland, October 3d, 1779.

His Excellency Benjamin Franklin.

Honoured and Dear Sir,—When I had the honour of
writing to you on the 11th of August, previous to my departure from the Road of Groaix, I had before me the
most flattering prospect of rendering essential service to
the common cause of France and America. I had a full
confidence in the voluntary inclination and ability of every
captain under my command to assist and support me in
my duty with cheerful emulation; and I was persuaded that
every one of them would pursue glory in preference to
interest.

Whether I was or not deceived will best appear by a
relation of circumstance.

The little squadron under my orders, consisting of the
Bon Homme Richard of 40 guns, the Alliance of 36 guns,
the Pallas of 32 guns, the Cerf of 18 guns, and the Vengeance of 12 guns, joined by two privateers, the Monsieur
and the Granville, sailed from the Road of Groaix at daybreak on the 14th of August.

On the morning of that day, the 23d, the brig from Holland not being in sight, we chased a brigantine that appeared laying to the windward. About noon we saw and
chased a large ship that appeared coming round Flamborough Head from the northward, and at the same time I
manned and armed one of the pilot boats to sail in pursuit
of the brigantine, which now appeared to be the vessel that
I had forced ashore. Soon after this a fleet of 41 sail appeared off Flamborough Head, bearing N.N.E. This
induced me to abandon the single ship which had then
anchored in Burlington Bay. I also called back the pilot
boat, and hoisted a signal for a general chase. When the
fleet discovered us bearing down, all the merchant ships
crowded sail towards the shore. The two ships of war that
protected the fleet at the same time steered from the land,
and made the disposition for the battle. In approaching the
enemy, I crowded every possible sail, and made the signal

for the line of battle, to which the Alliance showed no attention. Earnest as I was for the action, I could not reach the commodore's ship until seven in the evening. Being then within pistol shot, when he hailed the Bon Homme Richard, we answered him by firing a whole broadside.

The battle, being this begun, was continued with unremitting fury. Every method was practised on both sides to gain an advantage, and rake each other; and I must confess that the enemy's ship, being much more manageable than the Bon Homme Richard, gained thereby several times an advantageous situation, in spite of my best endeavors to prevent it. As I had to deal with an enemy of *greatly superior force*, I was under the necessity of closing with him, to prevent the advantage which he had over me in point of manoeuvre. It was my intention to lay the Bon Homme Richard athwart the enemy's bow, but, as that operation required great dexterity in the management of both sails and helm, and some of our braces being shot away, it did not exactly succeed to my wishes. The enemy's bowsprit, however, came over the Bon Homme Richard's poop by the mizzen mast, and I made both ships fast together in that situation, which by the action of the wind on the enemy's sails forced her stern close to the Bon Homme Richard's bow, so that the ships lay square alongside of each other, the yards being all entangled, and the cannon of each ship touching the opponent's side. When this position took place, it was 8 o'clock, previous to which the Bon Homme Richard had received sundry eighteen-pound shot below the water, and leaked very much. My battery of twelve-pounders, on which I had placed my chief dependence, being commanded by Lieut. Dale and Col. Weibert, and manned principally with American seamen and French volunteers, were entirely silenced and abandoned. As to the six old eighteen-pounders that formed the battery of the lower gun-deck, they did no service whatever. Two out of three of them burst at the first fire, and killed almost all the men who were stationed to manage them. Before this time, too, Col. de Chamillard, who commanded a party of 20 soldiers on the poop, had abandoned that station after having lost some of his men. These men deserted their quarters. I had now only two pieces of cannon, nine-pounders, on the quarter deck, that were not silenced; and not one of the heavier cannon was fired during the rest of

the action. The purser, Mr. Mease, who commanded the
guns on the quarter deck, being dangerously wounded in
the head, I was obliged to fill his place, and with great difficulty rallied a few men, and shifted over one of the lee
quarter-deck guns, so that we afterward played three
pieces of nine-pounders upon the enemy. The tops alone
seconded the fire of this little battery, and held out bravely
during the whole of the action, especially the main top,
where Lieut. Stack commanded. I directed the fire of one
of the three cannon against the main-mast, with double-
headed shot, while the other two were exceedingly well
served with grape and canister shot to silence the enemy's
musketry, and clear her decks, which was at last effected.
The enemy were, as I have since understood, on the instant
of calling for quarters when the cowardice or treachery of
three of my under officers induced them to call to the
enemy. The English commodore asked me if I demanded
quarters; and, I having answered him in the most determined negative, they renewed the battle with double fury.
They were unable to stand the deck; but the fire of their
cannon, especially the lower battery, which was entirely
formed of eighteen-pounders, was incessant. Both ships
were set on fire in various places, and the scene was dreadful beyond the reach of language. To account for the
timidity of my three under officers,—I mean the gunner,
the carpenter, and the master-at-arms,—I must observe
that the two first were slightly wounded; and, as the ship
had received various shots under water, and one of the
pumps being shot away, the carpenter expressed his fear
that she would sink, and the other two concluded that she
was sinking, which occasioned the gunner to run aft on the
poop without my knowledge to strike the colors. Fortunately for me, a cannon ball had done that before by carrying away the ensign staff. He was therefore reduced to the
necessity of sinking, as he supposed, or of calling for
quarter; and he preferred the latter.

All this time the Bon Homme Richard had sustained the
action alone, and the enemy, though much superior in
force, would have been very glad to have got clear, as appears by their own acknowledgments, and by their having
let go an anchor the instant that I laid them on board, by
which means they would have escaped, had I not made
them well fast to the Bon Homme Richard.

At last, at half-past 9 o'clock, the Alliance appeared, and I now thought the battle at an end; but, to my utter astonishment, he discharged a broadside full into the stern of the Bon Homme Richard. We called to him for God's sake to forbear firing into the Bon Homme Richard; yet he passed along the off side of the ship, and continued firing. There was no possibility of his mistaking the enemy's ship for the Bon Homme Richard, there being the most essential difference in their appearance and construction; besides, it was then full moonlight, and the sides of the Bon Homme Richard were all black, while the sides of the prizes were yellow; yet, for the greater security, I shewed the signal of our reconnoisance by putting out three lanthorns, one at the head (bow), another at the stern (quarter), and the third in the middle in a horizontal line. Every tongue cried that he was firing into the wrong ship, but nothing availed. He passed round, firing into the Bon Homme Richard's head, stern, and broadside; and by one of his volleys killed several of my best men, and mortally wounded a good officer on the forecastle. My situation was really deplorable. The Bon Homme Richard received various shot under water from the Alliance, the leak gained on the pumps, and the fire increased much on board both ships. Some officers persuaded me to strike, of whose courage and good sense I entertain a high opinion. My treacherous master-at-arms let loose all my prisoners without my knowledge, and my prospect became gloomy indeed. I would not, however, give up the point. The enemy's mainmast began to shake, their firing decreased, ours rather increased, and the British colors were struck at half an hour past 10 o'clock.

This prize proved to be the British ship of war the Serapis, a new ship of 44 guns, built on their most approved construction, with two complete batteries, one of them of eighteen-pounders, and commanded by the brave Commodore Richard Pearson. I had yet two enemies to encounter far more formidable than the Britons,—I mean fire and water. The Serapis was attacked only by the first, but the Bon Homme Richard was assailed by both. There were five feet of water in the hold, and, though it was moderate from the explosion of so much gunpowder, yet the three pumps that remained could with difficulty only keep the water from gaining. The fire broke out in various parts of the ship, in spite of all the water that could be thrown to quench it, and at length broke out as low as the powder magazine, and within a few inches of the powder. In that dilemma I took out the powder upon deck, ready to be thrown overboard at the last extremity; and it was 10 o'clock the next day, the 24th, before the fire was entirely extinguished. With respect to the situation of the Bon Homme Richard, the rudder was cut entirely off the stern frame, and the transoms were almost entirely cut away; the timbers, by the lower deck especially, from the main-mast to the stern, being greatly decayed with age, were mangled beyond my power of description; and a person must have been an eye-witness to form a just idea of the tremendous scene of carnage, wreck and ruin that every-where appeared. Humanity cannot but recoil from the prospect of such finished horror, and lament that war should produce such fatal consequence.

After the carpenters, as well as Capt. de Cottineau, and other men of sense, had well examined and surveyed the ship (which was not finished before five in the evening), I found every person to be convinced that it was impossible to keep the Bon Homme Richard afloat so as to reach a port if the wind should increase, it being then only a very moderate breeze. I had but little time to remove my wounded, which now became unavoidable, and which was effected in the course of the night and next morning. I was determined to keep the Bon Homme Richard afloat, and, if possible, to bring her into port. For that purpose the first lieutenant of the Pallas continued on board with a party of men to attend the pumps, with boats in waiting ready to take them on board in case the water should gain on them too fast. The wind augmented in the night and the next day, on the 25th, so that it was impossible to prevent the good old ship from sinking. They did not abandon her till after 9 o'clock. The water was then up to the lower deck, and a little after ten I saw with inexpressible grief the last glimpse of the Bon Homme Richard. No lives were lost with the ship, but it was impossible to save the stores of any sort whatever. I lost even the best part of my clothes, books, and papers; and several of my officers lost all their clothes and effects.

Having thus endeavored to give a clear and simple relation of the circumstances and events that have attended the little armament under my command, I shall freely submit my conduct therein to the censure of my superiors and the impartial public.

Upon the whole, the captain of the Alliance has behaved so very ill in every respect that I must complain loudly of his conduct. He pretends that he is authorized to act independent of my command. I have been taught the contrary; but, supposing it to be so, his conduct has been base and unpardonable. Either Capt. Landais or myself is highly criminal, and one or the other must be punished. I forbear to take any steps with him until I have the advice and approbation of your excellency. I have been advised by all the officers of the squadron to put M. Landais under arrest; but, as I have postponed it so long, I will bear with him a little longer until the return of my express.

We this day anchored here, having since the action been tossed to and fro by contrary winds. I wished to have gained the Road of Dunkirk on account of our prisoners, but was overruled by the majority of *my colleagues*. I shall hasten up to Amsterdam; and there, if I meet with no orders from my government, I will take the advice of the French ambassador. It is my present intention to have the Countess of Scarborough ready to transport the prisoners from hence to Dunkirk, unless it should be found more expedient to deliver them to the English ambassador, taking his obligation to send to Dunkirk, &c., immediately an equal number of American prisoners. I am under strong apprehensions that our object here will fail, and that through the imprudence of M. de Chaumont, who has communicated every thing he knew or thought on the matter to persons who cannot help talking of it at a full table. This is the way he keeps state secrets, though he never mentioned the affair to me.

I am ever, &c.,
John P. Jones.

Midway (1942)

William W. Smith

Historians quite generally speak of the battle of Midway, June 6, 1942, as the turning point of World War II in the Pacific. The Japanese attack on Pearl Harbor had destroyed much of the United States battle fleet, and subsequent successes, as at Singapore and Manila, gave the Japanese supremacy over a wide area of the Pacific. They expected to destroy or drive back the remaining United States naval power by an attack on Midway Island.

Carrier forces fortunately had been away from Pearl Harbor at the time of the attack, and now gathered to meet the new threat. The United States forces were commanded by Admiral Frank John Fletcher, and the Japanese by Admiral Yamamoto. The battle was almost entirely waged by air, marking the change in naval warfare: carrier and carrier-based planes became the dominant features. The sinking and damaging of the Japanese carriers at Midway not only meant the loss of the engagement, it ended the threat of attack on United States positions, and permanently weakened the Japanese in future combat.

The account of Midway is by Admiral William W. Smith, who commanded a cruiser force in the battle.

THE COUNTERATTACK

4 June, afternoon. At 1100, just as *Hiryu's* attack group of bombers and fighters formed up and started toward *Yorktown*, Fletcher began launching ten SBD's of the squadron kept in reserve for scouting purposes. He had finally learned from Gray that we were attacking three enemy carriers. He knew that there were to have been four carriers with Nagumo according to early reports. He had to find the fourth flattop. *Yorktown*'s ten planes, led by Lieutenant Wallace C. Short, Jr., took off with orders to search an arc of 110 degrees, from 280 (just north of west) to 20 degrees (east of north). While heading into the wind after the search planes cleared, Fletcher began relieving fighters of his combat air patrol, which were low on gas, when four of Thach's fighters and two damaged SBD's came in for landing. They were struck below as twelve fighters of Thach's squadron, those which had been held in reserve, were launched for combat air patrol.

The fighters just relieved from CAP were refueling, but before gasoline could be pumped into their almost empty tanks, the *Yorktown* radar officer, Lieutenant V. M. Bennett, saw a number of pips coming in on his screen. He diagnosed the situation, and at 1159 reported to Fletcher and to Captain Buckmaster that a large formation of planes was approaching from west-sou'west at high speed. This, of course, was *Hiryu*'s Lieutenant Kobayashi and his eighteen bombers plus six fighters. Some records to the contrary notwithstanding (*Yorktown*'s were lost), the distance as reported to me at the time was sixty-five miles.

The alarm was sounded immediately; the fueling operation was terminated. Fuel lines were drained and filled with carbon dioxide gas, pumped into them at 20 pounds pressure as part of the standard procedure to prevent fires if hit. A portable 800-gallon gasoline tank on the flight deck was heaved overboard; watertight doors were closed and securely dogged. *Yorktown* built up her speed to 30.5 knots, as did ships of the screen. They were listening in on Fletcher's voice radio and well knew what to expect.

Our Wildcat fighter planes, guided by orders from *Yorktown*'s fighter director officer, struck Kobayashi's formation, within our sight but still miles to the westward of *Yorktown*. Some engaged Jap fighters in dogfights but most concentrated on the bombers. Eleven of the eighteen Japs were shot down before they could release their bombs. Two were dropped by ship's A.A. fire; nine were shot down by pilots of VF-3. From *Astoria*'s flag bridge I saw the almost simultaneous splash of six enemy planes. The sky was filled with A.A. gunfire bursts and every gun that could bear was blazing.

Leslie, returning from the attack on *Kaga*, had assembled his SBD's, except two already safely on the carrier, over *Yorktown*. One section already was in the landing circle when he received a general signal to form combat air patrol but to keep out of antiaircraft gun range. His guns were hopelessly jammed; his wingman Holmberg's hydraulic system was punctured by enemy bullets and his landing gear was incapable of retraction. Leslie says, "There was suddenly very heavy A.A. fire from all ships and thus I first learned that an enemy attack was underway. The sky looked like a July Fourth fireworks display. Several planes around us fell flaming and I saw smoke and flames coming from *Yorktown*, the result of enemy bombs. It was sickening to see this ship under attack, all hands doing everything possible to protect her, while we were helpless, unable to do anything about it."

The first bomb dropped was a near miss on the starboard side, its plane shot down before the pilot could level off from his dive. The second bomb pierced *Yorktown's* flight deck close to the bridge as all hands "hit the deck." It detonated within the smokestack structure—the heart of the ship's propulsion system. The uptakes, which form an exit for combustion gases, were shattered and the concussion completely disabled two boilers and doused fires in the others. Choking, acrid fumes drove personnel from the firerooms and up the ladders. Officers and men, with gas masks, managed to keep two burners going under one boiler, but the ship rapidly lost speed and at 1220 stopped.

A third bomb—the second hit—exploded on the flight deck aft. It fell after the plane that dropped it was shot down, but its missile killed many men and started a fire in the hangar. One more hit was scored; this one exploded on the fourth deck down, starting a fire in a rag compartment which generated heat so intense that it endangered a nearby magazine.

For years every naval ship of size had included in its organization a damage control department. Men of this department, "those who also serve," spent many hours of drudgery at drills during peacetime general quarters. As damage was called from gunnery control, they restored broken electric lines by running "jumpers," shored up bulk-heads, and counterflooded when the ship took a list from pierced compartments by flooding compartments opposite them.

Yorktown's damage control team had been through many drills simulating battle conditions and had experi-enced the real thing at Coral Sea. Their performance was superb. As fire broke out on the hangar deck, endangering planes below, Lieutenant A. C. Emerson, who was respon-sible for that deck, promptly cracked the valve of the sprinkler system and doused the flames. The magazine adjoining the burning rag compartment was flooded with sea water. The gasoline tank stowage compartment was filled with gas from carbon dioxide gas bottles; and willing workers made feverish but effective efforts to clear the fire-rooms and get fires going under those boilers.

Yorktown came to a dead stop at 1220, her communi-cation facilities badly damaged. Fletcher signaled me to send a boat for himself and his staff. *Astoria* lowered a motor whaleboat which lost no time in reaching the stricken carrier. It is a long way from a carrier's deck to the sea below. It's possible to jump overboard, but haz-ardous, so Fletcher's staff went hand-over-hand down ropes thrown from the flight deck. Frank Jack gave it a try, but had to admit his arm muscles hadn't had sufficient ex-ercise for some time. A bowline was secured beneath his arms and he was lowered to the boat.

When *Yorktown* stopped, Leslie's SBD's were directed to land on carriers *Enterprise* and *Hornet*, then hull down but plainly visible. Spruance, who witnessed the attack on *Yorktown*, ordered heavy cruisers *Pensacola* and *Vin-cennes* and two destroyers, *Balch* and *Benham*, to reinforce *Yorktown*'s screen and furnish badly needed additional antiaircraft gun support in case of a second attack.

Leslie had started his squadron toward the two carriers but, sighting a downed torpedo plane, he and his wingman peeled off to investigate, then made a message drop on the deck of the nearest destroyer (a leaded memo that required skill for a successful drop on a narrow deck). Resuming his flight toward the carriers, Leslie observed the destroyer heading for a second downed and floating TBD, so he turned back to signal the same information to another destroyer. (The man sitting on the wing of the torpedo plane, rescued, proved to be Chief Aviation Pilot Esders; his gunner, however, was dead.)

By this time Leslie was too low on gas to make *Enterprise*. His wingman Holmberg was in worse shape because the friction of his unretractable wheels had required more fuel than normal just to keep pace with Leslie. Both planes had been in the air five and one-half hours. Before hitting the water, Leslie's gunner-radioman wrenched loose and threw overboard his machine gun, to prevent it breaking off and bashing Leslie's skull on impact with the sea.

The remaining planes of the squadron landed successfully on the flight decks of *Hornet* and *Enterprise*. *Hornet* had been unfortunate throughout the day. Her torpedo squadron had been annihilated; her dive bombers had failed to intercept the enemy and some of them were forced to ditch; and her fighter squadron had plunged into the sea because the Point Option furnished them was in error and they had run out of fuel. Now she was hit with another tragedy.

One of our SBD's, waved off because of a faulty approach, crash-landed on her deck. The wounded pilot, who evidently had his finger on the trigger of his energized machine guns, sprayed the deck and upper works with 50-caliber bullets, piercing bulkheads of half-inch steel, killing five of the ship's crew and wounding more than twenty others. Among those killed was Lieutenant Royal R. Ingersoll II, a brilliant young officer, serving as assistant gunnery control officer. Ingersoll's father, Admiral Royal E. Ingersoll, was at the time commander in chief, U.S. Atlantic Fleet; his grandfather, Rear Admiral Royal Rodney Ingersoll, had been an academy graduate of the class of 1868.

No sooner had Fletcher and staff climbed *Astoria*'s ladder and even before the boat could be hooked on, two of our dive bombers dropped unexpectedly from the sky and ditched within feet of *Astoria*'s gangway ladder. The occupants of the first plane threw over a rubber raft, stepped into it and from there to our whaleboat. The pilot and gunner of the second imitated that performance but were dunked briefly in the process. Both planes sank within seconds as their crews climbed on board. The two pilots reported to the bridge so calmly that I would not have been surprised if their leader had said, "Sir, I have delivered the mail." The pilots were Leslie and his wingman, Lieutenant "Lefty" Holmberg.

Fletcher's first step after shifting to *Astoria* had been to order cruiser *Portland* to take *Yorktown* in tow. Before Captain Laurence DuBose could begin passing the necessary lines, radar showed a second flight of enemy planes approaching at about fifty miles out.

Apparently, after Kobayashi and his bombers took off and even before the result of the attack had been reported, Yamaguchi learned that he was opposing not one but three American carriers. He had only ten torpedo planes ready for launching. He was determined to strike before being hit himself, so he ordered *Hiryu* to launch the ten torpedo planes plus six fighters at once. Tomonaga, who commanded the air armada that raided Midway several hours before, took off with this flight and was on his way by 1245.

Yorktown lay dead in the water for slightly more than an hour after being hit. The square yellow breakdown flag with crossed blue stripes flew at her masthead. We had no information at that time about the damage she had sustained. She was not burning. We knew that her damage control party, her officers, and crew were making every effort to restore her fighting mobility.

Just as we heard the alarm and saw the warning signal that a second attack was coming, down went the breakdown flag and up *Yorktown*'s yardarm went a flag signal meaning, "My speed five." A cheer, a spontaneous cheer, went up from every ship of the screen. There is at least one man in every gun crew who knows something of signals. Most of those on deck knew the descending breakdown flag, for it is distinctive and is flown only from the masthead.

"There is something about a sailor" is an old saying that no one can deny. I have always held the American bluejacket in esteem and admired him for his capability and his loyalty. At this hour I was very, very proud of him. His morale never faltered even during the sneak attack on Pearl Harbor, and at Midway it was at its peak. In a recent letter to me, *Yorktown*'s captain, now retired Vice Admiral Buckmaster, wrote, "I heard that cheer, I still hear it."

Soon *Yorktown*'s "My speed five" flag hoist was replaced with "My speed ten," then by "My speed nineteen" (the last speed signal hoisted) as we spotted the approaching torpedo planes.

There were ten fighters on *Yorktown*'s flight deck, each with only 20 to 25 gallons of gas in its tanks. These were quickly manned and, disregarding the direction of the little wind we had, eight of the ten fighters, led by Thach, managed to take off. Had they been weighted down by full fuel tanks, launching would have been impossible. Clearing the ship just in time, Thach made a sharp turn and shot down an enemy plane before it could drop its torpedo.

Some ten miles before reaching us, Tomonaga broke his formation and dispersed his flight so that the attackers seemed to come at us from all directions. Flying low, almost skimming the water like hungry sea birds, they presented a serious problem for our antiaircraft control.

Once they slipped within our outer screen our difficulty increased, for firing this low we were in danger of hitting each other. My cruisers fired main battery 8-inch guns into the sea in advance of the low-flying planes. Explosions of these shells on hitting the water threw up columns 100 feet high as a splash wall through which the planes could not safely pass.

Of Tomonaga's ten attacking planes, at least eight—including his own—were shot down by our fighters and A.A. guns. Two somehow got through and with deadly accuracy slipped two fish into *Yorktown*'s port side. The carrier had avoided two torpedoes before being hit. If she had been able to make thirty instead of nineteen knots, she might have combed the oncoming tracks as she had done at Coral Sea. At 1442, one hour after she had signaled "My speed five," the hard-fighting *Yorktown* went dead in the water for the second and last time. She took a list of seventeen degrees to port.

Yorktown's plight was well described by Buckmaster in a personal letter to me: "She was dead in the water for some time, but finally got up to about 20 knots. With this reduced speed I was unable to avoid the torpedo attacks and received two hits on the port side amidships. The ship stopped, took a list to port. It became difficult to stand up as the list increased.

"About this time and just after I had received reports

from below that the engine rooms were flooded, that nothing could be done to check the progressively increasing list, the auxiliary power diesel engine started up automatically. The exhaust outlet for this engine was on the starboard side just below the bridge. The loudspeaker system was inoperative, and the noise from the exhaust of the diesel engine was so great that no orders could be given. I sent a messenger below to have the diesel stopped but was informed that the controls were under water and could not be reached. The list, increasing to 26 degrees, made standing up most difficult. Capsizing seemed imminent. Large bubbles of air were being replaced by water entering the compartments below. The air could be heard escaping even above the sound of the diesel exhaust."

The shock of explosions had created havoc throughout the ship. Quick-acting watertight doors were so warped they could not be closed; the engine rooms were flooded; some fuel oil tanks were open to the sea and spreading a sticky, stinking oil film over the surface of the unusually calm waters. The port side of the canted flight deck was almost flush with the ocean surface.

Buckmaster reluctantly ordered the ship abandoned. His orders were obeyed with drill-like precision, calmly and with no indication of panic. The wounded—and after both bombing and torpedo attacks, there were many—were lowered into boats or rafts quickly provided by cruisers and destroyers of the screen. After an inspection of the ship Commander Dixie Kiefer, executive officer, reported all hands including the sick evacuated. Buckmaster ordered him over the side and Kiefer complied, but fell part of the way and broke an ankle.

The skipper, believing himself alone on this ship of which he was so proud, watched rescue-operations for a while, then started his inspection. Leaving the debris-cluttered bridge, he made his way with difficulty along the starboard side and finding all 5-inch gun platforms abandoned (except one at which the entire crew lay dead from the bombing attack), visited the battle dressing stations, the flag and captain's quarters, and descended a ladder leading to the hangar deck, the port side of which was at water level. Finding no living thing, Buckmaster worked his way aft, went hand-over-hand down a rope at the stern and into the water where he was picked up by destroyer *Ham-*

mann.

A question has been raised as to why we did not shoot down the ten enemy torpedo planes before they came within torpedo range, as the Japanese had done to the squadrons led by Waldron, Lindsey, and Massey a few hours before. The answer: *Yorktown*'s combat air patrol met the enemy about ten miles out, but a good part of that patrol had to engage Tomonaga's six protective Zero fighters. Our remaining fighters shot down many of the enemy torpedo planes but could not bag all of them. The remarkable last-minute launching of Thach and his eight F4F-4 planes mopped up the remainder, but some of the enemy pilots were able to drop their torpedoes before crashing.

Enterprise and *Hornet*, hull down on the horizon, knew from their radarscopes that an attack was on the way, but had problems of their own. Most of *Yorktown*'s records were lost, but *Enterprise*'s log shows the entry: "At 1205, twenty enemy planes bearing 310 degrees, coming in." Entries in the *Enterprise* log for the two hours following that of 1205 to the time when *Yorktown* had to be abandoned read:

    1210: Landed own attack group [that of McClusky, whose planes had hit Nagumo and had long been in the air].

    1233–1235: Launched eight fighters, fifth Combat Patrol.

    1237–1238: Landed two *Yorktown* bombers, 5-B-3 and 5-B-16. Pilot reported *Yorktown* in bad shape, unable to recover planes.

    1242–1248: Landed seven *Yorktown* SBD bombers, 5-B-7; 5-B-8; 5-B-9; 5-B-10; 5-B-12; 5-B-13; 5-B-14, and 5-B-15.

    12–1248: Landed seven more *Yorktown* SBD bombers [numbers recorded].

    1251–1259: Landed *Yorktown* four fighters and six SBD bombers [numbers recorded].

    1304–1305: Landed *Yorktown* fighters 5-F-10 and 5-F-15.

    1339–1341: Launched 6 VF [fighters], sixth Combat Patrol.

    1347–1359: Landed third and fourth Combat Patrols, 16 VF [fighters].

1410: Shot down enemy seaplane tracker, 50 miles south our force.

To conduct these operations, it was necessary for Task Force 16 to steam at high speed just south of east. Added to all this, our screening ships protecting the carriers at Midway were not adequately equipped with truly effective antiaircraft guns. They mounted excellent 5-inch A.A. weapons, but they had not yet been outfitted with the 40- and 20-millimeter rapid-fire guns that proved so effective throughout the rest of the war.

We had at Midway what was called the One-Point-One, a multibarreled piece developed at the Naval Gun Factory. The weapon got its name from the 1.1-pound projectile it fired. A five-man crew was needed for the complicated feeding the gun required. Because of the watchlike precision of so many of its tight-tolerance parts, the gun often jammed and gave us a great deal of trouble. Added to a multitude of other drawbacks, the 1.1's pedestal occupied so much deck space that it finally had to be removed and junked. The weapon turned out to be a complete flop. It was replaced but not forgotten by most gunnery officers, who thoroughly detested it.

Fortunately, at about this time the British touted us onto the Oerlicken machine gun, a Swiss design that featured enough tolerance in its moving parts to provide much-needed reliability and endurance. We soon began using this weapon in 20- and 40-millimeter versions.

Spruance, when *Yorktown* was damaged by the bombing attack, had reinforced Fletcher's screen with heavy cruisers *Pensacola* and *Vincennes,* destroyers *Balch* and *Benham.* We of the screen circled the carrier at 20 knots, radius about 2,000 yards, Fletcher with me on *Astoria*'s flag bridge. When Buckmaster's decision to abandon reached us, all ships stopped long enough to lower motor lifeboats, and destroyers moved in for rescue operations, in which they were superb.

Until *Balch* and *Benham* joined us, Captain R. G. Tobin, Destroyer Division 4, in *Russell,* commanded the destroyer screen. *Balch* carried Captain E. P. Sauer, '16, commanding Destroyer Squadron 6. Sauer, one year senior to Tobin, naturally assumed responsibility for the rescue. Each destroyer, after picking up survivors in its vicinity, was to replace another in the screen, because only destroyers carried underwater listening gear for the detection of enemy submarines. However, circumstances made rotation difficult and some of the DD's were in position to rescue more than others and furthermore could not avoid doing so.

Russell's skipper, Lieutenant Commander G. R. Hartwig, described the situation as he faced it: "I approached her [*Yorktown*'s] starboard side expecting to go alongside but, before I got there, they began abandoning ship. Had I closed in, hundreds could have been crushed between the two ships. I stopped about fifty yards off. Survivors swarmed down the *Yorktown*'s side and around my propellers. A new multiple radar contact at this time indicated the approach of planes believed to be hostile. Squadron Commander Sauer ordered all DD's to get clear. I could not comply because my props were fouled with *Yorktown* swimmers.

"I could not move a wheel without making hamburger of human flesh, so continued picking them up. Tobin [division commander] concurred in my decision to expedite the rescue. We had on board the first one hundred when it was learned that the radar contact was that of our own or Task Force 16 planes returning from combat. Just one of those lucky things. I did pick up Dixie Kiefer [*Yorktown* exec] but transferred him and eight of the most badly wounded to *Astoria* that night or next day."

Destroyer *Benham* (Lieutenant Commander J. M. Worthington), like *Russell*, surrounded by swimmers, could not comply with the order to move out; nor could *Balch*, Sauer's flagship. Under the circumstances, the order applied only to those who were free to turn a propeller. We witnessed the remarkable rescue operation from *Astoria*. Cargo nets were thrown over the sides of destroyers and used as ladders to safety. Carling life rafts were thrown overboard and as soon as filled were towed by motor lifeboats—also loaded with survivors pulled from the water —to the destroyer sides.

Some crew members dove overboard to help the helpless; stretchers were lowered for the wounded who were not already in lifeboat stretchers, which had been lowered from *Yorktown*'s deck as fast as they were brought up from the sick bay. The weather had been kind to us; the sea was almost as smooth as a rug. Had the sea kicked up, or had the carrier been ablaze when abandoned, there would have been heavy loss of life.

The ship was given time for an orderly demise; there were plenty of life preservers for those who had neglected to don them—as many, including officers, invariably did with action pending. Almost as if consciously striving to maintain order in the face of catastrophe, most of the crew members removed their shoes before going over the side and, for some unspoken reason, left them arranged in neat rows on the flight deck. The exact number left dead on board is not known definitely since the ship was not salvaged. In one hour and forty minutes, 2,280 men including the wounded were rescued and the destroyers returned to their assigned positions in the screen as Sauer circled the area to make certain no one had been left to drown.

The rescuing destroyers now were faced with additional problems. The complement assigned a modern destroyer of the time was 250 officers and men; messing and berthing facilities were provided for that number only, and there was no such thing as idle space in a ship designed for fighting. *Benham* found herself with 725 passengers; *Balch* with 541; *Russell,* 508; *Anderson,* 204; *Morris,* 193; *Hammann,* 85 including Captain Buckmaster; and *Hughes,* 24.

A large percentage of those rescued were coated with sticky, foul-odored fuel oil. They had brought with them nothing but the wet, stained, and tattered clothes in which they stood. Hoses were led out and turned on the refugees, while members of the regular crews, with the generosity somehow always shown by the American bluejacket, emptied their lockers and fitted the visitors with clean, dry duds. Galley facilities were taxed to the limit on those DD's carrying five hundred or more of the rescued, and officers and men could sit or bunk only in relays. Admittedly, sleeping in shifts will keep the mattresses warm, but these already had warmth enough in tropic latitudes.

Five hundred or more additional humans give a destroyer an added weight load in tonnage that is not static and threatens stability if the ship's metacentric height is dangerously reduced. The difference between center of gravity (determined by weight of ship and cargo) and center of buoyancy (weight of water displaced by the ship's hull) is known as metacentric height. It is very small, measured in feet. The center of gravity must be lower than the center of buoyancy. Should it be reduced to zero, the ship *could* capsize. In a typhoon, late in the war, three of Halsey's DD's, light because they were low on fuel, did capsize—with heavy loss of life.

Worthington, commanding *Benham,* the destroyer carrying the greatest number of rescued on board, had these men sent below, to engine and firerooms and even to the small steering engine compartment, to keep down his center of gravity. Hartwig, with 508 refugees, told me, "I tried to keep them below but you know how it is! I ballasted the ship by filling empty tanks with sea water, keeping the weight as low as possible." Again the sea was kind to us, placid and pleasant.

Japanese records do not tell whether any of Tomonaga's torpedo planes which attacked *Yorktown* escaped. I believe that none did; I believe I saw the last one shot down between *Astoria* and the carrier, as he sped past our bow, one of our fighters on his tail, and both passing through concentrated A.A. fire from our ships. Our fighter got him, then as our pilot attempted to gain altitude and get clear, his plane burst into flames—clearly a victim of our gunfire—and he bailed out. This pilot was Reserve Ensign Mortimer C. Tootle, IV, a towheaded twenty-one-year-old from St. Joseph, Missouri, whose total flying time in the Pacific had been less than two minutes. When Thach took off with his almost fuelless fighters just as the *Hiryu* planes moved in, Tootle, fresh from college and naval training, "somehow" got into one and took to the air for his first nontraining carrier flight. Just clear of the ship and even before he could get his wheels up, he made a sharp turn, got on the tail of a Jap torpedo plane, and shot it down. As he tried to get clear, he took a bullet from some place, burst into flame, and bailed out successfully at an altitude of less than 1,000 feet. He narrowly missed landing on a destroyer deck. The DD stopped and picked him up. Later questioned by a reporter, he was asked, "Were you frightened?" He replied, "Not until I got on board that destroyer; then I was scared to death it might sink."

THE SINKING OF HIRYU

4 June, evening, to 6 June. The ten SBD's sent out by

Fletcher to find the fourth enemy flattop were aloft for more than three hours searching to the outer limit of their fuel endurance. They sighted nothing, probably because of scattered clouds, and were making their way back when at 1445 Lieutenant Samuel Adams sighted the wakes of ships.

This lad did not go off half-cocked with a quick and alarming message of what appeared to be within his area; he went closer, studied the silhouettes, then radioed the *Yorktown:* "One carrier, two battleships, three heavy cruisers, four destroyers, latitude 31 degrees 15 minutes, longitude 179-05, course north, speed fifteen." The position given was only a few miles off, after hours of dead reckoning navigation. The contact position placed the enemy slightly more than one hundred miles west and north of Fletcher.

Adams could not know that at the time he sent his report *Yorktown* was stopped and hurt. The message was received by Fletcher on the bridge of *Astoria* and by Spruance on *Enterprise.* Spruance knew the plight of Task Force 17 and began launching from his flagship at 1530. He soon had in the air an attack mission of twenty-four SBD's, half of them loaded with 1,000-pound bombs, the others with 500-pound and 100-pound combinations.

The flight was led by Lieutenant W. E. Gallaher, whose squadron a few hours before had smeared *Akagi.* It was composed of ten dive bombers from *Enterprise* (six from VS-6 and four from VB-6) and fourteen from *Yorktown* (VB-3). All pilots were "veterans" of the forenoon attack; those from *Yorktown* had taken refuge on *Enterprise* when their mother carrier had been found disabled on their return. These were led by Lieutenant Commander Dewitt W. Shumway, executive officer of squadron VB-3. Leslie, the outfit's skipper, was grounded on the deck of *Astoria.*

While launching, Spruance signaled Fletcher: "Have you any instructions for me?" This called for a decision. Fletcher could not conduct an air battle from a cruiser. He did not have the communication and other facilities required for the job. His options were to transfer to *Hornet* or turn over command to Spruance, who was well qualified and had with him on *Enterprise* the entire aviation staff inherited from Halsey. Without hesitation, Fletcher replied: "None. Will conform to your movements." Thus,

Fletcher relinquished command, and Spruance took over. We continued to circle *Yorktown* until rescue operations were completed.

Japanese sources say that at this point *Hiryu*, with six fighters in the air on combat patrol, had a reserve of only a half-dozen dive bombers and four or five torpedo planes. However, Yamaguchi decided to launch a third attack before dark and wired Yamamoto of his intention to do so. After all, the survivors of Kobayashi's bombing attack had reported leaving one of our carriers dead in the water and burning fiercely. Tomonaga, before being shot down, also had radioed two sure torpedo hits on a fast-moving carrier of the *Enterprise* class.

The bold Japanese admiral, not knowing that the two carriers were one and the same and having been assured that we had only three of this type in the area, apparently was convinced that the American commander had been reduced to just one ship capable of launching planes for further combat. Furthermore, though at some distance still, Yamamoto with his heavy guns and light carrier *Hosho* and Kondo with his battleships, cruisers, and light carrier *Zuiho* were steaming to join him.

If relatively small *Hiryu*, in two raids, had sunk or disabled two of the American's three best carriers, and *Hosho* and *Zuiho* would soon arrive on the scene, backed up by the might of Japan's heavy ships, why not polish off the remaining enemy carrier, finish the job, congratulate the emperor, and serve rice wine to the troops tomorrow, after they had occupied the Midway base? "Mission accomplished! Remnants of the United States Pacific Fleet scattered and running for cover!"

But in the words of Robert Burns,

> The best-laid schemes o' mice an' men
> Gang aft agley,
> An' lea'e us nought but grief an' pain,
> For promis'd joy!

Yamaguchi did not have long to live after reaching his decision. Twenty-four U.S. dive bombers were heading toward him. His number was up.

Gallaher's air group, flying at 13,000 feet, sighted the enemy force at 1645 at a distance of thirty miles. The ships were in formation on a westerly course and appeared to be steaming at about 20 knots. Weather conditions were ideal with excellent visibility, unlimited ceiling, scattered clouds at 2,500 feet. The sea was smooth.

Gallaher expected—and found—a combat air patrol over the carrier. He led his group to a position from which he could strike down sun from 19,000 feet. He directed the planes from *Enterprise* to follow him in his dive on *Hiryu* and ordered Shumway and the *Yorktown* bombers to strike the nearer of the two battleships and to go on from there.

Spruance had been unable to furnish fighter coverage for this attack. *Hornet* had lost, through fuel exhaustion, the fighters she had sent with Ring on the morning mission. The CAP over the two carriers had been rotated throughout the day, and all remaining fighter planes were needed to patrol over *Enterprise* and *Hornet*.

Lookouts on the enemy cruiser *Chikuma*, at 1700, sighted planes just as Gallaher was about to push over for his attack. The alarm was sounded. All ships of the screen opened up with antiaircraft guns; reconnaissance fighters overhead spotted our dive bombers as they dove in for the kill. *Hiryu* threw her rudder hard over, putting the carrier in a 90 degree turn as bombs were released by the pilots of VB-6 and VS-6.

Shumway, observing no direct hits by Gallaher's bombs, and in the midst of intensive A.A. fire, coolly evaluated the situation and demonstrated competent leadership and outstanding judgment by shifting from his assigned battleship target to carrier *Hiryu*, Yamaguchi's flagship. The first four planes of *Yorktown*'s bombing squadron, piloted by Lieutenants Shumway and Bottomley and Ensigns Cooner and Merrill, were attacked in their dives by Japanese fighters. The four continued to bore in, as did the other ten *Yorktown* planes, and four direct hits were scored on *Hiryu*.

Two pilots, Ensigns Campbell and Benson, seeing *Hiryu* burning furiously when their turns came to push over, shifted to the battleship and claimed (not confirmed) one direct hit, one near miss. Shumway's squadron suffered the loss of two planes, one flown by Lieutenant (j.g.) O. B. Wiseman with radioman G. U. Dawn, ARM3/c, the other piloted by Ensign J. C. Butler with radioman ARM3/c D. D. Berg. The Navy later recognized their bravery by naming destroyer escorts: No. 667, USS *Wiseman* and No. 339, USS *Butler*. Three of the planes were so badly shot up they later had to be destroyed after landing safely on *Enterprise*.

Hiryu shook as she was hit by four bombs in rapid sucession. Her flight deck forward was destroyed, the elevator blown from its supports and slammed against the bridge structure. She burst into flames as planes on deck caught fire and bombs and torpedoes exploded, throwing men and debris into the air. Captain Kaku made every effort to save his ship; the crew battled the flames above and below decks, but the fires could not be brought under control. Most of the men trapped below perished. The ladders leading from engine and firerooms were useless because of smoke and flame.

One half hour after Gallaher and Shumway struck, *Hornet*'s group of sixteen dive bombers arrived. Finding *Hiryu* a flaming wreck, they dove on battleships and cruisers, but scored no hits. Later in the afternoon, squadrons of Army B-17's came from Midway, more from the island of Molokai, 1,300 miles to the eastward. Releasing their bombs from great altitudes, as was their practice, they did no damage to anyone, as usual.

By midnight the *Hiryu* had taken a list of about 15 degrees; her bilges were flooded, partly by water used in the fire-fighting effort; and destroyers were standing by. At about 0230 the following morning, it was admitted that the ship could not be saved. Japanese reports quote Yamaguchi as telling his assembled officers and men, "As Commanding Officer of this carrier division, I am fully and solely responsible for the loss of *Hiryu* and *Soryu*. I shall remain on board to the end. I command all of you to leave the ship and continue your loyal service to His Majesty, the Emperor."

A destroyer was called alongside for transfer of the emperor's portrait, and within two hours the ship was abandoned by all except those trapped below and Admiral Yamaguchi, who refused to leave. According to reports, he tied himself to the bridge and said, "The moon is so bright in the sky." Captain Kaku, knowing the meaning of this, is said to have replied, "We shall watch the moon together," determined to die with his admiral.

At 0510, 5 June, Japanese destroyers sent two torpedoes

into the ship but failed to scuttle her. *Hiryu* stubbornly remained afloat until 0900, when she turned over for her final dive. Meanwhile, between abandon ship and sinking, a number of crew members who had been trapped in engine room compartments somehow broke out and were seen on deck. A plane dispatched by Yamamoto from light carrier *Hosho*, which accompanied the fleet flagship, photographed the doomed ship and sighted men on board. She radioed that survivors were on board and efforts are reported to have been made for their rescue. Fearing the carrier might capsize at any moment, these men finally dove overboard and swam to an abandoned lifeboat at 0815. A Midway-based PBY sighted them thirteen days later on 18 June. Captain Simard immediately ordered out seaplane tender *Ballard,* which picked up twenty survivors. These POW's later were delivered to Nimitz at Pearl.

Yamamoto exchanged a series of messages with Nagumo and other force commanders during the afternoon of 5 June. He had received a heavy dose of bad news from Nagumo, but still hoped for the anticipated fleet engagement. At 1915 that evening he sent all division and force commanders a message of bold encouragement: "The enemy fleet, which has practically been destroyed, is retiring to the East. (2) Combined Fleet units in the vicinity are preparing to pursue the remnants and at the same time to occupy Midway. (3) The Main Body is scheduled to reach Lat. 32 degrees ten minutes N., Long. one seven five dash forty three E., on course 90 degrees, speed 20 knots, by midnight. (4) The Mobile Force, Occupation Force less Crudiv 7, and Advance Force [submarines] will immediately contact and attack the enemy." At the same time, he ordered his Aleutian landing forces to proceed with the occupation of Attu and Kiska.

We do not know whether Yamamoto, in issuing orders at this point, was confident, hopeful, or very desperate. His staff is reported to have found him sullen and uncommunicative. At 2030 he radioed submarine I-168, Lieutenant Commander Yahachi Tanabe, cruising in the Midway area, to surface and bombard the Midway airstrips until two the next morning. Then Rear Admiral Kurita's cruisers would take over and continue shelling, to make certain we could not use the airfield as a relay station for plane reinforcements from Hawaiian bases.

Nagumo, however, appears to have been going to pieces at about this time: When *Chikuma*'s plane returned with an erroneous contact report, he wired Yamamoto at 2130: "Total strength of the enemy is five carriers, six cruisers, and fifteen destroyers. They are steaming westward. Am offering protection to *Hiryu* and retiring to the northwest at eighteen knots."

Little more than an hour later, he radioed: "There still exist four enemy carriers, six cruisers, and sixteen destroyers. They are steaming westward. *None of our carriers operational.*"

Somewhat shocked, Yamamoto ordered Admiral Kondo, already speeding to join forces with Nagumo, to take over command. He ordered Nagumo rather testily to take charge of the sinking carriers and the ships standing by them.

Kondo immediately ordered all ships under his command to prepare for the night engagement that the Japanese at this time needed so desperately. With his air power gone, Yamamoto must hit our Pacific Fleet with everything he had—destroyer torpedoes and the main batteries of heavy ships—before daylight, or suffer an air attack from the several carriers reportedly left to his opponent and heading west during the night.

Kondo ordered ships formerly under Nagumo, except those standing by the still floating *Akagi* and *Hiryu,* to reverse course and join in the expected night battle, which he indicated would be at about one in the morning. He directed the disposition of forces from his flatship, heavy cruiser *Atago.* However, the concentration of forces could not be accomplished.

As further intelligence reports came in—all bad—Yamamoto began to realize the seriousness of his position. His carriers *Kaga* and *Soryu* definitely had been sunk. The *Akagi* and the *Hiryu* were burning hulks, abandoned or about to be abandoned. For the present, "enough was enough." Members of his staff concurred in his estimate of the situation and with his decision to "get the hell out." At five minutes before three in the morning a message was broadcast to all ships of the fleet: "Occupation of Midway is canceled."

Yamamoto directed the transports to head westward to get well out of range of Midway-based planes. He ordered his commanders to rendezvous with him for refueling next day, Latitude 33° North, Longitude 177° East, about seven hundred miles northwest of Midway atoll. Kondo and Nagumo joined him there at 1300, 5 June; Takasu, with his battleships and cruisers of the Aleutian screening force met the main body later in the day and further to the westward.

Yamamoto had lost and he knew it. Retiring toward home waters, he is said to have taken to his bed for days, complaining of stomach trouble and eating nothing but rice gruel. Japan had lost four modern—almost irreplaceable—aircraft carriers with all their planes and most of their pilots, those same pilots who had so skillfully blasted our Pacific Fleet on 7 December 1941. And Chuichi Nagumo, the vice admiral upon whom the emperor had bestowed almost every imperial honor and medal for having led the Pearl Harbor raid, was now a broken man.

IX
THE GENERALS
TELL IT

WATERLOO
ALESIA
BERLIN

Waterloo (1815)

Napoleon Bonaparte

The great alliance—principally Great Britain,
Austria, Prussia, and Russia—had worn out the
French armies, especially in the invasion and retreat
from Moscow, and brought about Napoleon's re-
linquishment of the crown and his exile. But in 1815
the exiled emperor returned from Elba, and gathered
a new force. The allies organized once more to
bring him down.

The critical encounter came at Waterloo, near
Brussels in present Belgium, in June, 1815. The
allied commander was the Duke of Wellington, who
had won victories in Spain and Portugal, but had
never before confronted Napoleon himself. The issue
depended not only on the tactics of the battlefield
but on the speed with which the cooperating forces
of Blucher (for Wellington) and Grouchy (for
Napoleon) should come up. Napoleon's defeat was
final, resulting in his exile to St. Helena and the re-
establishment of the French monarchy under Louis
XVIII.

The defeated emperor spent part of his time in
dictating his memoirs. They served not only to justify
his own career, but to develop the myth of Napoleonic greatness which was to influence the future
of France. The account of Waterloo is part of the
memoirs.

A battle is a dramatic action, which has its beginning, its
middle and its end. The order of battle which the two armies take up, the opening moves to come to grips, are the
exposition; the counter-moves, which the attacked army

makes, form the crux which imposes new dispositions and
brings on the crisis; from which springs the result, or de-
nouement. As soon as the attack by the centre of the
French army was revealed, the enemy general would make
counter-moves, either with his wings, or behind his line, in
order to provide a diversion, or rush to the support of the
point attacked; none of these movements could escape my
experienced eye in the central position which I had taken
up, and I had all my reserves under control to send them
according to my will or wherever the pressure of circumstances should demand their presence.

Ten artillery divisions, including three divisions of
twelve, came together, the left resting on the Charleroi
road on the hillock beyond La Belle-Alliance and in front
of the left-hand division of the 1st Corps. They were intended to support the attack on La Haie-Sainte, which two
divisions of the 1st Corps and the two divisions of the 6th
were to make, at the same time as the two other divisions
of the 1st Corps were moving on La Haye. By this means,
the whole left of the enemy would be turned.

While everything was going forward for this decisive
attack, Prince Jérôme's division, on the left, exchanged
shots at the Hougoumont wood. Soon the firing became
very brisk. The enemy having unmasked close on forty
guns, General Reille moved forward the artillery battery
of his 2nd Division, and I sent orders to General Kellermann to have his twelve light guns moved up. Soon the
cannonade became really hot. Prince Jérôme carried the
Hougoumont wood several times, and was several times
turned out of it.

This was defended by an English Guards division, the
enemy's best troops, which I was glad to see on his right,
which made the attack on the left all the easier. Foy's division supported Prince Jérôme's, and both sides performed
prodigies of valour. The English Guards covered the woods
and avenues of the château with their dead, but not without selling their lives dearly. After various vicissitudes,
which took up several hours of the day, the whole wood
remained in French hands; but the château, where several
hundred stout fellows were embattled, put up an unbreak-
able resistance. I gave orders to assemble a battery of
eight field howitzers which set fire to the barns and roofs,
and made the French masters of this position.

Marshal Ney received the honour of commanding the big attack in the centre. It could not be entrusted to a braver man, nor to one more accustomed to this kind of thing. He sent one of his aides-de-camp to announce that everything was ready and that he waited only for the signal. Before giving it, I wanted to cast a final look over the whole battlefield, and perceived in the direction of Saint-Lambert a cloud which looked to me like troops. I said to my chief of staff, 'Marshal, what do you see towards Saint-Lambert? I think I can see five to six thousand men there; that is probably a detachment of Grouchy's.'

All the glasses of the general-staff were fixed on this point. The weather was rather misty. Some maintained, as often happens on such occasions, that they were not troops, but trees; others that they were columns in position; some others that they were troops on the march. In this uncertainty, without further deliberation, I sent for Lieutenant-General Daumont, and ordered him to go with his division of light cavalry and General Subervic's to reconnoitre the right, get into touch speedily with the troops which were arriving at Saint-Lambert, effect a junction with them if they belonged to Marshal Grouchy, hold them if they belonged to the enemy. These 3,000 cavalrymen only had to do a right wheel in fours to get outside the lines of the army; they moved quickly and without confusion for three thousand toises, and there drew themselves up in battle array, as a cross-piece to the whole right of the army.

A quarter of an hour later, a Chasseur officer brought in a Prussian Black Hussar who had just been taken prisoner by the despatch-riders of a flying column of three hundred chasseurs, who were out scouting between Wavres and Planchenoit. This hussar was the bearer of a letter. He was extremely intelligent and gave by word of mouth all the information that could be desired. The column which was to be seen at Saint-Lambert was the advance-guard of the Prussian General Bülow, who was arriving with 30,000 men; it was the 4th Prussian Corps which had not been engaged at Ligny.

The letter was in fact the announcement of the arrival of this corps; the general was asking the Duke of Wellington for further orders. The hussar said that he had been at Wavres that morning, that the three other corps of the

Prussian army were camped there, that they had spent the night of the 17th to 18th there, that there were no Frenchmen in front of them, that he presumed the French to have marched on Planchenoit, that one patrol of his regiment had been as far as two leagues from Wavres during the night without encountering any French body. The Duke of Dalmatia immediately sent the intercepted letter and the hussar's report to Marshal Grouchy, to whom he repeated the order to march, without halting, on Saint-Lambert, and to take General Bülow's corps in the rear.

It was eleven o'clock; the officer had at most only five leagues to cover, on good roads all the way, to reach Marshal Grouchy; he promised to be there at one o'clock. From the most recent news received of this marshal, it was known that he was to move, at daylight, on Wavres. . . .

I immediately gave orders to Count de Lobau to cross the Charleroi road, by a change of direction to his right by divisions, and to go towards Saint-Lambert to support the light cavalry; to choose a good intermediate position where he could, with 10,000 men, hold up 30,000, if that became necessary; to attack the Prussians vigorously, as soon as he should hear the first cannon shots from the troops which Marshal Grouchy had detached in their rear.

These dispositions were carried out at once. It was of the utmost importance that Count de Lobau's movement should take place without delay. Marshal Grouchy must have detached from Wavres 6,000 to 7,000 men to search in the direction of Saint-Lambert, and these would find themselves compromised, since General Bülow's corps amounted to 30,000 men. In exactly the same way General Bülow's corps would be compromised and lost, if, at the moment when he was attacked in the rear by 6,000 to 7,000 men, he were attacked in front by a man of Count de Lobau's calibre.

Seventeen to eighteen thousand Frenchmen, disposed and commanded in this fashion, were worth a great deal more than 30,000 Prussians; but these events involved a change in my original plan. I found myself weakened on the battlefield by 10,000 men, whom I was obliged to send against General Bülow. I only had 59,000 men against 90,000; moreover, the enemy army, which I was to attack, had just been increased by 30,000 men, already on the battlefield. It was 120,000 strong against 69,000—two to one.

'This morning the odds were nine to one in our favour,' I said to the Duke of Dalmatia. 'Bülow's arrival deprives us of three; but that still leaves us with six to four in our favour, and, if Grouchy retrieves the horrible blunder he made yesterday of twiddling his thumbs at Gembloux, and sends his detachment with speed, victory will be all the more decisive, because Bülow's corps will be entirely destroyed.' . . .

It was noon, and the sharp-shooters were engaged all along the line; but the battle had only really begun on the left, in the wood and around the Château of Hougoumont. On the extreme right General Bülow's troops were still stationary. They appeared to be forming up and to be waiting for their artillery to come through the defile.

I sent orders to Marshal Ney to open fire with his batteries, to get hold of the farm of La Haie-Sainte and to put an infantry division in position there; also to get hold of the village of La Haye and turn the enemy out of it, in order to cut all communication between the Anglo-Dutch army and General Bülow's corps. Eighty pieces of artillery soon belched forth death upon the whole left of the English line; one of their divisions was entirely wiped out by the cannon-balls and grape-shot.

While this attack was being unmasked, I watched closely to see what would be the movement of the enemy's general. He made none on his right; but I saw that on his left he was preparing for a big cavalry charge; I dashed there at the gallop. The charge had taken place; it had repulsed a column of infantry which was advancing on the plateau, had taken two eagles from it, and put seven guns out of action.

I ordered a brigade of General Milhaud's cuirassiers, of the second line, to charge this cavalry. It went off with shouts of 'Vive l'Empereur'; the English cavalry was broken, most of the men were left behind on the battlefield; the guns were retaken; the infantry protected. . . .

During this engagement I went along the line of the infantry of the 1st Corps, the cavalry of Milhaud's cuirassiers, and the Guard in the third line, in the midst of the cannon-balls, grape-shot and shells; they ricocheted between the lines. Brave General Devaux, commanding the artillery of the Guard, who was beside me, was killed by a cannon-ball. This loss was keenly felt, especially at that moment, for he knew better than anyone the positions occupied by the artillery reserves of the Guard, ninety-six pieces strong. Brigadier-General Lallemand succeeded him, and was wounded soon afterwards.

Confusion reigned in the English army. The baggage trains, the transport, and the wounded, seeing the French approaching the Brussels highway and the principal exit of the forest, scrambled *en masse* to effect their retreat. All the English, Belgian and German fugitives, who had received sabre wounds from the cavalry, rushed towards Brussels. It was four o'clock. Victory ought from then on to have been assured; but General Bülow's corps carried out its powerful diversion at this moment. From two o'clock in the afternoon onwards General Daumont had reported that General Bülow was debouching in three columns, and that the French Chasseurs were keeping up their fire all the while they were retiring before the enemy, which seemed to him very numerous. He estimated them at more than 40,000 men. He said, moreover, that his despatch-riders, well mounted, had gone several leagues in different directions and had not reported any news of Marshal Grouchy; and that, therefore, he could not be counted on.

At this very juncture, I received extremely annoying news from Gembloux. Marshal Grouchy, instead of leaving Gembloux at first light, as he had announced in his despatch of two in the morning, had still not left this camp at 10 A.M. The officer attributed this fact to the horrible weather—a ridiculous reason. This inexcusable inertia, in circumstances of such delicacy, on the part of such a zealous officer, was inexplicable.

However, the exchange of artillery fire between General Bülow and Count de Lobau broke out with little delay. The Prussian army was marching in échelons, with the centre in front. Its line of battle was at right angles to the right flank of the army, parallel to the road from La Haie-Sainte to Planchenoit. The centre échelon unmasked about thirty pieces of artillery. Our artillery opposed an equal number to it.

After an hour's cannonade, Count de Lobau, seeing that the first échelon was not supported, marched up to it, broke into it, and pushed it back a long way; but the two other lines, which appeared to have been delayed by the bad roads, rallied to the first échelon, and, without trying to breach the French line, sought to outflank it by a left wheel in battle. Count de Lobau, fearing that he might be turned, carried out his retreat, chequerwise, approaching the army. The fire of the Prussian batteries redoubled; up to sixty pieces of artillery could be counted. The cannon-balls were falling on the roadway before and behind La Belle-Alliance, where I was with my Guard: it was the fighting zone of the army.

At the most critical moment the enemy got so close that his grape-shot raked this road. I thereupon ordered General Duhesme, commanding my Young Guard, to go to the right of the 6th Corps with his two infantry brigades and twenty-four pieces of artillery, belonging to the Guard. A quarter of an hour later, this formidable battery opened up; the French artillery did not take long to gain the advantage: it was better manned and placed. As soon as the Young Guard were in action, the movement of the Prussians seemed to be halted; one could see signs of wavering in their line; however, they still continued to extend it to their left, outflanking the French right and reaching as far as the heights of Planchenoit.

Lieutenant-General Morand thereupon proceeded with four battalions of the Old Guard and sixteen guns to the right of the Young Guard. Two regiments of the Old Guard took up positions in front of Planchenoit. The Prussian line was outflanked. General Bülow was repulsed, his left moved backwards, closed in, and imperceptibly his whole line fell back. Count de Lobau, General Duhesme and Marshal Morand marched forward; they soon occupied the positions which General Bülow's artillery had held. Not only had this general exhausted his attack, and brought into play all his reserves, but, held at first, he was now in retreat. The Prussian cannon-balls not only fell short of the Charleroi road, but did not even reach the positions which Count de Lobau had occupied; it was seven P.M.

It was two hours since Count d'Erlon had got possession of La Haye, had outflanked the whole English left and Gen-

eral Bülow's right. The light cavalry of the 1st Corps, pursuing the enemy infantry on the plateau of La Haye, had
been brought back by a superior force of cavalry. Count
Milhaud thereupon climbed the height with his cuirassiers
and warned General Lefebvre-Desnouettes, who started at
once at the trot to back him up.

It was five o'clock, the moment when General Bülow's
attack was at its worst, when, far from being held, he kept
on throwing in new troops, which extended his line to the
right. The English cavalry was repulsed by the bold cuirassiers and chasseurs of the Guard. The English abandoned
all the battlefield between La Haie-Sainte and Mont-Saint-
Jean, which their left had occupied, and were brought to
bay on their right. At the sight of these brilliant charges,
shouts of victory were heard on the battlefield. I said 'It is
an hour too soon; nevertheless what has been done must be
followed up.'

I sent an order to Kellermann's cuirassiers, who were
still in position on the left, to go at full trot to support the
cavalry on the plateau. General Bülow was at this moment
threatening the flank and rear of the army; it was important not to fall back at any point, and to hold the present
position which the cavalry had taken, although it was pre-
mature. This move at full trot by 3,000 cuirassiers who
passed by with shouts of 'Vive l'Empereur,' and under the
gunfire of the Prussians, created a fortunate diversion at
this critical moment. The cavalry were marching on as if
to pursue the English army, and General Bülow's army was
still making progress on the flank and in the rear. To know
whether we were victorious or in danger the soldiers, even
the officers, sought to divine the answer from the expression on my face; but it displayed only confidence. It was
the fiftieth pitched battle that I had conducted in twenty
years.

However, the heavy cavalry division of the Guard, under the orders of General Guyot, who was in second line
behind Kellermann's cuirassiers, followed at full trot and
proceeded to the plateau. I noticed this, and sent Count
Bertrand to recall it; it was my reserve. When this general
got there, it was already committed and any movement of
withdrawal would have been dangerous. From five P.M.
onwards, I was thus deprived of my cavalry reserve, of that

reserve which, skilfully employed, had so often brought me victory.

However, these 12,000 picked cavalrymen performed miracles; they overwhelmed all the more numerous enemy cavalry which sought to oppose them, drove in several infantry squares, broke them up, seized sixty pieces of artillery, and, in the middle of the squares, captured ten standards, which three Chasseurs of the Guard and three cuirassiers presented to me in front of La Belle-Alliance. The enemy, for the second time that day, thought the battle lost, and saw with apprehension to what extent the bad battle-site which he had selected was going to add to his difficulties in his retreat. Ponsonby's brigade, charged by the red lancers of the Guard under General Colbert, was broken into. Its general was pierced by seven lance thrusts, and fell dead. The Prince of Orange, on the point of being seized, was severely wounded; but, not being backed up by a strong mass of infantry, which was still contained by General Bülow's attack, this gallant cavalry had to confine itself to holding the battlefield which it had conquered.

At length, at seven o'clock, when General Bülow's attack had been repulsed and the cavalry was still holding its own on the plateau which it had carried, the victory was won; 69,000 Frenchmen had beaten 120,000 men. Joy was visible on every face and hearts were lifted high. This feeling followed on the shock that had been experienced during the flank attack, launched by an entire army, which, for an hour, had even threatened to bring about the retreat of the army. At this juncture Marshal Grouchy's gunfire could be heard distinctly. It had passed beyond Wavres at the most distant point and at the nearest point; it was behind Saint-Lambert.

Marshal Grouchy had only left his camp at Gembloux at ten in the morning, and was halfway to Wavres between noon and one o'clock. He heard the dreadful cannonade of Waterloo. No experienced man could have mistaken it: it was the sound of several hundred guns, and from that moment two armies were hurling death at each other. General Excelmans, commanding the cavalry, was profoundly moved by it. He went up to the Marshal and said to him: 'The Emperor is at grips with the English army; there can be no doubt about it, such a furious fire can be no skirmish. Monsieur le Maréchal, we must march towards the sound of the guns. I am an old soldier of the Army of Italy; I have heard General Bonaparte preach this principle a hundred times. If we turn to the left we shall be on the battlefield in two hours.' . . .

The Marshal appeared to be convinced; but at this moment he received the report that his light cavalry had arrived at Wavres and was at grips with the Prussians; that all their units were assembled there; and that they amounted to at least 80,000 men. At this news, he continued his move on Wavres: he reached there at four in the afternoon. Believing that he had in front of him the whole Prussian army, he took two hours to take up battle stations and make his dispositions. It was then that he received the officer sent from the battlefield at ten in the morning. He detached General Pajol with 12,000 men to go to Limate, a bridge on the Dyle, a league in the rear of Saint-Lambert. This general arrived there at seven P.M. and crossed the river. Meanwhile Grouchy attacked Wavres.

As soon as General Bülow's attack had been repulsed, I gave orders to General Drouot, who was doing the duties of aide Major-General of the Guard, to rally his whole guard in front of the farm of La Belle-Alliance, where I was with eight battalions drawn up in two lines; the other eight had marched on to support the Young Guard and defend Planchenoit. However, the cavalry, which continued to hold the position on the plateau from which it dominated the whole battlefield, saw General Bülow's move but, deriving confidence from the reserves of the Guard, which it saw there to hold them, did not feel any anxiety as a result, and gave vent to cries of victory when they saw this corps repulsed. They were only waiting for the arrival of the infantry of the Guard to decide the victory; but they were staggered when they perceived the arrival of the numerous columns of Marshal Blücher.

Some regiments drew back. I noticed this. It was of the highest importance to put the cavalry in countenance again; and, realizing that I still needed another quarter of an hour to rally my whole Guard, I put myself at the head of four battalions, and advanced to the left in front of La

Haie-Sainte, sending aides-de-camp along the line to announce the arrival of Marshal Grouchy, and to say that,
with a little determination, the victory was soon to be
decided.

General Reille assembled his whole corps on the left, in
front of the Château of Hougoumont, and prepared his attack. It was important that the Guard should be in action
all at once, but the eight other battalions were still in the
rear. Being at the mercy of events, and seeing the cavalry
put out of countenance, and realizing that a reserve of infantry was needed to support it, I ordered General Friant
to go with these four battalions of the Middle Guard to
meet the enemy's attack; the cavalry pulled itself together
again and marched forward with its accustomed dash. The
four battalions of the Guard repulsed everybody that they
encountered; cavalry charges struck terror into the English ranks. Ten minutes later, the other battalions of the
Guard arrived. I drew them up in brigades, two battalions
in battle array and two in columns on the right and the
left; the 2nd Brigade in échelons, which combined the advantage of the two types of formation.

The sun had gone down; General Friant, who had been
wounded, and was passing by at this moment, said that
everything was going well, that the enemy appeared to be
forming up his rear-guard to support his retreat, but that
he would be completely broken, as soon as the rest of the
Guard debouched. A quarter of an hour was needed!

It was at this moment that Marshal Blücher arrived at La
Haie [Haye] and overthrew the French unit defending it;
this was the 4th Division of the 1st Corps; it fell back,
routed, and only offered slight resistance. Although it was
attacked by forces four times as strong, if only it had
shown a little resolution, or had barricaded itself up in the
houses, since night had already fallen, Marshal Blücher
would not have had the time to carry the village. It is there
that the cry of 'Sauve qui peut' is said to have been heard.

The breach effected, the line having been broken owing
to the lack of vigour of the troops at La Haie, the enemy
cavalry swept over the battlefield. General Bülow marched
forward; Count de Lobau put on a bold front. The route
became such that it was necessary to give orders to the
Guard, which was formed up to go forward, to change direction. This move was carried out in good order; the

Guard faced about, with its left on the side of La Haie-Sainte and its right on the side of La Belle-Alliance, confronting the Prussians and the attack on La Haie. Immediately afterwards, each battalion formed itself into a square. The four squadrons detailed for action charged the Prussians. At this moment the English cavalry brigade, which arrived from Ohain, marched forward. These 2,000 horse got in between General Reille and the Guard.

The disorder became appalling over the whole battlefield; I only just had time to place myself under the protection of one of the squares of the Guard. If General Guyot's cavalry division of the reserve had not committed itself, without orders, to following up Kellermann's cuirassiers, it would have repulsed this charge, prevented the English cavalry from penetrating into the battlefield, and the Foot Guard would then have been able to hold all the enemy's efforts. General Bülow marched on his left, still outflanking the whole battlefield.

Night added to the confusion and obstructed everything; if it had been daylight, and the troops had been able to see me, they would have rallied: nothing was possible in the darkness. The Guard began to retreat, the enemy's fire was already a hundred toises behind and the roads were cut. I remained for a long time, with my general staff, with the regiments of the Guard on a hillock. Four guns which were there, fired briskly into the plain; the last charge wounded Lord Paget, the English cavalry general. At last, there was not a moment to lose. I could only effect my retreat across country; cavalry, artillery, infantry, were all mingled pell mell.

The general staff reached the little village of Gennapes; it hoped to be able to rally a rear-guard corps there; but the disorder was appalling, all efforts were in vain. It was eleven P.M. Finding it impossible to organize a defence, I pinned my hope on Girard's division, the 3rd of the 2nd Corps, which I had left on the battlefield at Ligny, and to which I had sent orders to move on to Quatre-Bras to support the retreat.

Alesia (52)

Julius Caesar

Julius Caesar, by political arrangement, was elected consul at Rome in 59 B.C. and at the end of his term made proconsul or governor of the province of Gaul—mainly what is now northern Italy. He extended Roman power into modern Switzerland, France, Belgium, Gallia Transalpina (Gaul across the Alps), threatened the German tribes across the Rhine, and invaded the island of Britain. In 52 B.C. the Gallic tribes rose in revolt, under Vercingetorix, chief of the Arverni.

Caesar besieged Vercingetorix at Alesia (Alise, near Dijon) and was himself surrounded. The success of the siege and the surrender of Vercingetorix marked the end of the revolt.

Caesar's victories in Gaul brought northern and western Europe, especially France, under Roman influence. They also gave him a superb army and a great reputation, which were foundations for his later absolute power in Rome. The account which follows, though written in the third person, is from Caesar's own Gallic War. *It opens with the battle at Gergovia and the Gallic withdrawal to Alesia.*

This was approved, and all were sworn, and on the morrow the horsemen were divided into three detachments. Two, in battle array, made a demonstration on the two flanks, and one began to hinder the march at the head of the column. On report of this Caesar divided his own cavalry likewise into three, and ordered it to advance against the enemy. The battle began simultaneously in every quarter. The column halted, and the baggage was drawn back inside the legions. At any point where our troops seemed to be distressed or too hard pressed Caesar would order the standards to advance and line of battle to be formed. This served to check the enemy in pursuit and to encourage our troops by hope of succour. At length the Germans on the right flank gained the top of a ridge and dislodged the enemy, drove them headlong as far as the river, where Vercingetorix had halted with the footmen of his force, and slew not a few. The rest remarked this and, fearing they might be surrounded, betook themselves to flight. Everywhere slaughter ensued.

When all his horsemen had been put to flight Vercingetorix drew his forces back from their position in front of the camps and at once began the march to Alesia, a town of the Mandubii, ordering the baggage to be brought speedily out of camp and to follow close after him. Caesar withdrew his baggage to the nearest hill and, leaving two legions to guard it, pursued as long as daylight allowed. Some three thousand of the enemy's rearguard were slain, and on the next day he pitched camp near Alesia. He reconnoitred the situation of the city, and as the enemy were terror-struck by the rout of their horsemen, the branch of their army on which they most relied, he urged his soldiers to the task and began the investment.

The actual stronghold of Alesia was set atop of a hill, in a very lofty situation, apparently impregnable save by blockade. The bases of the hill were washed on two separate sides by rivers. Before the town a plain extended for a length of about three miles; on all the other sides there were hills surrounding the town at a short distance, and equal to it in height. Under the wall, on the side which looked eastward, the forces of the Gauls had entirely occupied all this intervening space, and had made in front a ditch and a rough wall six feet high. The perimeter of the siege-works which the Romans were beginning had a length of eleven miles. Camps had been pitched at convenient spots, and three-and-twenty forts had been constructed on the line. In these, piquets [pickets] would be posted by day to prevent any sudden sortie: by night the same stations were held by sentries and strong garrisons.

When the siege-work had been started, a cavalry encounter took place in the plain. Both sides strove with the utmost vigour. When our men were distressed Caesar sent up the Germans, and posted the legions in front of the camp to prevent any sudden inrush on the part of the enemy's footmen. With the reinforcement of the legions behind them our men's spirit was increased; the enemy were put to flight, and, hampering one another by sheer numbers, as the gates were left too narrow, were crowded together in a press. The Germans pursued most vigorously right up to the fortification. A great slaughter ensued; some of the enemy abandoned their horses, and tried to cross the ditch and scale the wall. Caesar ordered the legions posted in front of the rampart to advance a short distance. The Gauls inside the fortifications were in just as great a confusion as the rest: believing that the enemy were coming on them at once, they shouted the call to arms, and some in panic burst into the town. Vercingetorix ordered the gates to be shut, lest the camp should be deserted. After much slaughter and the capture of many horses the Germans retired.

Vercingetorix now made up his mind to send away all his horsemen by night, before the Romans could complete their entrenchments. His parting instructions were that each of them should proceed to his own state and impress for the campaign all men whose age allowed them to bear arms. After giving these instructions he sent the horsemen silently away in the second watch, at a point where a gap was left in our works. He ordered all the corn to be brought into his headquarters; he appointed death as the penalty for any disobedience of the order; the cattle, of which great store had been driven together, he distributed man by man; he arranged that the corn should be measured out sparingly and gradually; he withdrew into the town all the force which he had posted in front of it. By such measures did he prepare for the conduct of the campaign, in anticipation of the succours from Gaul.

Caesar had report of this from deserters and prisoners, and determined on the following types of entrenchments. He dug a trench twenty feet wide with perpendicular sides, in such fashion that the bottom thereof was just as broad as the distance from edge to edge at the surface. He set back the rest of the siege-works four hundred paces from the trench; for as he had of necessity included so large an area, and the whole of the works could not easily be manned by a ring-fence of troops, his intention was to provide against any sudden rush of the enemy's host by night upon the entrenchments, or any chance of directing their missiles by day upon our troops engaged on the works. Behind this interval he dug all round two trenches, fifteen feet broad and of equal depth; and the inner one, where the ground was level with the plain or sank below it, he filled with water diverted from the river. Behind the trenches he constructed a ramp and palisade twelve feet high; all strong and firm, the earth was trodden down hard for one foot from the bottom, and the remainder of the pit was covered over with twigs and brushwood to conceal the trap. Eight rows of this kind were dug, three feet apart. From its resemblance to the flower the device was called a "lily." In front of all these, logs a foot long, with iron hooks firmly attached, were buried altogether in the ground and scattered at brief intervals all over the field, and these they called "spurs."

When all these arrangements had been completed Caesar constructed parallel entrenchments of the same kind facing the other way, against the enemy outside, following the most favorable ground that the locality afforded, with a circuit of fourteen miles. This he did to secure the garrisons of the entrenchments from being surrounded by a host, however large it might chance to be. And in order that he might not be constrained to dangerous excursions from camp, he ordered all his men to have thirty days' corn and forage collected.

While this was proceeding about Alesia, the Gauls summoned a council of chiefs and determined not to call up (according to the proposal of Vercingetorix) all who could bear arms, but to require of each chief a certain quota from his state; for they feared that with so large a host herded together they might not be able to preserve discipline, or to distinguish their several contingents, or to secure a supply of corn.

When eight thousand horsemen and about two hundred and fifty thousand footmen had been collected, the force was reviewed and a muster was taken in the country of the Aedui. Full of spirit and confidence, all started for Alesia; there was not a man of them all who thought the mere sight of so vast a host could be withstood, especially in a two-sided engagement, when there would be fighting with those who made a sortie from within the town, and outside the display of so vast an army of horse and foot.

They reached the neighbourhood of Alesia with all their force, and, seizing a hill outside, halted not more than a mile from our entrenchments. The day after they brought their horsemen out of camp and filled the whole of that plain which we have described as extending for a length of three miles; their force of footmen they posted a little way back from the spot, on the higher ground. There was a bird's eye view from the town of Alesia over the plain. At sight of these reinforcements the others hastened together with mutual congratulation, and all minds were stirred to joy. So they brought out their force and halted in front of the town; they covered over the nearest trench with hurdles and filled it in with earth, and prepared for a sally and for every emergency.

Caesar disposed the whole army on both faces of the entrenchments in such fashion that, if occasion should arise, each man could know and keep his proper station; then he ordered the cavalry to be brought out of camp and to engage. There was a view down from all the camps, which occupied the top of the surrounding ridge, and all the troops were intently awaiting the issue of the fight. The Gauls had placed archers and light-armed skirmishers here and there among the horsemen to give immediate support to their comrades if driven back and to resist the charge of our cavalry. A number of men, wounded unexpectedly by these troops, began to withdraw from the fight. When the Gauls were confident that their own men were getting the better of the battle, and saw ours hard pressed by numbers, with shouts and yells on every side—those who were confined by the entrenchments as well as the others who had come up to their assistance—they sought to inspirit their countrymen. As the action was proceeding in sight of all, and no deed, of honour or dishonour, could escape notice, both sides were stirred to courage by desire of praise and fear of disgrace. The fight lasted, and the victory was doubtful, from noon almost to sunset; then the Germans in one part of the field massed their troops of horse, charged the enemy and routed them, and when they had been put to flight the archers were surrounded and slain. Likewise, from the other parts of the field, our troops pursued the retreating enemy right up to their camp, giving them no chance of rallying. But the Gauls who had come forth

from Alesia, almost despairing of victory, sadly withdrew
again into the town.

After one day's interval, in the course of which they
made a great number of hurdles, ladders, and grappling-
hooks, the Gauls left camp silently at midnight and approached the entrenchments in the plain. Raising a sudden
shout, to signify their coming to the besieged inside the
town, they began to fling down the hurdles, to dislodge our
men from the rampart with slings, arrows, and stones, and
to carry out everything else proper to an assault. At the
same moment, hearing the shout, Vercingetorix gave his
troops the signal by trumpet, and led them out of the
town. Our troops, as on previous days, moved each to his
appointed station in the entrenchments; with slings, one-
pounders, stakes set ready inside the works, and bullets,
they beat off the Gauls. As the darkness made it impossible
to see far, many wounds were received on both sides. A
number of missiles were discharged by the artillery. Then
Marcus Antonius and Gaius Trebonius, the lieutenant-gen-
erals to whom the defence of these sections had been allotted, withdrew troops from forts farther away, and sent
them up to bring assistance wherever they remarked that
our men were hard pressed.

While the Gauls were some distance from the entrenchment they had more advantage from the quantity of their
missiles; then, when they came up closer, they were soon
caught unawares on the "spurs," or they sank into the pits
and were impaled, or they were shot by artillery pikes from
the rampart and the turrets, and so perished on every side.
Many a man was wounded, but the entrenchment was nowhere penetrated; and when daybreak drew nigh, fearing
that they might be surrounded on their exposed flank by a
sortie from the camps above them, they retired to their
comrades. Meanwhile the inner force brought out the appliances which had been prepared by Vercingetorix for a
sortie and filled in the nearer trenches; but they lingered
too long in the execution of the business, and, or ever they
could get near the entrenchments, they learnt that their
countrymen had withdrawn. So without success they returned to the town.

Twice beaten back with great loss, the Gauls took counsel what to do. They called in men who knew the locality
well, and from them they learnt the positions and the de-

fences of the upper camps. On the north side there was a
hill, which by reason of its huge circumference our troops
had been unable to include within the works; they had
been obliged to lay out the camp on ground gently sloping,
which put them almost at a disadvantage. Having reconnoitred the locality by means of scouts, the commanders
of the enemy chose out of the whole host sixty thousand
men belonging to the states which had the greatest reputation for courage: they determined secretly together what
should be done and in what fashion, and decided that the
advance should take place at the moment when it was
seen to be midday. In charge of this force they put Vercassivellaunus, a kinsman of Vercingetorix. He left camp
in the first watch, and having almost completed his march
just before dawn, he concealed himself behind the height
and ordered his soldiers to rest after their night's work.
When at last it was seen to be near midday he moved with
speed on the camp above mentioned and at the same moment the horsemen began to advance towards the entrenchments in the plain, and the rest of the force to make
a demonstration before the camp.

When from the citadel of Alesia Vercingetorix observed
his countrymen, he moved out of the town, taking with
him the hurdles, poles, mantlets, grappling-hooks, and all
the other appliances prepared for the sally. The fight went
on simultaneously in all places, and all expedients were
attempted, with a rapid concentration on that section
which was seen to be the least strong. With lines so extensive the Roman army was strung out, and at several points
defence proved difficult. The shouting which arose in rear
of the fighting line did much to scare our troops, as they
saw that the risk to themselves depended on the success of
others; for, as a rule, what is out of sight disturbs men's
minds more seriously than what they see.

Caesar found a suitable spot from which he could see
what was proceeding in each quarter. To parties distressed
he sent up supports. Both sides felt that this was the hour
of all others in which it was proper to make their greatest
effort. The Gauls utterly despaired of safety unless they
could break through the lines; the Romans anticipated an
end of all toils if they could hold their own. The hardest
struggle occurred by the entrenchments on the hill, whither,
as we have mentioned, Vercassivellaunus had been sent.

The unfavourable downward slope of the ground had great effect. Some of the enemy discharged missiles, others moved up in close formation under their shields; fresh men quickly replaced the exhausted. Earth cast by the whole body together over the entrenchments gave the Gauls a means of ascent and at the same time covered over the appliances which the Romans had concealed in the ground; and our troops had now neither arms nor strength enough.

When Caesar learnt this, he sent Labienus with six cohorts to support them in their distress. He commanded him if he could not hold his ground, to draw in the cohorts and fight his way out, but not to do so unless of necessity. He himself went up to the rest of the troops, and urged them not to give into the strain, telling them that the fruit of all previous engagements depended upon that day and hour. The enemy on the inner side, despairing of success on the level ground, because of the size of the entrenchments, made an attempt to scale the precipitous parts, conveying thither the appliances they had prepared. They dislodged the defenders of the turrets by a swarm of missiles, filled in the trenches with earth and hurdles, tore down rampart and breastwork with grappling-hooks.

Caesar first sent young Brutus with some cohorts, and then Gaius Fabius, lieutenant-general, with others; last of all, as the fight raged more fiercely, he himself brought up fresh troops to reinforce. The battle restored, and the enemy repulsed, he hastened to the quarter whither he had sent Labienus. He withdrew four cohorts from the nearest fort, and ordered part of the cavalry to follow him, part to go round the outer entrenchments and attack the enemy in rear. Labienus, finding that neither ramps nor trenches could resist the rush of the enemy, collected together forty cohorts, which had been withdrawn from the nearest posts and by chance presented themselves, and sent messengers to inform Caesar what he thought it proper to do. Caesar hurried on to take part in the action.

His coming was known by the colour of his cloak, which it was his habit to wear in action as a distinguishing mark; and the troops of cavalry and the cohorts which he had ordered to follow him were noticed, because from the upper levels these downward slopes and depressions were visible. Thereupon the enemy joined battle: a shout was raised on both sides, and taken up by an answering shout from the rampart and the whole of the entrenchments. Our troops discarded their pikes and got to work with their swords. Suddenly the cavalry was noticed in the rear; other cohorts drew near. The enemy turned to flee; the cavalry met them in flight, and a great slaughter ensued. Sedulius, commander and chief of the Lemovices, was killed; Vercassivellaunus was captured alive in the rout; seventy-four war-standards were brought in to Caesar; of the vast host few returned safe to camp. The others beheld from the town the slaughter and rout of their countrymen, and, in despair of safety, recalled their force from the entrenchments. Directly they heard what had happened the Gauls fled from their camp. And if the troops had not been worn out by frequent reinforcing and the whole day's effort, the entire force of the enemy could have been destroyed. The cavalry were sent off just after midnight and caught up the rearguard: a great number were taken and slain, the rest fled away into the different states.

On the morrow Vercingetorix summoned a council, at which he stated that he had undertaken that campaign, not for his own occasions, but for the general liberty; and as they must yield to fortune he offered himself to them for whichever course they pleased—to give satisfaction to the Romans by his death, or to deliver him alive. Deputies were despatched to Caesar to treat of this matter. He ordered the arms to be delivered up, the chiefs to be brought out. He himself took his seat in the entrenchments in front of the camp: the leaders were brought out to him there. Vercingetorix was surrendered, arms were thrown down. Keeping back the Aedui and the Arverni, to see if through them he could recover their states, he distributed the rest of the prisoners, one apiece to each man throughout the army, by way of plunder.

When these affairs were settled he started for the country of the Aedui and recovered the state. The Arverni sent deputies to him there who promised to carry out his commands: he required of them a great number of hostages. He sent the legions into cantonments. He himself decided to winter at Birbracte. When the despatches of the campaign were published at Rome a public thanksgiving of twenty days was granted.

Berlin (1945)

Marshal Vasili I. Chuikov

By the end of 1944 the Allies had begun to close their giant pincers on Nazi Germany. England and the United States were in France in the west, ready to march on the Rhine River. Russian forces were drawn up in the east.

Much bitter fighting raged that winter—attacks and counterattacks—but by spring 1945 the Rhine was crossed in the west. In the east the Russian troops having crossed Poland were in East Germany outside Berlin itself. Hitler, his mistress Eva Braun, and a few die-hard aides were hidden in a fortress within the city. Rather than surrender, Hitler decided to defend Berlin to the bitter end. Thousands of lives were lost needlessly. The Russians, crushing all opposition before them, moved into the city.

Marshal Vasili I. Chuikov, commander of Russia's famed 8th Guards, who had become heroes in the defense of Stalingrad, tells of the house-to-house combat in the city. He himself, never a behind-the-lines general, led his Guards in the fighting. Five days after the action depicted in this selection, from his book The Fall of Berlin, *Hitler and his mistress killed themselves. On May 7th, a week after Hitler's death, Nazi Germany surrendered unconditionally to the Allied forces—chief of whom were the United States, Russia, and England.*

THE GUARDSMEN

By the close of day on 25 April the Army's storm groups had advanced three, or on some sectors four, kilometres

nearer to the city centre. Almost everywhere the fighting
had been of exceptional ferocity. Every house, every block
of the defence areas and sectors, was packed with fire
points and nests of men wielding 'Faustpatronen'; the latter
had made good use of balconies and windows on upper
floors, as points from which to launch their weapons from
above against tanks and concentrations of men.

There are many railway lines in Berlin, intersecting the
city in various directions and forming very convenient defence positions. The approaches to stations, bridges and
level crossings were all turned into powerful strong points;
canals and the points at which they could be crossed became defence lines at which the enemy did his best to halt
our advance. Death-dealing fire met our men from every
point—from streets, alleys, basements and ruined buildings.

The assault detachment commanded by First Lieutenant
Vasili Chernyayev, of the 220th Guards Regiment, 79th
Guards Division, was about to get the enemy out of a
large stone-built house at the intersection of two streets—
Alt-Mark Str. and Tarkendorfstrasse.* The Nazis had fortified the building strongly. In the basement they had a small-
calibre gun and a group of men with sub-machine guns; on
the second floor there were riflemen and a heavy machine-
gun. The garrison had fire cooperation with the neighbouring building.

The detachment's commander told machine-gunner
Nikolai Vlasenko and two anti-tank gun crews to fire at
the windows of the house. At the same time Sergeant
Pyotr Vasil'ievski was to use his 45 mm gun to wipe out
the enemy machine-gun, and then to fire on any enemy fire
points which had come to life again. Under cover of the
fire from the anti-tank guns, machine-guns, and the 45 mm,
Chernyayev's detachment rushed in to storm the house.

The hail of heavy fire had made the Nazis take cover
behind the walls of the building, and weakened their fire.
Our men took advantage of it. Sergeant Ivan Trubachev's
storm group was the first to approach the house, firing as
they went. Grenades were sent flying in at the doors and
windows of the basement. The Guardsmen broke into the
lower floor, killing the crew of the enemy gun and several

* This street not located; possibly that meant is the Thorwald-
senstrasse.

Germans with automatics. Behind the storm group came soldiers from the support group under Sergeant Fyodor Nikitin.

Meanwhile another detachment, under Lieutenant Mikhail Belyavski and Junior Lieutenant Viktor Romanov, acting in close concert with guns and mortar crews, had occupied the second house on the corner.

The Germans went over to the counter-attack repeatedly, bringing in tanks and self-propelled guns. They made use of the following trick: making it look as though a counter-attack had failed, they would withdraw. But in the houses they had 'abandoned' they would leave groups of men with automatics, whose job it was to open fire suddenly on our men from the flanks and rear. Our Guardsmen soon grasped this idea. They reinforced their reconnoitring parties, and when approaching 'empty' houses they would fire in at the windows, attics and entrances, and throw grenades in. The German tommy-gunners would have to come out of ambush.

On the way to the Tempelhof airfield our units reached the Teltow canal. The first men to reach its bank were those of an assault detachment under Lieutenant Dmitri Nesterenko, from the 39th Guards Division. The smoke from burning buildings was so thick that it was hard to distinguish anything on the far bank. So the enemy, too, reasoned Nesterenko, could not see from the other bank that our men had reached the canal. He ordered the first storm group of his detachment to force the canal and get possession of a multi-storey building.

There was a bridge which had been blown up and had collapsed into the water, but it was still possible to make one's way over it, though with difficulty. But the enemy snipers and machine-gunners did not let our men get to the bridge. Then Nesterenko decided to organize an artillery blow. Our artillery's shells obliged the enemy to cease their fire. A storm group led by Senior Sergeant Andrei Anis'yev, a Communist Party member, rushed the bridge. The party's commander was the first man to reach the building, and he hurled a grenade in at a window from which a machine-gun was firing; the firing ceased. After throwing two more grenades in at the window Anis'yev got inside the building, and cleared three rooms of their Nazi occupants.

The Guardsmen's attack had been made with such speed and élan that the Nazis gave way and retreated. Our supporting group opened up heavy fire on them. Under cover of this Anis'yev and his men went into the neighbouring building, hard on the retreating enemy's heels, and gained possession of that too.

And here is yet another page from the chronicle of the 8th Guards Army's fighting progress; it was written by Guards Sergeant-Major of Signals Alexei Burmashev. Here in Berlin he repeated the remarkable deed of the famous signalman Titayev, who during the fighting for Mamayev Kurgan held the broken ends of a communication line together in his teeth as he lay dying.

I knew Alexei Burmashev well, I had met him on the Dnieper, on the Vistula and on the Oder. He was a broad-shouldered, broad-cheekboned Siberian. Eye-witnesses of his feat in Berlin told us this of it: Guards Sergeant-Major Burmashev was standing on the gently sloping bank of the river Spree; he was examining with interest this foreign river of which he had heard so much, and it evidently reminded him of other times, for he remarked to his friends, 'Well, we've crossed some bigger than that!'

Small boats rocked on the water, moored by the bank; the Germans had not had time to destroy them. The signals platoon under Burmashev was to be among the first groups to go over to the far bank.

The Germans were putting up stiff resistance. Shells and mortar bombs were bursting in the river; columns of water rose up and fell cascading back. The little fisherman's rowboat in which the platoon's commander and telephonist Koshelyov were making the crossing looked likely to turn turtle at any moment. But it got across in spite of the shell-fire, and hit the bank with a thud. Rifles and rolls of wire in their hands, the signallers jumped out and began to lay their line. The Germans saw them, and directed gunfire on them. Koshelyov was killed. The Sergeant-Major was left alone on the enemy-held shore. Sometimes crawling, sometimes running, he went on, laying his cable behind him. And soon at the unit's command post they heard a familiar voice—'Eagle, Eagle, can you hear me? This is Rowan. . . .'

The regiment entered Berlin. Stubborn fighting was in progress for Tempelhof, the central airport of the city.

Guards Sergeant-Major Burmashev was seen up telegraph poles, on the roofs of burning buildings, down in deep, dank cellars. A man needs fantastic will-power and courage to climb up a telegraph pole under a hail of shell-splinters and bullets, and connect up wire there on top!

Alexei Burmashev ran through the streets of Berlin. Only ten metres to go before he reached a building for which our assault groups were struggling, only ten metres . . . but just then a splinter struck him. Pressing his hand over the wound, Burmashev shouted to his men, 'Keep the line!' —and fell on the roadway.

Those few metres of wire were the last of a thousand kilometres of line that Burmashev had laid during the years of war. And those last metres were laid along the streets of the German capital. Soon good news sped over them— 'The aerodrome has been completely surrounded!'

Thus it was, in the thick of an especially complex operation—to cut off and gain control of Tempelhof aerodrome —that Guards Sergeant-Major Alexei Burmashev did his duty to the end.

I repeat—this was an especially complex operation: for Tempelhof was now the last and only airfield in Berlin from which German planes could still take off. So, naturally, the enemy did everything he could to retain this last 'window on the sky.' The aerodrome was defended by anti-aircraft units, SS troops, and tanks, the latter being drawn up in an L-shape along the southern and eastern edges of the field. Most of them were dug into the ground, and thus made into invulnerable fire points. It looked as though the Berlin garrison had no more fuel supplies for their tanks; all the petrol and diesel fuel, according to depositions from captured tank crews, had been taken by the air force for their planes.

Depositions from prisoners shed light on yet another aspect of affairs, which could not be ignored. In the underground hangars of the aerodrome planes were standing ready, tanks filled with fuel, able to take off at any minute; beside them were their crews, standing on duty every hour in the twenty-four, and among these men were pilots and navigators who in the past had been entrusted with the duty of flying Hitler, Goebbels, Bormann and other Nazi leaders to destinations all over Germany. From this information one might conclude that Hitler and his closest associates were still in Berlin, and might—who knows what the devil has up his sleeve!—slip out through this last loop-hole. So we had to do everything possible to ensure that this did not happen. It would not do to scare the bird away too soon; on the other hand, too great delay also held the possibility of permitting the impermissible—letting the chief war criminal escape.

For this reason regiments of the 39th and 79th Guards Divisions were given orders to get right round the aerodrome from west and east, before battle was joined on the southern perimeter. The artillery was given the task of keeping the runways covered. We did not know the precise location and other details of the exit gates from the underground hangars, so storm groups reinforced with tanks were assigned to the job of cutting off all access to the runways themselves by fire from guns and machine-guns, and so keeping the planes bottled up underground.

The plan worked perfectly. From the evening of 25 April on, not a single plane took off from the field, and by midday of 26 April the aerodrome itself, and the whole airport complex of Tempelhof—hangars, communications installations, and the main 'Flughafen' building—were in our hands.

The good news arrived accompanied by sorrow: the commander of the 117th Guards Rifle Regiment, 39th Division, Lieutenant-Colonel of Guards Yefim Dmitrievich Gritsenko, a man of wisdom, resolution and outstanding courage, had been killed. He died on the night between 25 and 26 April.

After it had happened a nursing sister from the 117th Division, Tat'iana Gubaryova, came to me carrying an envelope containing Yefim Dmitrievich's papers, which he always carried in his left breast pocket; it was holed by bullets. A German machine-gunner had got him right through the heart. What a hero was lost to us!

. . . The assault had been in progress for more than two days and nights. The area left to the Berlin garrison was shrinking, but their resistance was stiffening all the time. Our dispositions were becoming ever closer. The possibilities of fire and movement were reduced to the utmost. Everything was shut in to the narrow bounds of actual streets. Now our advance could be compared only to the work of miners driving an underground gallery. A break-

through from one street to the next could be made only
through gaps in thick brick or stone walls, or over heaps
of ruins, over piled-up masses of shattered ferro-concrete,
with jagged ends of metal protruding from them. Sensing
the approach of the end, the Nazis were now wrecking
all there was in the city, taking no heed of the numbers of
ordinary citizens they killed in the process, if only they
could inflict on us the greatest possible losses of men and
materials.

The most ferocious resistance of all was that put up by
SS detachments on the square in front of the church which
stands on the Kurfürstenstrasse. Remember that square,
historians! It is now in the American sector of Berlin.

During the night preceding 27 April 1945 a storm group
from the 34th Heavy Tank Regiment broke through to this
point. They achieved this by a bold dash across two sets of
railway lines which run across the south part of the city
almost to the centre itself. On the square in front of the
church one tank hit a mine and was left with only one
track working. Seeing that the Soviet machine could no
longer manœuvre, the SS men cut off the way of retreat
for the tank's crew and for the tommy-gunners who were
covering them, and then set about wiping out the whole
group. There were about a hundred of them, and twelve of
our men. An unequal fight began.

In this fight Sergeant of Guards Herman Shashkov distinguished himself by signal valour, skill and determination
in action. He took the place first of the gun-loader, when
the latter was wounded, and then of the crew's commander,
who was killed outright. The tank kept up its fire undimin-
ished. A 'Faustpatrone' exploded just in front of the driver's
turret; a second later the crew's commander fell dead.
Shashkov was now alone. He pressed the starter, and the
tank jerked and began to rotate on its axis. Another direct
hit from a 'Faustpatrone,' and the engine was on fire.
Shashkov put it into reverse and drove into a half-ruined
wall; this collapsed on to the engine unit and put out the
flames. After a few more minutes Shashkov had used up
all his ammunition except hand-grenades. He was then
wounded for the second time, in the chest. The tank began
to burn once more. Nazi soldiers were hammering on the
armour, calling on him to surrender. But Herman Shashkov, soldier of the Guards and true to his oath, chose to

die in his burning tank. When his comrades got to him, they saw around the tank over thirty dead or wounded German soldiers, armed with automatics or 'Faustpatronen,' and wearing the uniform of the Gestapo. Shashkov, half-burnt and wounded, lay on the bottom of the tank with a knife in his hand. He was still alive. He breathed on for long enough to tell the tale of what had happened, and his last words were 'Thanks, brothers, for not letting the Nazis have my body.'

Eternal glory to a hero of the land of Russia, Herman Petrovich Shashkov, who fell in the storming of Berlin!

In the course of those days I was again attacked by that burning itch on the arms, like thousands of red-hot needles pricking the skin. It came on after I had heard a report made by General Ryzhov, commanding the 28th Corps. He informed me that on the far side of the Heinrich von Kleist Park, in a corner building which had been turned into a major strong point, a besieged garrison of enemy soldiers remained which was keeping up a continual fire from heavy machine-guns. Apparently these men were self-condemned to kill on till they themselves were killed; they were firing along the streets, killing medical orderlies, wounded, women and children who tried to cross from one side of the street to the other—anyone who came into their sights. What was to be done about them?

Prior to this I had been hesitant for some time over whether to make use of the detachments armed with flame-throwers which our Army included, or whether to leave them in reserve. Now my mind was made up. I gave orders to bring up to the front line teams with portable flame-throwers, from the 41st brigade of sappers.

The sappers made their way right up to the objective and sent streams of flame in at all the openings and windows of the building's basement. One would have thought that now the enemy would cease resistance and surrender. But before long the machine-guns were stuttering again. So we would have to break in and annihilate the Nazis where they were. Private Nikolai Popov, a brave soldier whose native ground was Argun' in Chita Region, hurled a stick of grenades in at the door and went into the building through a gap in the first-floor wall. There were Nazi soldiers in the corridors on that floor. They did not have time to start firing, the flame-thrower blasted them in a moment. But

the main enemy force was down in the basement. Popov
threw several grenades down there, then jumped down
himself—and found himself surrounded by Nazis. There
were about thirty of them, he said later. He shouted 'Hands
up!' The response was a burst of machine-gun fire, and then
another. He had to take cover behind a dividing wall and
direct the jet of the flame-thrower from there.

The whole building began to burn. The Nazis tried to
run for it, but our men were waiting for them outside.

In this episode it was a single man, in effect, who turned
the tide. But when the enemy has established himself in a
building with thick brick-built walls, the efforts of several
arms simultaneously are as a rule required to get him out.
The experience of street fighting in Berlin shows that every
storm group needs to be supported by not less than three
or four guns, not counting the infantry's own heavy arms.
Our artillerymen would 'frame' an objective with fire,
cutting it off from the flanks and the rear, isolating it from
its neighbours and so excluding support to its garrison from
outside. Our own guns were used to suppress the fire points
within the fortified buildings and to prevent the enemy
counter-attacking.

Here is a notable example from the Berlin fighting.
Senior Sergeant Fyodor Cherpachenko and the crew of his
gun were given the job of supporting the infantry who
were to storm a large building. On the second floor of this
building the Germans had a machine-gun, and in the basement there was a concentration of men with automatics
and grenades. The Senior Sergeant picked a position in the
courtyard of the house opposite. A gap was made in the
wall, and a supply of ammunition brought up. Cherpachenko arranged agreed signals for opening fire, transferring
fire, and indicating targets, with the commander of the
storm group. The gun was run into position before dawn.
As soon as morning broke, Cherpachenko opened fire.
Two shells put the enemy machine-gun out of action, and
Cherpachenko transferred his fire to the basement windows.
Supported by artillery fire, and that of mortars and machine-guns attached to the storm group, the infantrymen
rushed in to storm the building, and fighting broke out inside it. Now Cherpachenko's gun could no longer fire on
the building, so he began to hammer the next-door house,

thus preventing the enemy from assisting the beleaguered garrison from there.

I repeat once again that comradeship in action, mutual assistance between infantry, artillery, engineers, signals, tanks and reconnaissance, became the decisive factor at this stage. Nowhere, under no other circumstances, is there or can there be such constant contact between the men of various arms of the service, as there is during the storming of cities and their fortifications. The commander of a storm group thus becomes the chief organizer of the tactical manœuvre of fire-power and man-power. On his ability to follow and make sense of the fighting as it progresses, and to take the right decision quickly, depends the continued battle-worthiness of the detachment as a whole and of each soldier individually.

Every attack, every assault, was preceded by careful reconnaissance. The men engaged in this work had to possess exceptional coolness, initiative and resource. A reconnaissance man in city fighting has to be listening post, observation post and scout, all rolled into one. If you can't get the information you need by simple observation, then you must make your way unnoticed right up to the objective to be stormed and find out what you can by ear. If you don't succeed in hearing what you need, you must penetrate the enemy disposition.

Throughout the whole period of the Berlin fighting excellent work was done by the reconnaissance group led by Senior Lieutenant Viktor Lisitsyn. His men penetrated the enemy's dispositions, made their way into places which might have been considered safe from all observation, and showed great intelligence and guile in all they did.

In Berlin many buildings and blocks were connected by passages. These were utilized by our reconnaissance men. They would operate as follows: part of the group would go forward, with one or two men using torches. Very often the Nazis, seeing the light of torches, would take it that those approaching were their own men—which was what our men were counting on.

X
SECONDHAND
REPORT

SYRACUSE
CRÉCY

Syracuse (413 B.C.)

Thucydides

*In the years after the failure of the Persian attack,
Athens became the leader of an alliance of Greek
states, and a great naval power. Her power and
wealth helped rouse the opposition of other Greek
states, especially of Sparta, the traditional military
power, whose warriors were the heroes of
Thermopylae.*

*The succeeding war, between Athens with her
allies and Sparta with hers, is usually known as the
Peloponnesian War (the southern peninsula, on which
Sparta was located, was the Peloponnesus). It lasted
almost thirty years, and included most of Greece and
the islands.*

*After the death of Pericles, the great Athenian
leader, the Athenian popular assembly accepted the
scheme of Alcibiades for an attack on Syracuse, a
Greek colony on the island of Sicily. The description
of the expedition and of its failure is from the
Athenian historian Thucydides. He himself had been
a general in the Athenian forces early in the war
and collected accounts from men on both sides as
the war proceeded.*

THE DEPARTURE

The departure for Sicily took place, it being now about
midsummer. Most of the allies, with the corn transports
and the smaller craft and the rest of the expedition, had
already received orders to muster at Corcyra, to cross the
Ionian sea from thence in a body to the Iapygian promontory. But the Athenians themselves, and such of their

allies as happened to be with them, went down to Piraeus upon a day appointed at daybreak, and began to man the ships for putting out to sea. With them also went down the whole population, one may say, of the city, both citizens and foreigners; the inhabitants of the country each escorting those that belonged to them, their friends, their relatives, or their sons, with hope and lamentation upon their way, as they thought of the conquests which they hoped to make, or of the friends whom they might never see again, considering the long voyage which they were going to make from their country. Indeed, at this moment, when they were now upon the point of parting from one another, the danger came more home to them than when they voted for the expedition; although the strength of the armament, and the profuse provision which they remarked in every department, was a sight that could not but comfort them. As for the foreigners and the rest of the crowd, they simply went to see a sight worth looking at and passing all belief.

Indeed this armament that first sailed out was by far the most costly and splendid Hellenic force that had ever been sent out by a single city up to that time. The present expedition was formed in contemplation of a long term of service by land and sea alike, and was furnished with ships and troops so as to be ready for either as required. The fleet had been elaborately equipped at great cost to the captains and the state; the treasury giving a drachma a day to each seaman, and providing empty ships, sixty men of war and forty transports, and manning these with the best crews obtainable; while the captains gave a bounty in addition to the pay from the treasury to the crews generally, besides spending lavishly upon figureheads and equipments, and one and all making the utmost exertions to enable their own ships to excel in beauty and fast sailing. Meanwhile the land forces had been picked from the best muster-rolls, and vied with each other in paying great attention to their arms and personal accoutrements. From this resulted not only a rivalry among themselves in their different departments, but an idea among the rest of the Hellenes that it was more a display of power and resources than an armament against an enemy. For if any one had counted up the public expenditure of the state, and the private outlay of individuals, it would have been found that many talents in all were being taken out of the city. Indeed the expedition became not less famous for its wonderful bold-ness and for the splendour of its appearance, than for its overwhelming strength as compared with the peoples against whom it was directed, and for the fact that this was the longest passage from home hitherto attempted, and the most ambitious in its objects considering the re-sources of those who undertook it.

The ships being now manned, and everything put on board with which they meant to sail, the trumpet com-manded silence, and the prayers customary before putting out to sea were offered, not in each ship by itself, but by all together to the voice of a herald; and bowls of wine were mixed through all the armament, and libations made by the soldiers and their officers in gold and silver goblets. In their prayers joined also the crowds on shore, the citi-zens and all others that wished them well. The hymn sung and the libations finished, they put out to sea, and first sail-ing out in column then raced each other as far as Aegina, and so hastened to reach Corcyra, where the rest of the allied forces were also assembling.

EDITOR'S NOTE

Alcibiades, who had urged the expedition, was re-called on charges of irreligious behavior, and fled to Sparta. The Athenian forces, under Nicias and Demosthenes, nearly surrounded Syracuse, but a Spartan force prevented this. Thucydides tells the story of the last days of the expedition—the sea fight in the harbor of Syracuse, and the ensuing land battles.

It should be clear from the account that the main fighting at sea took either the form of ramming the enemy's ship, or of coming alongsides and boarding. In the latter case, what followed amounted to an infantry battle on shipboard.

THE END OF THE CAMPAIGN

Syracusan generals and Gylippus now perceived that the Athenians were manning their ships, and immediately pro-ceeded to man their own also. Meanwhile Nicias, appalled by the position of affairs, realising the greatness and the

nearness of the danger now that they were on the point
of putting out from shore, reminded them of their country,
the freest of the free, and of the unfettered discretion allowed in it to all to live as they pleased; and added other
arguments such as men would use at such a crisis, and
which, with little alteration, are made to serve on all occasions alike—appeals to wives, children, and national gods
—without caring whether they are thought commonplace,
but loudly invoking them in the belief that they will be of
use in the consternation of the moment. Having thus admonished them, Nicias withdrew and led the troops to the
sea, and ranged them in as long a line as he was able, in
order to aid as far as possible in sustaining the courage of
the men afloat; while Demosthenes, Menander, and Euthy-
demus, who took the command on board, put out from
their own camp and sailed straight to the barrier across the
mouth of the harbour and to the passage left open, to try
to force their way out.

The Syracusans and their allies had already put out with
about the same number of ships as before, a part of which
kept guard at the outlet, and the remainder all round the
rest of the harbour, in order to attack the Athenians on all
sides at once; while the land forces held themselves in
readiness at the points at which the vessels might put into
the shore. When the rest of the Athenians came up to the
barrier, with the first shock of their charge they overpowered the ships stationed there, and tried to undo the
fastenings; after this, as the Syracusans and allies bore
down upon them from all quarters, the action spread
from the barrier over the whole harbour, and was more
obstinately disputed than any of the preceding ones. On
either side the rowers showed great zeal in bringing up
their vessels at the boatswains' orders, and the helmsmen
great skill in manoeuvring, while the ships once alongside,
the soldiers on board did their best not to let the service
on deck be outdone by the others; in short, every man
strove to prove himself the first in his particular department. And as many ships were engaged in a small com-
pass (for these were the largest fleets fighting in the
narrowest space ever known, being together little short
of two hundred), the regular attacks with the beak were
few, there being no opportunity of backing water or of
breaking the line; while the collisions caused by one ship

chancing to run foul of another, either in flying from or attacking a third, were more frequent. So long as a vessel was coming up to the charge the men on the decks rained darts and arrows and stones upon her; but once alongside, the heavy infantry tried to board each other's vessel, fighting hand to hand. In many quarters also it happened, by reason of the narrow room, that a vessel was charging an enemy on one side and being charged herself on another, and that two, or sometimes more ships had got entangled round one, obliging the helmsmen to attend to defence here, offence there, not to one thing at once, but to many on all sides; while the huge din caused by the number of ships crashing together not only spread terror, but made the orders of the boatswains inaudible. The boatswains on either side in the discharge of their duty and in the heat of the conflict shouted incessantly orders and appeals to their men; the Athenians they urged to force the passage out, and now if ever to show their mettle and lay hold of a safe return to their country; to the Syracusans and their allies they cried that it would be glorious to prevent the escape of the enemy, and conquering, to exalt the countries that were theirs. The generals, moreover, on either side, if they saw any in any part of the battle backing ashore without being forced to do so, called out to the captain by name and asked him: the Athenians, whether they were retreating because they thought the thrice hostile shore more their own than that sea which had cost them so much labour to win; the Syracusans, whether they were flying from the flying Athenians, whom they well knew to be eager to escape in whatever way they could.

Meanwhile the two armies on shore, while victory hung in the balance, were a prey to the most agonising and conflicting emotions; the natives thirsting for more glory than they had already won, while the invaders feared to find themselves in even worse plight than before. The Athenians' fear for the event was like nothing they had ever felt; while their view of the struggle was necessarily as chequered as the battle itself. Close to the scene of action and not all looking at the same point at once, some saw their friends victorious and took courage, and fell to calling upon heaven not to deprive them of salvation, while others who had their eyes turned upon the losers, wailed and cried aloud, and, although spectators, were more overcome than the actual combatants. Others, again, were gazing at some spot where the battle was evenly disputed; as the strife was protracted without decision, their swaying bodies reflected the agitation of their minds, and they suffered the worst agony of all, ever just within reach of safety or just on the point of destruction. In short, in that one Athenian army as long as the sea-fight remained doubtful there was every sound to be heard at once, shrieks, cheers, "We win," "We lose," and all the other manifold exclamations that a great host would necessarily utter in great peril; and with the men in the fleet it was nearly the same; until at last the Syracusans and their allies, after the battle had lasted a long while, put the Athenians to flight, and with much shouting and cheering chased them in open rout to the shore. The naval force, one one way, one another, as many as were not taken afloat now ran ashore and rushed from on board their ships to their camp; while the army, no more divided, but carried away by one impulse, all with shrieks and groans deplored the event, and ran down, some to help the ships, others to guard what was left of their wall, while the remaining and most numerous part already began to consider how they should save themselves. Indeed, the panic of the present moment had never been surpassed. They now suffered very nearly what they had inflicted at Pylos; as then the Lacedaemonians with the loss of their fleet lost also the men who had crossed over to the island, so now the Athenians had no hope of escaping by land, without the help of some extraordinary accident.

The sea-fight having been a severe one, and many ships and lives having been lost on both sides, the victorious Syracusans and their allies now picked up their wrecks and dead, and sailed off to the city and set up a trophy. The Athenians, overwhelmed by their misfortune, never even thought of asking leave to take up their dead or wrecks, but wished to retreat that very night. Demosthenes, however, went to Nicias and gave it as his opinion that they should man the ships they had left and make another effort to force their passage out next morning; saying that they had still left more ships fit for service than the enemy, the Athenians having about sixty remaining as against less than fifty of their opponents. Nicias was quite of his mind; but when they wished to man the vessels, the sailors refused to go on board, being so utterly overcome by their defeat as no longer to believe in the possibility of success.

Accordingly they all now made up their minds to retreat by land. Meanwhile the Syracusan Hermocrates, suspecting their intention, and impressed by the danger of allowing a force of that magnitude to retire by land, establish itself in some other part of Sicily, and from thence renew the war, went and stated his views to the authorities, and pointed out to them that they ought not to let the enemy get away by night, but that all the Syracusans and their allies should at once march out and block up the roads and seize and guard the passes.

Nicias and Demosthenes now thinking that enough had been done in the way of preparation, the removal of the army took place upon the second day after the sea-fight. It was a lamentable scene, not merely from the single circumstance that they were retreating after having lost all their ships, their great hopes gone, and themselves and the state in peril; but also in leaving the camp there were things most grievous for every eye and heart to contemplate. The dead lay unburied, and each man as he recognised a friend among them shuddered with grief and horror; while the living whom they were leaving behind, wounded or sick, were to the living far more shocking than the dead, and more to be pitied than those who had perished. These fell to entreating and bewailing until their friends knew not what to do, begging them to take them and loudly calling to each individual comrade or relative whom they could see, hanging upon the necks of their tent-fellows in the act of departure, and following as far as they could, and when their bodily strength failed them, calling again and again upon heaven and shrieking aloud as they were left behind. So that the whole army being filled with tears and distracted after this fashion found it not easy to go, even from an enemy's land, where they had already suffered evils too great for tears and in the unknown future before them feared to suffer more. Dejection and self-condemnation were also rife among them.

Nicias, seeing the army dejected and greatly altered, passed along the ranks and encouraged and comforted them as far as was possible under the circumstances, raising his voice still higher and higher as he went from one company to another in his earnestness, and in his anxiety that the benefit of his words might reach as many as possible.

As he made his address, Nicias went along the ranks, and brought back to their place any of the troops that he saw straggling out of the line; while Demosthenes did as much for his part of the army, addressing them in words very similar. The army marched in a hollow square, the division under Nicias leading, and that of Demosthenes following, the heavy infantry being outside and the baggage-carriers and the bulk of the army in the middle. When they arrived at the ford of the river Anapus they there found drawn up a body of the Syracusans and allies, and routing these, made good their passage and pushed on, harassed by the charges of the Syracusan horse and by the missiles of their light troops. On that day they advanced about four miles and a half, halting for the night upon a certain hill. On the next they started early and got on about two miles further, and descended into a place in the plain and there encamped, in order to procure some eatables from the houses, as the place was inhabited, and to carry on with them water from thence, as for many furlongs in front, in the direction in which they were going, it was not plentiful. The Syracusans meanwhile went on and fortified the pass in front, where there was a steep hill with a rocky ravine on each side of it, called the Acrean cliff. The next day the Athenians advancing found themselves impeded by the missiles and charges of the horse and darters, both very numerous, of the Syracusans and allies; and after fighting for a long while, at length retired to the same camp, where they had no longer provisions as before, it being impossible to leave their position by reason of the cavalry.

Early the next morning they started afresh and forced their way to the hill, which had been fortified, where they found before them the enemy's infantry drawn up many shields deep to defend the fortification, the pass being narrow. The Athenians assaulted the work, but were greeted by a storm of missiles from the hill, which told with the greater effect through its being a steep one, and unable to force the passage, retreated again and rested.

During the night Nicias and Demosthenes, seeing the wretched condition of their troops, now in want of every kind of necessity, and numbers of them disabled in the numerous attacks of the enemy, determined to light as many fires as possible, and to lead off the army, no longer by the same route as they had intended, but towards the

sea in the opposite direction to that guarded by the Syracusans. The whole of this route was leading the army not
to Catana, but to the other side of Sicily, towards
Camarina, Gela, and the other Hellenic and barbarian
towns in that quarter. They accordingly lit a number of
fires and set out by night. Now all armies, and the greatest most of all, are liable to fears and alarms, especially
when they are marching by night through an enemy's country and with the enemy near; and the Athenians falling
into one these panics, the leading division, that of Nicias,
kept together and got on a good way in front, while that of
Demosthenes, comprising rather more than half the army,
got separated and marched on in some disorder. By morning, however, they reached the sea, and getting into the
Helorine Road, pushed on in order to reach the river
Cacyparis, and to follow the stream up through the interior, where they hoped to be met by the Sicels whom
they had sent for. Arrived at the river, they found there
also a Syracusan party engaged in barring the passage of
the ford with a wall and a palisade, and forcing this guard,
crossed the river and went on to another called the Erineus,
according to the advice of their guides.

Meanwhile, when day came and the Syracusans and allies found that the Athenians were gone, most of them
accused Gylippus of having let them escape on purpose,
and hastily pursuing by the road which they had no difficulty in finding that they had taken, overtook them about
dinner-time. They first came up with the troops under
Demosthenes, who were behind and marching somewhat
slowly and in disorder, owing to the night-panic above
referred to, and at once attacked and engaged them, the
Syracusan horse surrounding them with more ease now
that they were separated from the rest, and hemming them
in on one spot. The division of Nicias was five or six miles
on in front, as he led them more rapidly, thinking that
under the circumstances their safety lay not in staying and
fighting, unless obliged, but in retreating as fast as possible,
and only fighting when forced to do so. On the other hand,
Demosthenes was, generally speaking, harassed more incessantly, as his post in the rear left him the first exposed
to the attacks of the enemy; and now, finding that the
Syracusans were in pursuit, he omitted to push on, in order
to form his men for battle, and so lingered until he was

surrounded by his pursuers and himself and the Athenians
with him placed in the most distressing position, being
huddled into an enclosure with a wall all round it, a road
on this side and on that, and olive-trees in great number,
where missiles were showered in upon them from every
quarter. This mode of attack the Syracusans had with good
reason adopted in preference to fighting at close quarters,
as to risk a struggle with desperate men was now more for
the advantage of the Athenians than for their own; besides,
their success had now become so certain that they began
to spare themselves a little in order not to be cut off in the
moment of victory, thinking too that, as it was, they would
be able in this way to subdue and capture the enemy.

In fact, after plying the Athenians and allies all day long
from every side with missiles, they at length saw that they
were worn out with their wounds and other sufferings; and
Gylippus and the Syracusans and their allies made a proc-
lamation, offering their liberty to any of the islanders who
chose to come over to them; and some few cities went
over. Afterwards a capitulation was agreed upon for all
the rest with Demosthenes, to lay down their arms on condition that no one was to be put to death either by violence
or imprisonment or want of the necessaries of life. Upon
this they surrendered to the number of six thousand in all,
laying down all the money in their possession, which filled
the hollows of four shields, and were immediately conveyed by the Syracusans to the town.

Meanwhile Nicias with his division arrived that day at the
river Erineus, crossed over and posted his army upon
some high ground upon the other side. The next day the
Syracusans overtook him.

Nicias surrendered himself to Gylippus, whom he trusted
more than he did the Syracusans, and told him and the
Lacedaemonians to do what they liked with him, but to
stop the slaughter of the soldiers. Gylippus, after this, immediately gave orders to make prisoners; upon which the
rest were brought together alive, except a large number
secreted by the soldiery, and a party was sent in pursuit of
the three hundred who had got through the guard during
the night, and who were now taken with the rest. The number of the enemy collected as public property was not
considerable; but that secreted was very large, and all
Sicily was filled with them, no convention having been

made in their case as for those taken with Demosthenes. Besides this, a large portion were killed outright, the carnage being very great, and not exceeded by any in this Sicilian war. In the numerous other encounters upon the march, not a few also had fallen. Nevertheless many escaped, some at the moment, others served as slaves, and then ran away subsequently. These found refuge at Catana.

The Syracusans and their allies now mustered and took up the spoils and as many prisoners as they could, and went back to the city. The rest of their Athenian and allied captives were deposited in the quarries, this seeming the safest way of keeping them; but Nicias and Demosthenes were butchered against the will of Gylippus, who thought that it would be the crown of his triumph if he could take the enemy's generals to Lacedaemon.

EDITOR'S NOTE

The war lasted nine years after the disaster in Syracuse, but ended in victory for Sparta. In 404 B.C. Athens agreed to destroy the walls that protected her connection with the port of Piraeus, the "Long Walls," and surrender the navy. Though Athenian independence was restored, and the city remained a center of literature, philosophy, and art, her empire was gone. Greece was divided and weakened, and finally open for the conquests of Philip of Macedon (father of Alexander the Great) from 358 to 336.

Crécy (1346)

Jean Froissart

The Hundred Years' War, fought between 1339 and 1453, was actually not a continuous war but a series of wars between England and France. The wars were fought over English claims to the French throne as well as the rivalry for control of the wool trade in the Low Countries. England also had a long tradition of feudal holdings in France, which were a constant source of friction between the two countries.

Edward III claimed the throne of France, which Philip VI (of Valois) held. Edward defeated the French in a sea battle at Sluys in 1340. In 1346 he invaded France and met Philip at Crécy. (Froissart calls it Cressy.) The English won an outstanding victory. As a result of this and subsequent victories, they won much territory but not the throne. The battle was notably, tactically, for the successful use of infantry and archers against knights. It was also one of the earliest European battles in which cannons were used, though Froissart does not speak of them.

Jean Froissart (1337–1410) was nine years old at the time of the battle of Crécy. In later life he knew intimately many of the men who fought there. Froissart was a native Frenchman who was also at home in the courts of England. Besides being a chronicler, he was a poet and courtier of note. His chronicles cover most of the first half of the Hundred Years' War. Froissart's work depicts the color and vitality of the times. Most historians do not rate him too highly for accuracy or depth.

The first important battle after landing took place at Caen, which town made an obstinate resistance, and upward of 500 English were killed in the narrow streets by the stones and benches which were thrown upon them from the tops of the houses. The King was so much enraged at his loss, that he gave orders that all the inhabitants should be put to the sword and the town burned; but Sir Godfrey de Harcourt prevailed with him to reverse this order, and with the inhabitants to submit to a quiet surrender. Much wealth and many prisoners were taken and sent over to England under charge of the Earl of Huntingdon, with 200 men-at-arms and 400 archers.

After the taking of Caen, the English committed serious ravages in Normandy; Sir John Chandos and Sir Reginald Cobham became greatly distinguished for their bravery, and also for their humane treatment of the sufferers. For a time the King of England avoided as much as he could any open engagement with the army of France, and contented himself with plundering the country through which he passed. The two armies, however, now arrived near to Cressy, and it was told Edward that the King of France desired to give him battle. "Let us post ourselves here," said King Edward to his people, "I have good reason to wait for the enemy on this spot; I am now on the lawful inheritance of my lady-mother, which was given her as her marriage portion, and I am resolved to defend it against Philip of Valois." As Edward had not more than an eighth part of the forces which the King of France had, he was, of course, anxious to fix on the most advantageous position; and after he had carefully disposed his forces, he lost no time in sending scouts toward Abbeville to learn if the King of France meant to take the field that day; these, however, soon returned, saying, that they saw no appearance of it; upon which the King dismissed his men to their quarters with orders to be in readiness betimes in the morning, and to assemble at the same place. The King of France remained all Friday at Abbeville, waiting for more troops; during the day he sent his marshals, the Lord of St. Venant and Lord Charles of Montmorency, out of the town to examine the country and get some certain intelligence respecting the English. They returned about vespers with information that the English were encamped on the plain. That night the King of France entertained at supper, in

Abbeville, all the princes and chief lords of his army. There was much conversation relative to the war; and after supper the King entreated them always to remain in friendship with each other; "to be friends without jealousy, and courteous without pride." All the French forces had not yet arrived, for the King was still expecting the Earl of Savoy, who ought to have been there with a thousand lances, as he had well paid for them at Troyes in Champaign, three months in advance. That same evening the King of England also gave a supper to his earls and barons, and when it was over he withdrew into his oratory, where, falling on his knees before the altar, he prayed to God that if he should combat his enemies on the morrow, he might come off with honor. About midnight he retired to rest, and rising early the next day, he and the Prince of Wales heard mass and communicated. The greater part of his army did the same. After mass the King ordered his men to arm themselves and assemble on the ground which he had before fixed upon.

There was a large park near a wood, on the rear of the army, which King Edward enclosed, and in it placed all his baggage, wagons, and horses; for his men-at-arms and archers were to fight on foot. He afterward ordered, through his constable and his two marshals, that the army should be divided into three battalions. In the first, he placed the young Prince of Wales, and with him the Earls of Warwick and Oxford, and many other knights and squires whom I cannot name. There might be, in this first division, about 800 men-at-arms, 2,000 archers, and 1,000 Welshmen; all of whom advanced in regular order to their ground, each lord under his banner and pennon, and in the centre of his men. In the second battalion were the Earl of Northampton, the Earl of Arundel, and many others, amounting in the whole to about 800 men-at-arms, and 1,200 archers. The third battalion was commanded by the King in person and was composed of about 700 men-at-arms and 2,000 archers. The King was mounted on a small palfrey, having a white wand in his hand, and attended by his two marshals. In this manner he rode at a foot's pace, through all the ranks, encouraging the army and entreating that they would guard his honor and defend his right; so sweetly and with such a cheerful countenance did he speak, that all who had been before dispirited were directly comforted by hearing him. By the time he had thus visited all the battalions it was nearly ten o'clock; he then retired to his own division, having ordered the men to regale themselves, after which all returned to their own battalions, according to the marshals' orders, and seated themselves on the ground, placing their helmets and bows before them, in order that they might be the fresher when their enemies should arrive.

That same Saturday the King of France also rose betimes, heard mass in the monastery of St. Peter's in Abbeville, where he lodged; and having ordered his army to do the same, left that town after sunrise. When he had marched about two leagues from Abbeville and was approaching the enemy, he was advised to form his army in order of battle, and to let those on foot march forward that they might not be trampled on by the horses. This being done, he sent off four knights, who rode so near to the English that they could clearly distinguish their position. The English plainly perceived that these knights came to reconnoitre; however, they took no notice of it, but suffered them to return unmolested.

When the King of France saw them coming back, he halted his army, and the knights pushing through the crowds came near to the King, who said to them, "My lords, what news?" Neither chose to speak first; at last the King addressed himself personally to the Lord Moyne, who said, "Sir, I will speak, since it pleases you to order me, but under correction of my companions. We have advanced far enough to reconnoitre your enemies. Know, then, that they are drawn up in three battalions, and are waiting for you. I would advise, for my part (submitting, however, to your better counsel), that you halt your army here and quarter them for the night; for before the rear shall come up, and the army be properly drawn up, it will be very late, and your men will be tired and in disorder, while they will find your enemies fresh and properly arrayed. On the morrow you may draw up your army more at your ease, and may at leisure reconnoitre on what part it will be most advantageous to begin the attack, for be assured they will wait for you." The King commanded that it should be so done; and the two marshals rode, one to the front and the other to the rear, crying out, "Halt banners, in the name of God and St. Denis." Those that were in front halted;

but those that were behind said they would not halt until they were as forward as the front. When the front perceived the rear pressing on, they pushed forward; and as neither the King nor the marshals could stop them, they marched on without any order until they came in sight of their enemies. As soon as the foremost rank saw the English they fell back at once in great disorder, which alarmed those in the rear, who thought they had been fighting. All the roads between Abbeville and Cressy were covered with common people, who, when they were come within three leagues of their enemies, drew their swords, bawling out, "Kill, kill!" and with them were many lords eager to make a show of their courage.

There is no man, unless he had been present, that can imagine or describe truly the confusion of that day, especially the bad management and disorder of the French, whose troops were out of number. What I know, and shall relate in this book, I have learned chiefly from the English, and from those attached to Sir John of Hainault, who was always near the person of the King of France. The English, who, as I have said, were drawn up in three divisions, and seated on the ground, on seeing their enemies advance, rose up undauntedly and fell into their ranks. The prince's battalion, whose archers were formed in the manner of a portcullis, and the men-at-arms in the rear, was the first to do so. The Earls of Northampton and Arundel, who commanded the second division, posted themselves in good order on the prince's wing to assist him if necessary.

You must know that the French troops did not advance in any regular order, and that as soon as their King came in sight of the English his blood began to boil, and he cried out to his marshals, "Order the Genoese forward and begin the battle in the name of God and St. Denis." There were about 15,000 Genoese cross-bow men; but they were quite fatigued, having marched on foot that day six leagues, completely armed and carrying their cross-bows, and accordingly they told the constable they were not in a condition to do any great thing in battle. The Earl of Alençon hearing this, said, "This is what one gets by employing such scoundrels, who fall off when there is any need for them." During this time a heavy rain fell, accompanied by thunder and a very terrible eclipse of the sun; and, before this rain, a great flight of crows hovered in the air over all the battalions, making a loud noise; shortly afterward it cleared up, and the sun shone very bright; but the French had it in their faces, and the English on their backs. When the Genoese were somewhat in order they approached the English and set up a loud shout, in order to frighten them; but the English remained quite quiet and did not seem to attend to it. They then set up a second shout, and advanced a little forward; the English never moved. Still they hooted a third time, advancing with their cross-bows presented, and began to shoot. The English archers then advanced one step forward, and shot their arrows with such force and quickness that it seemed as if it snowed. When the Genoese felt these arrows, which pierced through their armor, some of them cut the strings of their cross-bows, others flung them to the ground, and all turned about and retreated quite discomfited.

The French had a large body of men-at-arms on horseback to support the Genoese, and the King, seeing them thus fall back, cried out, "Kill me those scoundrels, for they stop up our road without any reason." The English continued shooting, and some of their arrows falling among the horsemen, drove them upon the Genoese, so that they were in such confusion they could never rally again.

In the English army there were some Cornish and Welsh men on foot, who had armed themselves with large knives; these advancing through the ranks of the men-at-arms and archers, who made way for them, came upon the French when they were in this danger, and falling upon earls, barons, knights, and squires, slew many, at which the King of England was exasperated. The valiant King of Bohemia was slain there; he was called Charles of Luxembourg, for he was the son of the gallant King and Emperor, Henry of Luxembourg, and, having heard the order for the battle, he inquired where his son the Lord Charles was; his attendants answered that they did not know, but believed he was fighting. Upon this, he said to them, "Gentlemen, you are all my people, my friends, and brethren at arms this day; therefore, as I am blind, I request of you to lead me so far into the engagement that I may strike one stroke with my sword." The knights consented, and in order that they might not lose him in the crowd, fastened all the reins of their horses together, placing the King at their head that he

might gratify his wish, and in this manner advanced toward
the enemy. The Lord Charles of Bohemia, who already
signed his name as King of Germany, and bore the arms,
had come in good order to the engagement; but when he
perceived that it was likely to turn out against the French
he departed. The King, his father, rode in among the
enemy, and he and his companions fought most valiantly;
however, they advanced so far that they were all slain, and
on the morrow they were found on the ground with all
their horses tied together.

The Earl of Alençon advanced in regular order upon the
English, to fight with them, as did the Earl of Flanders in
another part. These two lords, with their detachments,
coasting, as it were, the archers, came to the prince's battalion, where they fought valiantly for a length of time.
The King of France was eager to march to the place where
he saw their banners displayed, but there was a hedge of
archers before him; he had that day made a present of a
handsome black horse to Sir John of Hainault, who had
mounted on it a knight of his, called Sir John de Fusselles,
who bore his banner; the horse ran off with the knight and
forced his way through the English army, and, when about
to return, stumbled and fell into a ditch and severely
wounded him; he did not, however, experience any other
inconvenience than from his horse, for the English did not
quit their ranks that day to make prisoners: his page
alighted and raised him up, but the French knight did not
return the way he came, as he would have found it difficult
from the crowd. This battle, which was fought on Saturday, between La Broyes and Cressy, was murderous and
cruel; and many gallant deeds of arms were performed
that were never known; toward evening, many knights
and squires of the French had lost their masters, and,
wandering up and down the plain, attacked the English in
small parties; but they were soon destroyed, for the English
had determined that day to give no quarter, nor hear of
ransom from anyone.

Early in the day some French, Germans, and Savoyards
had broken through the archers of the prince's battalion,
and had engaged with the men-at-arms; upon this the second battalion came to his aid, and it was time they did so,
for otherwise he would have been hard pressed. The first
division, seeing the danger they were in, sent a knight off

in great haste to the King of England, who was posted
upon an eminence near a windmill. On the knight's arrival,
he said, "Sir, the Earl of Warwick, the Lord Stafford, the
Lord Reginald Cobham, and the others who are about
your son, are vigorously attacked by the French, and they
entreat that you will come to their assistance with your
battalion, for, if numbers should increase against him, they
fear he will have too much to do." The King replied, "Is
my son dead, unhorsed, or so badly wounded that he cannot support himself?" "Nothing of the sort, thank God,"
rejoined the knight, "but he is in so hot an engagement that
he has great need of your help." The King answered,
"Now, Sir Thomas, return to those that sent you, and tell
them from me not to send again for me this day, nor expect that I shall come, let what will happen, as long as my
son has life; and say that I command them to let the boy
win his spurs, for I am determined, if it please God, that all
the glory of this day shall be given to him, and to those into
whose care I have entrusted him." The knight returned to
his lords and related the King's answer, which mightily encouraged them, and made them repent they had ever sent
such a message.

It is a certain fact, that Sir Godfrey de Harcourt, who
was in the prince's battalion, having been told by some of
the English that they had seen the banner of his brother
engaged in the battle against him, was exceedingly anxious
to save him; but he was too late, for he was left dead on
the field, and so was the Earl of Aumarle, his nephew. On
the other hand, the Earls of Alençon and Flanders were
fighting lustily under their banners with their own people;
but they could not resist the force of the English, and
were there slain, as well as many other knights and
squires, who were attending on or accompanying them.

The Earl of Blois, nephew to the King of France, and the
Duke of Lorraine, his brother-in-law, with their troops,
made a gallant defence; but they were surrounded by a
troop of English and Welsh, and slain in spite of their prow-
ess. The Earl of St. Pol and the Earl of Auxerre were also
killed, as well as many others. Late after vespers, the King
of France had not more about him than sixty men, everyone included. Sir John of Hainault, who was of the number, had once remounted the King, for his horse had been
killed under him by an arrow; and seeing the state he was

in, he said, "Sir, retreat while you have an opportunity, and do not expose yourself so simply; if you have lost this battle, another time you will be the conqueror." After he had said this he took the bridle of the King's horse and led him off by force, for he had before entreated him to retire. The King rode on until he came to the castle of La Broyes, where he found the gates shut, for it was very dark; he ordered the governor of it to be summoned, who, after some delay, came upon the battlements, and asked who it was that called at such an hour. The King answered, "Open, open, governor, it is the fortune of France." The governor hearing the King's voice immediately descended, opened the gate, and let down the bridge; the King and his company entered the castle, but he had with him only five barons: Sir John of Hainault, the Lord Charles of Montmorency, the Lord of Beaujeu, the Lord of Aubigny, and the Lord of Montfort. It was not his intention, however, to bury himself in such a place as this, but having taken some refreshments, he set out again with his attendants about midnight, and rode on under the direction of guides who were well acquainted with the country, until about daybreak he came to Amiens, where he halted. This Saturday the English never quitted their ranks in pursuit of anyone, but remained on the field guarding their position and defending themselves against all who attacked them. The battle ended at the hour of vespers, when the King of England embraced his son and said to him, "Sweet son, God give you perseverance; you are my son; for most loyally have you acquitted yourself; you are worthy to be a soyereign." The prince bowed very low, giving all honor to the King, his father. The English during the night made frequent thanksgivings to the Lord for the happy issue of the day; and with them there was no rioting, for the King had expressly forbidden all riot or noise.

On the following day, which was Sunday, there were a few encounters with the French troops; however, they could not withstand the English, and soon either retreated or were put to the sword. When Edward was assured that there was no appearance of the French collecting another army, he sent to have the number and rank of the dead examined. This business was entrusted to Lord Reginald Cobham and Lord Stafford, assisted by three heralds to examine the arms, and two secretaries to write down the names. They passed the whole day upon the field of battle, and made a very circumstantial account of all they saw: according to their report it appeared that 80 banners, the bodies of 11 princes, 1,200 knights, and about 30,000 common men were found dead on the field.

XI
AFTERMATH

SOLFERINO

Solferino (1859)

J. Henry Dunant

*The Italian movement for independence and unity
met a main obstacle in the Austrian possessions and
influence in Italy. In 1859 the Kingdom of Pied-
mont (in northern Italy) made an alliance with
Napoleon III of France against the Austrian empire, and the allied forces won some success. At
Solferino, in Lombardy, northern Italy, June 24,
1859, the battle between Austrians on one side and
French and Piedmontese on the other was itself not
decisive, though the Austrians withdrew. The horrors and bloodshed, however, so affected Napoleon
III that he began to arrange a separate truce and
then a peace treaty with the Austrians. He probably
had other motives, too. The settlement, though re-
sented by the Piedmontese, was a step on the road to
the Kingdom of Italy.*

*Among the witnesses to Solferino and its after-
math was a Swiss civilian, J. Henry Dunant. His account tells not only of the fighting but especially of
the suffering of the wounded and of his efforts to
relieve it. The experience of Solferino led Dunant
directly to his life work of promoting the Red Cross,
and his* Memory of Solferino, *from which this report
is taken, persuaded many to support his work.*

In the French Army, after the Marshals and Generals,
mention cannot be omitted of the glorious deeds of the
brave Brigadiers, the brilliant Colonels, the fearless Majors and valiant Captains, who did so much to bring about
the victory of that famous day. It was, indeed, no small
honour to have fought and defeated such warriors as Prince

Alexander of Hesse, Stadion, Benedek, or Karl von Windisch—Greats!

"It seemed as if the wind was carrying us forward," a simple soldier picturesquely expressed it, trying to give an idea of the spirit and enthusiasm of the comrades who went with him into battle.

When the sun came up on the twenty-fifth, it disclosed the most dreadful sights imaginable. Bodies of men and horses covered the battlefield; corpses were strewn over roads, ditches, ravines, thickets and fields; the approaches of Solferino were literally thick with dead. The fields were devastated, wheat and corn lying flat on the ground, fences broken, orchards ruined; here and there were pools of blood. The villages were deserted and bore the scars left by musket shots, bombs, grenades and shells. Walls were broken down and pierced with gaps where cannonballs had crushed through them. Houses were riddled with holes, shattered and ruined, and their inhabitants, who had been in hiding, crouching in cellars without light or food for nearly twenty hours, were beginning to crawl out, looking stunned by the terrors they had endured. All around Solferino, and especially in the village cemetery, the ground was littered with guns, knapsacks, cartridge-boxes, mess tins, helmets, shakos, fatigue-caps, belts, equipment of every kind, remnants of blood-stained clothing and piles of broken weapons.

The poor wounded men that were being picked up all day long were ghastly pale and exhausted. Some, who had been the most badly hurt, had a stupefied look as though they could not grasp what was said to them; they stared at one out of haggard eyes, but their apparent prostration did not prevent them from feeling their pain. Others were anxious and excited by nervous strain and shaken by spasmodic trembling. Some, who had gaping wounds already beginning to show infection, were almost crazed with suffering. They begged to be put out of their misery, and writhed with faces distorted in the grip of the death-struggle.

There were poor fellows who had not only been hit by bullets or knocked down by shell splinters, but whose arms and legs had been broken by artillery wheels passing over them. The impact of a cylindrical bullet shatters bones into a thousand pieces, and wounds of this kind are always very serious. Shell-splinters and conical bullets also cause agonizingly painful fractures, and often frightful internal injuries. All kinds of splinters, pieces of bone, scraps of clothing, equipment or footgear, dirt or pieces of lead, often aggravate the severity of a wound and double the suffering that must be borne.

Anyone crossing the vast theatre of the previous day's fighting could see at every step, in the midst of chaotic disorder, despair unspeakable and misery of every kind. Some regiments had dropped their knapsacks, and the contents had been rifled by Lombard peasants and men of the Algerian Sharp-shooters, who snapped up whatever came their way. Thus, the Light Infantry of the Guard had left their packs near Castiglione, so that they could march light when they went to the help of Forey's Division attacking Solferino. They fought all day long, pushing further and further ahead, and finally spent the night near Cavriana. Next morning at daybreak they went back for their knapsacks, only to find them empty; everything had been stolen in the night. The loss was a cruel one for those poor soldiers. Their underclothes and uniforms were dirty and stained, worn and torn, and now they found all their clothing gone, perhaps all their small savings with it, besides things of sentimental value that made them think of home or of their families—things given them by their mothers, or sisters, or sweethearts. Looters stole even from the dead, and did not always care if their poor wounded victims were still alive. The Lombard peasants seemed especially greedy for boots, and wrenched them ruthlessly off the swollen feet of the dead.

The lack of water was more and more cruelly felt; the ditches were drying up, and the soldiers had for the most part only polluted and brackish water to quench their thirst. Wherever springs had been found, armed sentries were posted to keep the water for the sick. Near Cavriana, a swamp that had become foul served for two days to water twenty thousand artillery and cavalry horses. Some wounded, riderless beasts, after wandering all night long, dragged themselves towards the horse-lines as if asking their fellows for help, and were shot to put them out of their misery. One noble, beautifully caparisoned charger strayed into the middle of a French detachment, the saddle-bag he carried still fixed to his saddle. It contained letters

and objects that showed he must have belonged to the valiant Prince of Isenburg. A search for his master was begun, and the Austrian Prince was discovered among the
dead bodies, wounded and unconscious from loss of blood.
But he was immediately treated by the French surgeons
and was eventually able to go home to his family, who had
given him up for dead and had been wearing mourning for
him for several weeks.

Some of the soldiers who lay dead had a calm expression,
those who had been killed outright. But many were disfigured by the torments of the death-struggle, their limbs
stiffened, their bodies blotched with ghastly spots, their
hands clawing at the ground, their eyes staring widely, their
moustaches bristling above clenched teeth that were bared
in a sinister convulsive grin.

It took three days and nights to bury the dead on the
battlefield, but in such a wide area many bodies which lay
hidden in ditches, in trenches, or concealed under bushes
or mounds of earth, were found only much later; they,
and the dead horses, gave forth a fearful stench.

In the French Army a certain number of soldiers were
detailed from each company to identify and bury the dead.
Usually they picked out the men of their own units. They
took the regimental number on the dead man's belongings,
and then, with the help of the Lombard peasants paid for
the purpose, laid the body, clothed, in a common grave.
Unhappily, in their haste to finish their work, and because
of the carelessness and gross negligence of some of the
peasants, there is every reason to believe that more than
one live man was buried with the dead. The decorations,
money, watches, letters and papers found on the officers
were later sent to their families; but it was not always possible to fulfill this duty properly, with such a vast number
of bodies to be buried.

A son idolized by his parents, brought up and cherished
for years by a loving mother who trembled with alarm
over his slightest ailment; a brilliant officer, beloved by
his family, with a wife and children at home; a young soldier who had left sweetheart or mother, sisters or old father, to go to war; all lie stretched in the mud and dust,
drenched in their own blood! The handsome manly face is
beyond recognition, for sword or shot has done its dis-
figuring work. The wounded man agonizes, dies, and his

dear body, blackened, swollen and hideous, will soon be thrown just as it is into a half-dug grave, with only a few shovelfuls of lime and earth over it! The birds of prey will have no pity for those hands and feet when they protude, as the wet earth dries, from the mound of dirt that is his tomb. Later someone will perhaps come back, throw on some more earth, set up a wooden cross over his resting place—and that will be all!

Austrian bodies lay in thousands on hills and earth-works, on the tops of mounds, strewn in groves and woods, or over the fields and plains of Medola. Over the torn cloth jackets, the muddy grey great coats, or once white tunics, now dyed red with blood, swarmed masses of greedy flies; and birds of prey hovered above the putrefying corpses hoping for a feast. The bodies were piled by the hundred in great common graves.

How many young Hungarians, Bohemians, or Roumanians, enrolled only a few weeks earlier, had thrown themselves down, worn out and hungry once they were out of the range of guns, never to rise again! Some were only slightly wounded, but so weakened by loss of blood that they died miserably from exhaustion and hunger.

From Castiglione the wounded were supposed to go on to hospitals in Brescia, Cremona, Bergamo and Milan, to be given regular care, or undergo any amputations that might be necessary. But the Austrians had requisitioned and removed all the carts in the neighbourhood, and since the French army's means of transport were absolutely insufficient for such a fearful number of wounded, they had to be kept waiting in the field ambulances for two or three days before they could be taken to Castiglione.

The crowding in Castiglione became something unspeakable. The town was completely transformed into a vast improvised hospital for French and Austrians. On the Friday, hospital headquarters had been established there, and wagons full of lint, equipment and medicines had been unpacked. The townspeople gave all the blankets, linen and mattresses they could spare. The hospital of Castiglione, the Church, the San Luigi monastery and barracks, the Capuchin Church, the police barracks, the churches of San Maggiore, San Giuseppe, and Santa Rosalia, were all filled with wounded men, piled on one another and with nothing but straw to lie on. Straw had also been spread in the

streets, courtyards and squares, and here and there wooden
shelters had been thrown up or pieces of cloth stretched,
so that the wounded pouring in from all directions might
have a little shelter from the sun. Private houses were very
soon taken over; the more well-off among their owners
welcomed officers and soldiers, and busied themselves in
providing what little they could to relieve their pain. Some
ran wildly through the streets, looking for a doctor for
their guests. Others went to and fro in the town distraught,
begging to have the dead taken from their houses, for they
did not know how to get rid of them.

On the Saturday the number of convoys of wounded increased to such proportions that the local authorities, the
townspeople, and the troops left in Castiglione, were absolutely incapable of dealing with all the suffering. Scenes as
tragic as those of the day before, though of a very different
sort, began to take place. There was water and food, but
even so, men died of hunger and thirst; there was plenty of
lint, but there were not enough hands to dress wounds;
most of the army doctors had to go on to Cavriana, there
was a shortage of medical orderlies, and at this critical time
no help was to be had.

Oh, the agony and suffering during those days, the
twenty-fifth, twenty-sixth, and twenty-seventh of June!
Wounds were infected by the heat and dust, by shortage of
water and lack of proper care, and grew more and more
painful. Foul exhalations contaminated the air, in spite of
the praiseworthy attempts of the authorities to keep hospital areas in a sanitary condition. The convoys brought a
fresh contingent of wounded men in Castiglione every
quarter of an hour, and the shortage of assistants, orderlies
and helpers was cruelly felt. In spite of the activity of one
army doctor and two or three other persons in organizing
transportation to Brescia by ox-cart, and in spite of the
spontaneous help given by carriage-owners in Brescia,
who came to fetch officer patients with their carriages,
cases could not be evacuated nearly as quickly as new ones
came in, and the congestion grew worse and worse.

Men of all nations lay side by side on the flagstone floors
of the churches of Castiglione—Frenchmen and Arabs,
Germans and Slavs. Ranged for the time being close together inside the chapels, they no longer had the strength
to move, or if they had there was no room for them to do

so. Oaths, curses and cries such as no words can describe
resounded from the vaulting of the sacred buildings.

With faces black with the flies that swarmed about their
wounds, men gazed around them, wild-eyed and helpless.
Others were no more than a worm-ridden, inextricable
compound of coat and shirt and flesh and blood. Many
were shuddering at the thought of being devoured by the
worms, which they thought they could see coming out of
their bodies (whereas they really came from the myriads of
flies which infested the air). There was one poor man,
completely disfigured, with a broken jaw and his swollen
tongue hanging out of his mouth. He was tossing and trying to get up. I moistened his dry lips and hardened tongue,
took a handful of lint and dipped it in the bucket they were
carrying behind me, and squeezed the water from this improvised sponge into the deformed opening that had been
his mouth. Another wretched man had had a part of his
face—nose, lips and chin—taken off by a sabre cut. He
could not speak, and lay, half-blind, making heart-rending
signs with his hands and uttering guttural sounds to attract
attention. I gave him a drink and poured a little fresh water on his bleeding face. A third, with his skull gaping wide
open, was dying, spitting out his brains on the stone floor.
His companions in suffering kicked him out of their way,
as he blocked the passage. I was able to shelter him for the
last moments of his life, and I laid a handkerchief over his
poor head which still just moved.

Although every house had become an infirmary, and
each household had plenty to do in taking care of the
wounded officers within its doors, I succeeded, by the Sunday morning, in getting together a certain number of
women who helped as best they could with the efforts made
to aid the wounded. It was not a matter of amputations or
operations of any kind. But food, and above all drink, had
to be taken around to men dying of hunger and thirst;
then their wounds could be dressed and their bleeding,
muddy, vermin-covered bodies washed; all this in a scorch-
ing, filthy atmosphere in the midst of vile, nauseating
odours, with lamentations and cries of anguish all around.

Before long a group of volunteer helpers was formed.
The Lombard women went first to those who cried the
loudest—not always the worst cases. I sought to organize
as best I could relief in the quarters where it seemed to

be most lacking, and I adopted in particular one of the
Castiglione churches, on a height on the left coming from
Brescia, and called, I think the Chiesa Maggiore. Nearly
five hundred soldiers were there, piled in the church, and a
hundred more lay outside on straw in front of the church,
with strips of canvas to protect them from the sun. The
women entered the churches, and went from one man to
another with jars and canteens of pure water to quench their
thirst and moisten their wounds. Some of these improvised
nurses were beautiful and charming girls. Their gentleness
and kindness, their tearful and compassionate looks, and
their attentive care helped revive a little courage among
the patients. The boys of the neighbourhood ran back and
forth between the churches and the nearest fountains with
buckets, canteens and watering pots.

Meantime, we had obtained some new recruits, first an
ex-naval officer, then a couple of English tourists who came
into the church from curiosity, and whom we seized and
held practically by force. On the other hand, two more Englishmen showed the utmost helpfulness from the beginning
and distributed cigars among the Austrians. We were also
given help by an Italian priest, two or three casual travellers
and onlookers, a Paris journalist—who afterwards assumed
responsibility for the relief work in another church nearby
—and a few officers whose detachment had been ordered
to stand by in Castiglione.

Before long, one of these latter found that the scene
made him ill, and our other volunteer helpers withdrew
one by one, for they could no longer bear to look upon
suffering which they could do so little to relieve. The priest
followed the rest, but came back again, thoughtfully bringing aromatic herbs and flasks of salts to place under our
noses.

Some of the soldiers of the detachment left to garrison
the town tried to help their comrades, but they also could
not bear a spectacle which told upon their morale, making
too deep an impression on their imagination.

An Engineer Corporal, who had been wounded at
Magenta and had practically got over his wounds (he was
now returning to his battalion, and his orders left him a few
days' grace) went with us, and helped us bravely, though
he fainted twice in quick succession. The French Quartermaster, who had just taken up his quarters in Castiglione,

finally authorized the use of unwounded prisoners for hospital work; and three Austrian doctors came to help a young Corsican military surgeon who came and asked me several times for a certificate placing on record the zeal with which I had seen him work. A German surgeon, who had deliberately remained on the battlefield to bandage the wounds of his compatriots, devoted himself to the wounded of both armies. In recognition of this the Quartermaster's department sent him back to rejoin the Austrians at Mantua three days later.

"Don't let me die!" some of these poor fellows would exclaim—and then, suddenly seizing my hand with extraordinary vigour, they felt their access of strength leave them, and died. An old sergeant, with several service stripes on his sleeve, said to me with the utmost suddenness, with conviction, and with cold bitterness: "If I had been looked after sooner I might have lived, and now by evening I shall be dead!" And by evening he was dead.

"I don't want to die, I don't want to die!" shouted a Grenadier of the Guard fiercely. This man who, three days earlier, had been a picture of health and strength, was now wounded to death. He fully realized that his hours were inexorably counted, and strove and struggled against that grim certainty. I spoke to him, and he listened. He allowed himself to be soothed, comforted and consoled, to die at last with the straightforward simplicity of a child.

Up at the end of the church, in the altar recess on the left, a trooper of the African Light Infantry lay on straw, uttering no complaint and hardly moving any longer. Three bullets had struck him, one in the right side, one in the left shoulder, and the third in the right leg, where it had remained. It was Sunday night, and he said he had had nothing to eat since Friday morning. He was a revolting spectacle, covered with dry mud and clotted blood, his clothing torn and his shirt in shreds. We washed his wounds and gave him a little soup, and I covered him with a blanket. He carried my hand to his lips with an expression of inexpressible gratitude. At the entrance to the church was a Hungarian who never ceased to call out, begging for a doctor in heartbreaking Italian. A burst of grapeshot had ploughed into his back, which looked as if it had been furrowed with steel claws, laying bare a great area of red quivering flesh. The rest of his swollen body was all black and green, and he could find no comfortable position to sit or lie in. I moistened great masses of lint in cold water and tried to place this under him, but it was not long before gangrene carried him off.

Close by was a Zouave, who wept and wept and had to be comforted like a little child. The fatigue following their exertions and the lack of food and rest joined with morbid excitement and the fear of dying unaided, developed at this stage, even in soldiers who knew no fear, a nervous and sensitive condition which led them to burst into moans and sobs. One of their uppermost thoughts, when their pain was not too dreadful, was the recollection of their mothers, and the fear of the grief their mothers would feel when they heard what had become of them.

AMERICAN HERITAGE
SHORT HISTORY OF
THE CIVIL WAR

BY BRUCE CATTON

A concise presentation of the Civil War by its most famous living student. This fast moving narrative covers both the political and military aspects of the war and succeeds in capturing the feelings of a nation during the years of its greatest peril.

Here too is the ordinary soldier who, speaking for all America, North and South, says something this country can never forget.

LAUREL LEAF LIBRARY   60c

THE SIEGE AND FALL OF TROY

ROBERT GRAVES

This exciting narrative spans the incidents leading up to the Trojan War, the events of the epic clash itself, and the return of the victorious Greeks to their homes. The author supplements the great works of Homer, the ILIAD and the ODYSSEY, with accounts by various Greek and Latin authors. The result is perhaps the first modern attempt to put the whole story into a single short book for young readers.

LAUREL-LEAF LIBRARY 45c

A complete catalog of Laurel-Leaf Library titles may be requested from Dell Publishing Co., Inc., 750 Third Avenue, New York, New York 10017, Attn: Educational Sales Department.